The
Sarajevo
Olympics

The
Sarajevo
Olympics

A History of the 1984
Winter Olympic Games

Jason Vuic

University of Massachusetts Press
Amherst and Boston

Copyright © 2015 by University of Massachusetts Press
All rights reserved
Printed in the United States of America

ISBN 978-1-62534-165-5 (paper); 164-8 (hardcover)

Designed by Jack Harrison
Set in Adobe Minion Pro with Helvetica display type

Library of Congress Cataloging-in-Publication Data

Vuic, Jason, 1972–
The Sarajevo Olympics : a history of the 1984 Winter Olympic Games / Jason Vuic.
    pages cm
Includes bibliographical references and index.
ISBN 978-1-62534-165-5 (paper : alk. paper) —
ISBN 978-1-62534-164-8 (hardcover : alk. paper)
1. Olympic Winter Games (14th : 1984 : Sarajevo, Bosnia and Hercegovina)
2. Winter Olympics—History—20th century. I. Title.
GV842 1984 . V84 2015
796.9809—dc23

                        2014047522

British Library Cataloguing-in-Publication Data
A catalogue record for this book is available from the British Library.

Epigraph: Edin Numankadić quoted in Mark Ira Hooks, "A Tale of Two Olympic Cities,"
EurasiaStories (2013).

To Kara

*It is sad, really. Sarajevo is known for only three things . . .
the assassination of Franz Ferdinand and the start of World
War I, the siege of Sarajevo and ethnic war, and the 1984
Olympics. Only one of those things was something positive.*

EDIN NUMANKADIĆ, Director, Sarajevo Olympic Museum

Contents

Illustrations follow page 128

Acknowledgments

This book was several years in the making. It started in 2010 with a very generous Post Graduate Research Grant from the Olympic Studies Centre in Lausanne, Switzerland, and grants from Bridgewater College and the Virginia Foundation of Independent Colleges. It involved interviews, phone and e-mail conversations, and other forms of help, large and small, from dozens of people, including (but not limited to) Marie Alkire, Debbie Armstrong, Marvin Bader, Dragan Bisenić, Jada Blinn, Igor Boras, Regula Cardinaux, Arthur Chidlovski, Esmer Ćosić, Charles Crawford, Clark Dougan, Said Fazlagić, Bob Fitzgerald, Phil Griffin, Yana Hashamova, Jeff Hastings, Ahmed Karabegović, Johann Olav Koss, Geoffrey Mason, Nick Miller, Pere Miró, John Morton, Edin Numankadić, Dan Pennell, Russell O. Pickett, Nuria Puig, Elvira Rameni, Ron Rossi, Juan Antonio Samaranch, Miki Savičević, Jack Scovil, Sabahudin Selesković, Chet Simmons, Cindy Slater, Dudley Strosnider, Josh Thompson, Robert Tout, Lou Vairo, Wayne Wilson, Greg Windsperger, and Branka and Goran Živković. I wish to acknowledge, too, the help I received from the staff at the Olympic Studies Centre in Lausanne, the LA'84 Foundation Library in Los Angeles, the Lake Placid Olympic Museum, the Sarajevo Olympic Museum, and the Olympic Committee of Bosnia and Herzegovina. Many thanks also to my mapmaker, Mary Williams. Finally, I wish to thank my wife, Kara, my mother, Nancy, and my sister Kelly, all of my friends and family members, John Treadway, Charles Jelavich, Joseph Prestia, Halina Stephan, David Reis, Brian Chmura, Barry Hargreaves, the Periškić and Živković families, and all of my colleagues at Indiana University, Ohio State University, High Point University, and Bridgewater College.

Guide to Pronunciation

The former joint Serbo-Croatian language, or Bosnian/Croatian/Serbian as it is today known, uses a Latin alphabet in parts of western former Yugoslavia, that is, Croatia and Bosnia, and a Cyrillic alphabet in parts of eastern former Yugoslavia, that is, Serbia. The following is a pronunciation guide for the language's Latin alphabet:

A, a	a as in father	L, l	l as in like
B, b	b as in body	Lj, lj	ly as in billion
C, c	c as in chance	M, m	m as in map
Č, č	ch as in reach	N, n	n as in night
Ć, ć	tch as in patch	Nj, nj	ny as in canyon
D, d	d as in dog	O, o	o as in vote
Dž, dž	j as in John	P, p	p as in part
Đ, đ	j as in juice	R, r	r as in rag (slightly rolled)
E, e	e as in gray	S, s	s as in sun
F, f	f as in fig	Š, š	sh as in shop
G, g	g as in go	T, t	t as in top
H, h	h as in head	U, u	u as in juke
I, I	i as in police	V, v	v as in vat
J, j	y as in you	Z, z	z as in zed
K, k	k as in kid	Ž, ž	z as in seizure

The
Sarajevo
Olympics

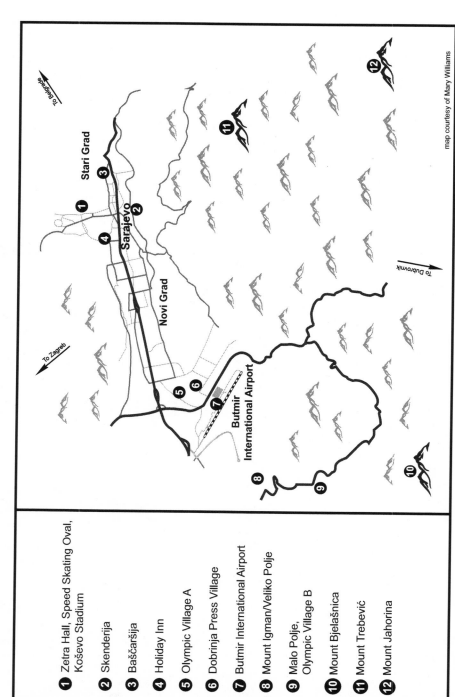

1 Zetra Hall, Speed Skating Oval, Koševo Stadium

2 Skenderija

3 Baščaršija

4 Holiday Inn

5 Olympic Village A

6 Dobrinja Press Village

7 Butmir International Airport

8 Mount Igman/Veliko Polje

9 Malo Polje, Olympic Village B

10 Mount Bjelašnica

11 Mount Trebević

12 Mount Jahorina

Map of Olympic Sites, 1984 Winter Olympics, Sarajevo, Yugoslavia

map courtesy of Mary Williams

Introduction

Remember Sarajevo

IGOR BORAS was a member of the Bosnian bobsled team traveling from Sarajevo, by a circuitous route, to the 1993 World Bobsleigh Championships in Innsbruck, Austria. There were no planes, no buses or trains leaving Sarajevo to take Boras to Austria. Sarajevo was under siege. Since 1992 Serb forces had held the ridges above the city and controlled territory on both sides of Butmir International Airport, which belonged to the United Nations (UN). The Serbs allowed the UN to use the airport for humanitarian flights, but passenger flights for ordinary Bosnians like Boras were forbidden. To leave Sarajevo, he had just one option: to sprint across the runway, which meant risking his life by braving sniper fire. On the other side, maybe eight hundred yards out, was Bosnian territory. Complicating matters was the UN itself. French peacekeepers drove sport utility vehicles (SUVs) back and forth across the tarmac, shining spotlights on people trying to leave the city. The UN did this "in order to appear neutral," for if the UN allowed Bosnians free passage in and out of the city, the Serbs would close down the airport and Sarajevo would starve.[1] Caught between a rock and a hard place, the UN patrolled the runway to pacify the Serbs. "The problem with that," said Boras, "was that you'd be standing there like a deer in headlights. The light would come on, and the Serbs would shoot."[2]

To better their chances, Boras and his two compatriots hired a guide, a smuggler whose job it was to run back and forth across the tarmac between Bosnian lines. "It was dark, as I remember it, and foggy. You couldn't see thirty feet in front of you. And this guide . . . could've taken us anywhere. We went back and forth, toward the Serbs, away from the Serbs, toward the French, away from the French. At one point an SUV passed us, but its spotlight was pointed the other way. We ducked down until it went by, then made it to the other side." The "other side" was free Bosnia, a territory extending up and over Mount Igman that was under the control of a Muslim warlord named Juka. Juka was a sociopath, a street-toughened paramilitary leader from Sarajevo who, in the early stages of the war, had defended the city from the Serbs. However, Juka and his men, who were called Wolves, also looted the city, confiscating apartments, houses, cars, and other so-called surplus property in the name of civic defense. The Bosnian government "need[ed] men like Juka to fight," one observer explained. "But [it couldn't] control them."[3] At one point, in June 1992, Juka laid siege to the Bosnian Presidency Building and that October had a physical altercation with the president himself. When the Bosnian government tried to arrest Juka, he fled the city with two hundred men and took up position on Mount Igman. He promised to liberate Sarajevo by December but found it easier to extort or simply rob refugees and siphon a percentage of whatever food and weaponry he found. Juka, in short, was a war criminal and profiteer.

"I was scared of the guy, totally," Boras said. "But my teammate Zdravko Stojnić knew him from the old days in Sarajevo. Juka liked Stojnić and wanted to impress him, I guess. So he had his troops pick us up in a van . . . a purple American van. Weird, I know. The driver was stoned. You could smell it. And he drove us up this snowy mountain road with no headlights on, because if the Serbs saw you, even from a great distance, they'd shoot. It was in the van, I think, that Stojnić said to us, 'Whatever Juka says, don't reply. Just nod. He's crazy. If he gets mad or if you say the wrong thing, he could kill you.'" The next morning the Bosnian bobsled team woke with a start. Juka's troops had just received (or stolen) a load of machine guns and had raced outside, like crazed children, to try them out. RAT-TAT-TAT-TAT-TAT . . . RAT-TAT-TAT-TAT-TAT . . . over and over. Then Juka appeared. He said hello to the team and made small talk with Stojnić while a group of young, voluptuous women milled about. They were Juka's nurses, no explanation necessary. But while Boras was trying to stay invisible, one of the nurses exclaimed, "Igor!" "She was a girl from my neighborhood," Boras related, "a friend I knew casually from high school. But as soon as she said, 'Igor' I thought: 'Shit, I'm dead.'" She asked Igor how he was, if he'd heard from anyone back home, and so on, while Juka, a potentially jealous, sociopathic criminal, stood nearby. "I answered, 'yes' . . . 'no' . . . 'yes' . . . 'no,' as quietly and curtly as possible until finally she left. My heart was racing. I thought to myself: 'Now *that* was close.'"

At length, Juka said good-bye to the three bobsledders and ordered that they be driven to nearby Konjić, a small town west of Sarajevo controlled by the Croatians. From there they hitchhiked to Split, Croatia, and then flew to Austria. The strange part of the story is that Igor Boras had never bobsledded before. Not once. He risked his life at least three times—on the runway, on a treacherous mountain road in a beat-up van driven with the headlights off by a stoned driver, and at the headquarters of Commander Juka—because, he says, "I wanted to be in the Olympics." Under Olympic rules, each country with a recognized National Olympic Committee could send a team to the games provided that the team had participated in a world cup event sanctioned by the Fédération Internationale de Bobsleigh et de Tobogganing. The team didn't have to win the event or even finish in the top ten. It could be last. But to qualify for the Olympics the Bosnian bobsled team had to compete, which is why Boras, Stojnić, and a third teammate named Denis, traveled to Austria. "You couldn't leave Sarajevo without a pass," Boras said. "They needed soldiers. So Denis joined the team in order to escape the city. He trained with us for a few days in Austria, then left. It didn't bother me. Denis saw a chance and took it. And who could blame him? He ended up with family in Germany."

Boras and Stojnić stayed on in Innsbruck to compete. They were housed by the German Olympic Committee, which gave them a nine-year-old sled, painted black, which was "missing several screws."[4] Stojnić showed Boras how to use it. The thirty-six-year-old Stojnić had competed for Yugoslavia in the 1984 Winter Olympics, and was now the coach and driver of the Bosnian bobsled team. He'd chosen Boras, then twenty-four, because he had been a very good one-hundred-meter runner. He was tall and strong and could help Stojnić push. "The sled was loud," Boras remembered, "and you had to breathe a certain way and push your head up into the turns or the G-forces would mash you into the floor. It was brutal. I saw my back in the mirror after one race and it was black and green and blue. That's when I thought: 'This is crazy!'" But even crazier was Boras's decision to return to Sarajevo after the Innsbruck race, that is, to make it back through Bosnia, down Mount Igman, across the runway, and into the city. By this time Commander Juka was gone, his tiny force having been chased out and replaced by progovernment paramilitaries under the control of Zulfikar Ališpaga, Zuka. Yes, a warlord named Zuka had replaced a warlord named Juka. Although Boras insists that Zuka's men were "even worse than the other guys," they allowed him to cross the runway in late February 1993. Stojnić was with him. "Why'd we go back?" Boras asked. "Where else was there to go? Sarajevo was our home, and me personally, I had my mother to worry about. I had things to do."

Boras's job before the world championships was to collect books and other rare artifacts from museums and libraries throughout Sarajevo to store them underground. One item his unit moved was the *Sarajevo Haggadah,* a medieval Sephardic religious text made famous by Geraldine Brooks in her bestseller of 2008, *People of the Book.* He then worked as a clerk at the front desk of the Bosnian Presidency but was transferred when he returned from Austria to a partially destroyed Supreme Court building abutting the front lines. His new job was security guard, but since few people came to the building he spent most of his time doing wind sprints up and down its long, carpeted corridors or doing explosion exercises on its steps. He wanted to train, so what else could he do? There was no bobsled run in Sarajevo. The one on Mount Trebević, just above the city, had been destroyed in the fighting, and its curvy track was now being used "as a firebase for Serbian mortars."[5] Boras's only option was to run and jump in the hallways, to lift weights, and to stay alive. However, in April 1993 disaster struck. That month Croat forces in Herzegovina attacked local Muslims, igniting a Croat–Muslim war that made it impossible for Boras to escape Sarajevo by traveling to the sea. Like other Olympic qualifiers trying to get to the 1994 Winter Olympics in Lillehammer, Boras was trapped. "I could cross the airport like last time," he said, "but once I made it over Mount Igman the Croat territory to the west of Sarajevo was off-limits. I had no choice but to stay."

Trapped, too, were close to a dozen Bosnian athletes who had to bribe or beg every friend-of-a-friend-of-a-friend who maybe knew a friend who could somehow get them out. The only real route was by plane. You could leave if you were an official member of a Bosnian state delegation, a politician, or a diplomat, even a bodyguard. Therefore, athletes who had links to the government or who could bribe someone in the government got out. Boras tried everything. He asked the Bosnian Olympic Committee to help him. It said no. He asked a Bosnian Croat politician to help him, but since Boras was a Croat, the politician said, "It's too political." Then, when CNN's Christiane Amanpour came to interview him, he says, she too said no. "I was stuck," Boras remembered. "I was ready to give up. It's now January 1994, two weeks before the Olympics, and there's no way out. But then Hilary Brown from ABC came to interview me, and with her was this Italian guy from the UN press office. I told her about my situation, and she said to this guy, 'Why don't you help him? What's wrong with you?' She was a tough lady. She gave me a letter on ABC letterhead that said I was an affiliate from Cyprus. The Italian guy approved it, grudgingly, and the UN let me go."

On 3 February 1994, Igor Boras flew from Sarajevo, Bosnia, to Ancona, Italy. From there he went to Milan, and from Milan he went by plane to Oslo, Norway, where he passed through customs and made his way to the airport's Olympic reception area. What he saw looked surreal to him: food—lots of food—bread and cheese and meat and fruit. Fresh juice! The room was bright and clean. It was snowing outside, and everyone was relaxed. "You know, living in Sarajevo your body is in survival mode," he said. "You're always tense and you're super aware of what's happening around you. You have to be. So when I sat down I thought, 'I'm gonna relax. I'm here, I made it, and I'm gonna relax. I'm gonna put the war behind me.' But then, on this giant TV they had, I saw a CNN news report from Sarajevo." There was a massacre, the infamous Markale massacre, in which a single mortar shell landed in the middle of a crowded market in Sarajevo. The footage was perhaps the most graphic ever to appear on television. In one clip a man with a severed leg drags himself toward the camera, pleading. People are crying; some sit quietly, in a daze, but the carnage is so great no one knows what to do. And everywhere there is blood, pools of blood, the market is bathed in it. The death toll was 68, with another 144 wounded.

"I froze," Boras said, "and then, without warning, I wept. I wept, and I wept, and I wept. I couldn't control it. I couldn't stop. My lips trembled, and my chest was heaving. All those years in Sarajevo . . . all the fear and all the killing and all the suffering. It just came out at once. I'd been there like ten minutes, and here I was sobbing. It went on and on. I cried for a good forty minutes, while the other athletes asked, 'Who is that guy? What's wrong with him? Why's he crying?' And then a camera crew from CBS wanted to interview me, and I kept saying, 'No, later . . . later.' When finally I calmed down, I went to the desk and said, 'OK, I can go. Take me to Lillehammer.'" Boras emerged from the lounge to find other reporters were waiting. Light bulbs flashed. "Mr. Boras! Mr. Boras! What can you tell us about the market massacre?" He didn't say anything. He stepped into a special taxi, a Volvo station wagon, and made the two-hour drive to Lillehammer. By this point, he and his teammates were celebrities. Stojnić had made it out, as had eight other athletes who either fled Sarajevo just prior to the games or who'd been living abroad as refugees. The team included five Muslims, two Croats, and three Serbs.

"We did dozens of interviews," Boras said. "Dozens." The press wanted to know, for example, if anyone knew anything about the market. Did you shop there? How did you train? What did you eat? Did you serve in the army? Where is your family? What is your ethnicity? What sport do you play? Will you go home? One possibly brain-dead reporter asked Boras about blood doping. "You ask me about doping?" he laughed. "I went a year without fruit."[6] The most common question, perhaps, involved the 1984 Sarajevo Olympics. It was, after all, the games' tenth anniversary, and journalists wanted to know how "the same people who [had] made [the] Games such a sweet occasion ten years ago [were] killing each other today." William Oscar Johnson, the Olympics correspondent at *Sports Illustrated*, wrote, "This is the single most unbearable truth I face in trying to reconcile Sarajevo 1984, Olympic city of brotherly love, with Sarajevo 1994, human slaughterhouse."[7] This dichotomy—Sarajevo 1984 and Sarajevo 1994—was a recurring theme in the press. "Could it be? Ten years?" a reporter for the *Baltimore Sun* asked. "Torvill and Dean sealing a gold with a kiss. . . . The first Winter Olympics held in a communist country had somehow turned beautiful. There were brownouts in the rest of Yugoslavia, but Sarajevo was illuminated and alive."[8]

The writer Jane Leavy covered the Sarajevo Olympics for the *Washington Post*. "I remember Sarajevo," she wrote. "I remember a city painted in shades of gray, the color in the peoples' faces, in their ever-present smiles, in their diversity. . . . I remember the bridge where the [Austrian] Archduke [Franz] Ferdinand was shot, beginning World War I. And that Sarajevo's Olympic ambition was less lofty than most host cities: to build a ski resort, now a battleground, and to be remembered for something other than the assassination, now a foregone conclusion. I remember at one intersection there was a cathedral, a synagogue and a mosque. . . . Yes, I remember Sarajevo."[9] Remember Sarajevo. This is what CBS, the American broadcaster of the Lillehammer games, urged its viewers to do. Remember Sarajevo. It began its coverage, even before the opening ceremonies, with a documentary contrasting the Sarajevo of 1984 with the Sarajevo of 1994. The narrator intoned, "The world reveled in Sarajevo then, saying it would remember, but when Sarajevo needs it most, the world has forgotten."[10]

For the rest of the games, Remember Sarajevo was Lillehammer's leitmotif: fans and athletes lit candles, the Norwegian speed skater Johann Olav Koss set three world records and donated his entire bonus, $32,000, to the

Olympic Aid Relief Fund, which had been set up specifically for Sarajevo. He also "urged his 4.3 million countrymen to each donate ten Kroner—about $1.50—for every gold medal won by a Norwegian."[11] While this was going on, Juan Antonio Samaranch, the president of the International Olympic Committee (IOC), was in Sarajevo. "I came from Lillehammer with a message of friendship," he said, wearing a blue helmet and a flak jacket. "I remember the very successful games here" and wanted to tell Sarajevans that "they are not alone."[12] Samaranch renewed calls for an "Olympic Truce," in effect a one-month cease-fire, and promised to rebuild Sarajevo's sports facilities when the war was over. He then returned to Lillehammer and closed the Olympic Games with the words, "*Drago* Sarajevo, dear Sarajevo. We do not forget you."[13] By this point, it was impossible to forget. CBS had spent the previous two weeks barraging viewers with retrospective vignettes—Scott Hamilton remembers Sarajevo, Katarina Witt remembers Sarajevo, Torvill and Dean remember Sarajevo. At the closing ceremonies every person in Olympic Stadium, forty thousand in all, was given a flashlight with the inscription "Remember Sarajevo."

Critics claimed CBS had taken "advantage of [Sarajevo's] 10-year anniversary . . . to attract viewers." Its "motives were almost wholly commercial," they insisted, and audiences of future games "could expect increasingly impassioned and ennobled telecasts . . . manufactured to generate ratings."[14] So what's new? Death + charity + sport = good television. But certainly there's a story here, a way to remember Sarajevo that includes the wars of the nineties but that tells us the who, what, when, where, and why of the 1984 Winter Olympic Games. These were, after all, the first Olympic Games to feature Soviet and American athletes since the Americans had boycotted the 1980 Summer Olympics in Moscow. They were the only Winter Olympics ever held in a communist country, and the only Winter Olympics ever held in the Balkans. In all, the Sarajevo Olympics featured a record 1,272 competitors from 49 countries. An estimated 640,000 spectators attended its events, while over 2 billion people tuned into the games on television. What they saw was amazing: a city, considered to be out of the way even by Balkan standards, that had never been a winter sports center or even a tourist center and that was wildly, almost indescribably mixed. It was an ancient, modern, Austrian, Ottoman, Eastern, Western, capitalist, communist, Orthodox, Catholic, Jewish, Muslim Jerusalem that was perhaps the most interesting city to have ever hosted the Olympics.

It was "an amalgam of periods and cultures," one journalist wrote, "and its seams [were] easy to find. . . . Where one row of palatial Austro-Hungarian official buildings end[ed], 12th century Turkey with its stoop-shouldered roofs and cobbled streets [began]."[15] Sarajevo "was the first place I ever skied where there were mosques and minarets," one athlete said. "It was like Saudi Arabia or something."[16] Others saw Sarajevo as "Eastern Bloc-ish," a modern dictatorship that was part communist, part capitalist, but a city where the Iron Curtain was at least "partially rolled up."[17] Pictures of Yugoslavia's late dictator, Marshall Josip Broz Tito, were everywhere—in schools, restaurants, bars, factories, government buildings—but so was Coke. The Atlanta-based company had been in Yugoslavia since 1968 and had paid $2.9 million to be the "Official Soft Drink" of the 1984 Winter Games.[18] A theater on Marshall Tito Boulevard showed *Rough Cut* with Burt Reynolds, while signs at the airport read, "Merrill Lynch Welcomes You!" and "Only the Best Go to the Olympics! Mitsubishi." There wasn't yet a McDonald's in Sarajevo, but there was a short-order grill owned by a man named Asim Musić, who offered customers a "Big Mek," a "burger," wrote the Associated Press (AP), "on an oversized, crusty bun, garnished with onions, white Yugoslavian cheese, and a pink 'special sauce.'"[19]

Then, of course, there were the sports. The British ice dancers Jayne Torvill and Christopher Dean received nine perfect scores for artistic impression. The Soviet hockey team rebounded from 1980 to win all seven of its matches by a total score of forty-eight to five. In alpine skiing, the American Mahre brothers finished one-two in the men's slalom. Debbie Armstrong won the women's giant slalom, while a cocky twenty-three-year-old, Bill Johnson, promised to win the men's downhill and then did so. The American Scott Hamilton won in figure skating, as did a captivating East German named Katarina Witt, who received thirty-five thousand pieces of fan mail. Witt's compatriot Karin Enke won two golds and two silvers in women's speed skating, while in the men's competition the Canadian Gaetan Boucher nearly matched Enke's feat by winning two golds and a bronze. The Finnish star Marja-Liisa Haemaelaeinen won the five-, ten-, and twenty-kilometer events in women's cross-country, the Norwegian Eirik Kvalfoss won a complete set of medals in biathlon, while in the ski-jumping events Jens Weissflog of East Germany and Matti Nykaenen of Finland each won a silver and a gold.

The most touching moment at Sarajevo, perhaps, came when Jure Franko, a Yugoslav skier from Slovenia, won a silver medal in the men's giant slalom.

It was Yugoslavia's only medal in Sarajevo and its first medal ever in a Winter Olympics. "It was getting toward the end of the games, and we had no medals," Franko remembered. "People had climbed the lift towers, and they were yelling and reaching to touch me as I rode by. There were thousands on the hill and at the finish. When I won my medal, people began jumping on me, kissing me, practically tearing me apart, and all I did was laugh and laugh. Because of my medal, a medal for Yugoslavia, it suddenly all made sense that the country had pulled together to put on these Games. It made sense then that we were feeling such harmony, such peace, such brotherhood as Yugoslavians."[20] The next day there were signs and posters throughout Sarajevo that read, "We Love Jurek More than Burek!" (*Volimo Jureka više od bureka*), a reference to a Bosnian cheese-pie dish that everyone loved to eat.

So what happened? How did Sarajevo go from hosting the Olympics to fighting a civil war? It's a good question because no host, winter or summer, has ever staged the Olympic Games then fought a civil war. But why did Sarajevo even host the games in the first place? By any real measure, the IOC couldn't have chosen a stranger venue. Sarajevo was poor, dirty, and remote, Yugoslavia was failing financially, and just two years after the city won its Olympic bid, many people, including President Lord Killanin of the IOC, were predicting its demise. The games were "an ironic climax that wrung the last benefits from an increasingly obsolete and dysfunctional sociopolitical system," one expert wrote. Yet for those Sarajevans who lived through the games they were "the high point of [that] city's history."[21] So how do we remember Sarajevo? How do we remember a games held in what became a war-torn city in a divided republic in a country that no longer exists? It's simple. For two weeks in 1984, Sarajevo—a multiethnic, prewar, Yugoslavian Sarajevo—was at the very "center of the winter sports world."[22]

Bid for and hosted by Sarajevo for the sole purpose of creating a winter tourist trade in Bosnia, the 1984 Winter Olympic Games were in organizational terms a success. Financing, construction, transportation, security: contrary to all expectations, and in spite of a snowstorm, everything worked.

However, Sarajevo's Olympic Games actually involved *two* games: those that were bid for and organized, and those that were played. Therefore, this book is divided into two parts. Part 1, "Background and Organization," begins with the first chapter, "Athens, 1978," a brief history of the IOC from the early 1970s through spring 1978, when Sarajevo was chosen to host the 1984 Winter Games.

Chapter 2, "The Swedish Prince," is a short description of Bosnia's status within Yugoslavia, the republic's decision to bid for the games, and the reasons it ultimately won. Chapter 3, "Nobody Changes Light Bulbs," follows the Sarajevo Olympic Organizing Committee through the early 1980s, a turbulent period when domestic and foreign politics and issues of finance threatened to derail the games. Chapter 4, "No Amount of Slivovitz," is a review of each Olympic venue, the beleaguered test competitions of 1982–83, and the opening ceremonies of 1984. And finally, chapter 5, "Up Close and Personal," describes such wide-ranging topics as security, the controversy over press accreditation for Radio Free Europe / Radio Liberty, and the ratings fiasco of the games' biggest contributor, ABC.

Part 2, "Citius, Altius, Fortius," examines the sports. Beginning with chapter 6, it includes four vignettes. The first, titled "Do You Believe in Debacles?," is a detailed account of the most anticipated matchup of the 1984 Winter Games, a meeting of the American and Soviet hockey teams that never was. Chapter 7, "Nine Times First Place," is the tale of Sarajevo's figure skating competitions and the megawatt superstars Katarina Witt, Scott Hamilton, and Jayne Torvill and Christopher Dean. Chapter 8, "The *Nasenbohrer*," is the story of alpine skiing in Sarajevo and the meteoric rise of Bill Johnson, the troubled American downhiller who raced to the gold. The final chapter, "The 'Minor Sports,'" is the bizarre, yet fascinating tale of what, in the 1980s, were America's most neglected winter sports: biathlon, bobsled, speed skating, cross-country skiing, ski jumping, and luge. Finally, the book ends with an epilogue, a postscript of war and suffering titled "The Seats of Zetra Hall."

I

Background and Organization

1

Athens, 1978

In the late 1970s the IOC was a secretive organization. It was also an exclusive organization. In the words of its president, Lord Killanin, the IOC was "a self-electing, self-perpetuating body," whose "membership [was] invited."[1] In 1978 it had some eighty voting members, all male, including the Marquess of Exeter, the Prince Regnant of Liechtenstein, the Grand Duke of Luxembourg, Raja Bhalindra Singh of India, Sheikh Gabriel Gemayel of Lebanon, Vice-Admiral Pyrros Lappas of Greece, Chief Justice Ade Ademola of Nigeria, General Vladimir Stoytchev of Bulgaria, and Julian Roosevelt, a relative of Theodore Roosevelt. The Illuminati they were not, but these IOC members were powerful men. They were millionaires, billionaires, blue bloods, industrialists, the sons and brothers of dictators, and, in a few instances, former Olympians. To critics, IOC members were "lapse[d] Hapsburgs," the "distant relatives of robber barons" who had "a 1920s political awareness" in the 1970s.[2] "Crusty, self-righteous, fiercely independent and arrogant," IOC members, the *Washington Post* wrote, ruled the Olympic movement as a "private board of trustees."[3] They answered to no one. They conducted their affairs in private, and they served not as representatives of their home countries to the Olympics, but as IOC representatives to their home countries. The IOC was not a democracy. In the words of one journalist, it was "an unashamed autocracy" whose goal it was to defend the Olympic Charter.[4]

Written in 1908 by the French aristocrat and educator Pierre de Coubertin, the Olympic Charter was a surprisingly short document that defined the rules and principles of the Olympic movement. Its very first principle was as follows: "The aims of the Olympic Movement are to promote the development of those fine physical and moral qualities which are the basis of amateur sport and to bring together the athletes of the world in a great qua-drennial festival of sports thereby creating international respect and goodwill and thus helping to construct a better and more peaceful world."[5] There you have it: the goal of the IOC was (and is) international understanding through sport. This is what Coubertin wanted when he revived the Olympics in 1894, and this is why he staffed his Olympic Committee with people of means.[6] Coubertin "was determined to make his Olympic Games independent of governments and to protect them from all shades of political meddling," one expert wrote, "so he formed the [IOC] and filled it with titled men, on the principle that the greater the standing and respect its members enjoyed the less likely politicians were to interfere with them."[7] As a result, Coubertin's IOC was, from the very beginning, a veritable who's who of European elites. The committee's first one hundred members, for example, included eighteen counts, two dukes, eight princes, five barons, three marquis, and two lords. Barring a war or some other unexpected catastrophe, they met each year in a general assembly called a session. In May 1978 the IOC's eightieth session was held in Athens at the luxurious Hotel Caravel.

The "principal purpose of our meeting in Athens," said Lord Killanin, "is to select the sites of the 1984 [Winter and Summer] Games."[8] The candidate cities for the Winter Games included Sapporo, Japan, Gothenburg, Sweden, and Sarajevo, Yugoslavia. The site for summer was Los Angeles, period. Al-though Tehran, Glasgow, Algiers, Nice, and Riyadh had all considered a bid, the smoggy American metropolis was the only city to apply. The reason: cash. In 1976 the Summer Olympics in Montreal had left the city over $1 billion in debt.[9] The games themselves had turned a profit, but the costs of capital improvements and facilities had utterly dwarfed what monies came in. The Olympic Stadium, or the "Big O," for example, where the opening ceremo-nies were held and where the old Montreal Expos baseball team played, was known pejoratively as the Big Owe. The games are "too big, too expensive, [and] too politically diseased," one observer stated. They've "become hassles for everyone—the organizers, the athletes, [and] the press," and they aren't "fun anymore."[10]

Even Lord Killanin would admit that in 1978 the Olympics were "at a low ebb." The jovial Irishman had been president of the IOC since 1972 and had overseen perhaps the most disastrous period in the history of the Olympic movement. "I had more major crises to worry about during my eight years of presidency," wrote Killanin, "than my predecessor, Avery Brundage, had in his twenty."[11] Killanin took office on 11 September 1972, the day after the Munich games ended. They had been marred by the brutal murder of eleven Israeli athletes and one German police officer by a Palestinian terrorist organization known as Black September.

Although Killanin was president-elect at the time, he was caught up in the callous administration of Brundage, the truculent IOC leader whom critics called "the world's leading shamateur." Brundage collected insults "the way a light bulb attracts moths," one journalist wrote. He's been called "pompous, sanctimonious, asinine, archaic, unbending, autocratic, a tyrant, a jerk, and an anachronism," and his final, most highly resented act as IOC president was to tell Munich that the games "must go on."[12]

Less than twenty-four hours after the killings, Brundage announced a one-day delay of the games and ordered that Munich's massive Olympic flag and the flags of other competing nations be flown at half mast. He then told a packed memorial service at the Olympiastadion that he wouldn't allow "a handful of terrorists" to disrupt the Olympic Games or destroy "the nucleus of international understanding and good will" that was the Olympic movement.[13] Not everyone agreed. Citing safety, several national teams decided to leave the Olympics, and many athletes refused to compete. "Should there be a XXI Olympics?" the reporter Red Smith asked. "Should Montreal try to do this all over again four years hence? No . . . unless there is a thorough housecleaning first." The "incredible insensitivity with which [IOC officials] reacted to murder should disqualify them permanently from further participation in sports. The body count was hardly completed when they raised the rallying cry: 'On with the dance.'"[14]

In retrospect, Brundage's decision to continue with Munich probably saved the Olympic movement, but soaring costs and creeping politicization would threaten the IOC throughout the 1970s. Just two months after Munich, in November 1972, the new IOC president, Lord Killanin, faced his first big test. Denver, the host city of the 1976 Winter Olympics, announced it was withdrawing its bid. A group there known as Citizens for Colorado's Future (CCF) had collected over seventy-seven thousand signatures and had forced a referendum over whether or not state funds could be used for the Olympics.[15] Since federal funding was tied to state funding, and since very little private money had been raised or collected, the referendum amounted to a yes or no vote: Did Colorado want the Olympics? The answer was a resounding no.[16] Clifford Buck, a Denver resident and head of the U.S. Olympic Committee, said, "I think it's a tragedy for the state and a tragedy for the nation that the people of Colorado were not aware of the great privilege [it is] to host the 1976 Winter Games. But the majority has spoken and I don't think there's any more to add."[17]

Buck could have added that staging the Olympic Games was exorbitantly expensive. When the IOC awarded the Olympics to Denver in May 1970, officials there claimed they could stage them for a mere $14 million. By November 1972 that figure had risen to $35 million, and many expected the final price to be substantially higher. "The people behind the Olympics are the same ones who stand to profit," the CCF leader Dick Lamm said. "[They're] the airlines, hotels, banks and ski resorts. . . . We're starting to realize that growth isn't necessarily good."[18] Lamm was right. Of the 140 or so people involved in Denver's bid, 69 were presidents or board members of corporations, while no fewer than 60 were millionaires. One CCF supporter said, "Just about everybody who profits from a crowd is in there."[19]

Denver's organizing committee argued that the city's hosting of the games would bring long-term benefits to Colorado, such as low-income housing, an improved mass transit system, and attractive new sports facilities for its residents. But voters, informed by the CCF, took a different view. Bumper stickers that read, "Don't Californicate Colorado" proliferated, as the citizenry came to see the Denver Olympics as "sport for the rich paid for by the poor," an event whose sole purpose was to "Sell Colorado."[20] In November they carried the referendum with a 60 percent vote. As one resident explained, "Some voted against the Olympics because of the cost. Some voted against [them] because of the devastating effect on our ecology." And some "like myself voted against [them] because we sincerely believe the Olympic philosophy is passé. . . . How sweet our victory would be if the citizens of Montreal would also realize how wasteful the . . . Games are."[21]

Unfortunately, Mayor Jean Drapeau of Montreal didn't get the memo. As the chief supporter of the 1976 Summer Olympics, Drapeau, one author joked, was "possessed by Baron-de-Coubertin-ism," and his mouth "was permanently pursed" in "the letter O," as in *Olympics.*[22] The mayor planned to spend $125 million, an exceptionally low figure for a summer games, and in February 1973, in the wake of the Denver fiasco and claims that he too was over budget, Drapeau insisted the Montreal Olympics could "no more have a deficit than a man [could] have a baby."[23] The people of Quebec needed reas-

suring. The Munich games had cost over $600 million, three times the origi-
nal estimate and four times more expensive than the games held in Mexico
City in 1968.[24]

But Drapeau had a plan. His Olympics would be self-financing, that is,
they would pay for themselves. First, he'd raise money through the sale
of commemorative stamps and coins, and then he'd hold a Canada-wide
Olympic lottery. This formula would cover 75 percent of the Olympics. The
remaining money would come from ticket sales, sponsorships, hotel and
restaurant taxes, and television rights. This assumed, however, that Drapeau
had a budget—a clear-cut, transparent, publicly available budget. He did
not. The flamboyant mayor refused to tell anyone anything, claiming his
$125-million estimate wasn't really an estimate but "a budgetary envelope,"
in other words, a blank check.[25] Drapeau's greatest expense was the ultramodern Olympic Park, which included a seventy-two-thousand-seat stadium with a column-free elliptical roof, a ten-thousand-seat swimming facility, and a seventy-five-hundred-seat velodrome. The cost: an estimated $800
million, which didn't include a $70-million Olympic Village in the form of
two interconnected pyramids. As one person put it, they were "an obscene
monument to a vain man."[26]

The buildings were so grandiose that Lord Killanin actually drew up a
special contingency plan to move the Olympics to Germany if necessary. He
feared that Montreal wouldn't be ready. "My worries began almost as soon as
I became President," Killanin wrote. "There had been long delays in setting
up the Organizing Committee in Montreal so . . . work [there] had already
fallen behind."[27] Montreal had won the Olympic bid in May 1970, but by late
1972 it had no plan of construction and had yet to build even a single Olympic venue. As of mid-1974, the games' great centerpiece, Olympic Stadium,
was still a muddy field. Then came strikes, blizzards, riots, several deadly ac-
cidents, a world oil crisis, charges of graft and corruption, and inflation. The
result was a "billion-dollar photo finish," with over four thousand men working six days a week in two eleven-hour shifts, plus overtime. At one point
there were thirty-five cranes in and around Olympic Stadium. "It's a racket,"
one electrician said. "They're just gluing it together now, cutting corners all
over the place. . . .[You're going to] see a lot of big defects showing up in a
couple of years."[28] He was right. In 1991 a fifty-five-ton concrete slab the size
of a big rig crashed to the concourse below. The stadium closed briefly, and
the hapless Montreal Expos spent the rest of the season on the road.[29]

Although the work in Montreal proceeded apace, the IOC considered moving the games as late as January 1976. In a grueling ten-hour session just prior to the 1976 Winter Olympics in Innsbruck, officials from Montreal convinced the IOC that they'd be ready. "We discussed virtually everything," said one official. "We spoke of other cities, other stadiums, even other countries, but when it came right down to it there [was] no practical alternative to staging the Games in Montreal."[30] As matters stood, nineteen of twenty-one venues were ready, but missing were the Olympic Stadium, where the opening ceremonies would be held, and the swimming pool. Officials tried to hurry the process by jettisoning the stadium's roof and tower and relocating the in-stadium press center to an office building downtown. They even replaced the athletes' dressing rooms and bathrooms with portable pods. Still, IOC officials were worried. Some predicted disaster, while Killanin himself joked that instead of five interlocking rings, the Olympic symbol for 1976 should be "crossed fingers."[31]

Meanwhile, at Innsbruck the IOC prayed for even a hint of good news. It had awarded the 1976 Winter Games to Innsbruck following a rushed competition in February 1973 in which the famed Tyrolean resort outbid Lake Placid, New York, Chamonix, France, and Tampere, Finland. Innsbruck had already hosted the 1964 Winter Olympics and therefore most of its facilities were intact. Its mayor, Alois Lugger, promised a simple Olympics, one that respected the environment and kept costs to a minimum. But Lugger spent $148 million in three years, over four times his initial budget. "We thought the old Olympic rings would only have to be dusted off and repainted," said one resident.[32] They were, but Lugger also built a power plant, a highway, a school, a bridge, an indoor swimming pool with sauna baths, and a bus depot. His new Olympic Village included thirty-five housing blocks. Instead of limiting expenses, Lugger used the Olympic Games to finance key infrastructure improvements "five or more years ahead of schedule."[33]

The press ate it up. "Innsbruck Residents Unmoved by Games," read one headline. "Four Times Estimate, Winter Games Costly Too."[34] What with Montreal approaching the $1-billion mark, Innsbruck brought derision. "These were to be the 'simple' Olympics," wrote one editorial, but while Austria "could afford the Innsbruck Games," the average Austrian "couldn't afford a ticket."[35] Journalists described the Olympics as "exorbitant," "overpriced," "scandal-ridden," "grossly parochial," "pseudo-patriotic goodie-two shoes drivel" with "the appetite of a forest fire." The "more it eats, the hungrier it becomes."[36] Arthur Daley, a Pulitzer Prize–winning sports reporter with the *New York Times,* suggested that the first step toward fighting "Olympic gigantism" was to eliminate the Winter Olympics altogether. He called them "the Frostbite Follies" and claimed that instead of moving the games from Denver to Innsbruck the IOC should have buried the Winter Olympics in "a bottomless crevasse alongside some convenient glacier."[37]

But Daley wasn't the games' greatest opponent. Avery Brundage was.[38] During his entire career the aging IOC president had tried to torpedo the Winter Olympics. Brundage "attacked his target from all angles," wrote one author. He despised their "commercialism, sham amateurism, and inordinate cost." He berated them "so fiercely that one felt he had come to hate skiing and skating and was bent on killing them off as Olympic sports" before he retired.[39] In fact, one of Brundage's last acts as IOC president was to publicly call for an end to the Winter Games. "The Winter Olympics are dead," he told an IOC congress in 1972. "May they receive a decent burial at Denver."[40] Although certainly smaller, the Winter Olympics weren't that different from the Summer Olympics. They were expensive, bloated, and insanely nationalistic, and they featured professional athletes parading as amateurs. But Brundage's strongest argument, perhaps, was that the Winter Olympics simply weren't universal. You can't ski without snow.

In 1976 there were over one hundred National Olympic Committees, but only thirty-seven sent teams to Innsbruck. They were the usual suspects: the USSR took twenty-seven medals, followed by East Germany with nineteen, the United States with ten, West Germany with ten, Norway with seven, Finland with seven, Austria with six, and Switzerland with five. A shocker: the Nordic countries dominated the Nordic events, while the Alpine countries dominated the alpine events. Turkey, Taiwan, Lebanon, and Iran failed to medal. To Brundage, this was proof that the Winter Games were too parochial. Only "a score of nations [are] seriously interested," he wrote, "and by far most of the medals have been won and will continue to be won by competition from only a dozen countries. . . . We should never have created the Winter Olympics," he lamented, "but how can we stop them now?"[41]

How indeed? Judging from ABC's Nielsen Ratings, the 1976 Winter Olympics were, in a word, popular, drawing at one point a 35 percent market share, which meant that 35 percent of all televisions in the United States were tuned to the Olympics.[42] Americans liked what they watched. They cheered when the Austrian Franz Klammer rocketed to gold in the men's downhill, and they booed when the Soviet Union went 6 and 0 in ice hockey and outscored its opponents 56 to 14. The most popular women's haircut in 1976 was "the wedge," a boyish hairdo worn by the American figure skater Dorothy Hamill. Women went crazy for it after Hamill won the gold. "They may not be able to do a Hamill Camel," one reporter wrote, "but hundreds of women are getting the Hamill haircut."[43] ABC paid a record $10 million for the broadcast rights to the Innsbruck games and $25 million for the rights to Montreal. It was one of twenty networks that broadcast Olympic sports that year to over a 1½ billion fans. To produce the games ABC built a $5-million, fifty-one-room "control complex" in New York that it then dismantled and shipped to Montreal. The complex had two production control rooms, six videotape editing rooms, a studio, a set, and two announcing booths. In addition there were six mobile units, including five trucks and a helicopter, nineteen on-site cameras, four handheld cameras, and four miniature cameras powered by backpack. In all, ABC planned a whopping seventy-four hours of coverage and sent 450 workers to Montreal.[44] By the opening ceremony they were ready. "I declare open the Olympic Games of Montreal," Queen Elizabeth II intoned in French and in English, "celebrating the 21st Olympiad of the modern era." Above the queen and visible from one end of the stadium was a giant yellow crane, "a stark reminder," one observer wrote, "of the troubles the Canadians had" in preparing for the games.[45]

But the Canadians were ready, and, as promised, they had finished the Big O[we]. The only problem was that twenty-three national teams who had come to Montreal refused to participate. The first was Taiwan, the tiny island country off the coast of mainland China. Known as the Republic of China (ROC), Taiwan was established in 1949 when anticommunist forces under Chiang Kai-shek fled mainland China to form a new government on Taiwan. However, Taiwan continued to claim sovereignty over the communist-controlled mainland, which by then was the People's Republic of China (PRC). In turn, the PRC claimed sovereignty over Taiwan, which it insisted was one of twenty-three communist provinces controlled by Beijing. Thus, there were two Chinas: the ROC and the PRC. One was an island, the other a densely populated, continent-wide behemoth the size of Canada. Both claimed to be China, and what ensued was a decades-long "political deadlock over names."[46]

In 1952 the IOC allowed both the ROC and the PRC to send teams to the Olympics. "The Olympic organization must ignore questions of race, religion, or politics," Sigfrid Edström, then-president of the IOC, said. The

Olympic goal, above all else, "is to unite the youth of the world."[47] But Taiwan didn't see it that way and claimed to be "the only legal National Olympic Committee" in China and therefore the only entity authorized to send Chinese athletes to the Olympics.[48] Rather than compete with unauthorized, that is, communist, athletes, Taiwan sent its delegation home. In 1954 the IOC attempted to solve the problem by recognizing two Chinese committees, but this time the PRC walked out. The communists boycotted the Melbourne Olympics in 1956; then in 1958 the PRC's lone IOC member, Tung Shou-yi, resigned. "[You] are a faithful menial of the U.S. imperialists," Tung told Brundage, concluding that he was "bent on serving their plot of creating 'two Chinas.' A man like you . . . has no qualifications whatsoever to be the IOC president."[49]

With that, Beijing left the Olympic movement. However, in 1970 Canada became one of forty-six states to break off relations with Taiwan in order to recognize communist China. In 1971 the two countries exchanged ambassadors, and in 1973 signed a multibillion-dollar deal in which Beijing agreed to purchase 224 million bushels of Canadian wheat.[50] The contract was so lucrative that in May 1976 the prime minister of Canada, Pierre Trudeau, announced that Taiwanese athletes would be refused visas to Canada as long as they competed as the ROC. The IOC cried foul because denying access to athletes from a recognized National Olympic Committee violated not only the Olympic Charter but also the terms of Montreal's bid application, which had been guaranteed in writing by Trudeau. "China is not really the issue here," Lord Killanin said. "It is the principles of the Olympics that are at stake." ["When the games] were awarded to Montreal," he continued, "we had a firm guarantee [from Trudeau] that athletes . . . would be given free entry into Canada."[51] They weren't.

Killanin called it "an extremely dangerous precedent," for if Canada reneged on its commitment, what would the Soviets do? Ban Israel? (The 1980 Summer Olympics were to be held in Moscow.) Therefore, Killanin considered at one point canceling the Montreal games. He also considered withdrawing the IOC's official sanction from Montreal, which meant no Olympic medals, no Olympic symbols, and no Olympic rings. Both options were bad. As the journalist Geoffrey Miller put it, "If the Games were abandoned the athletes would suffer; if they went on unofficially, disowned by the IOC . . . its control would be lost completely."[52] Faced with two difficult options, but seeking to preserve the Olympics at all costs, Killanin did nothing. "This is an extremely unfortunate day in Olympic history," he said, "[and] I'm sorry it should happen at the beginning of the Games in Montreal." The IOC has suffered "a very heavy blow . . . [and] I hope we'll never be put in such a damnable position again."[53]

Killanin made his pronouncement on June 11, 1976. Just five days later and two days before the opening ceremony, Nigeria pulled out. It was joined by nineteen other African countries as well as Iraq and Guyana, who had tried unsuccessfully to have New Zealand banned from the Olympics for allowing its rugby team to tour South Africa. Rugby wasn't an Olympic sport, but the protesting countries wanted the IOC to censure New Zealand for its "open approval" of apartheid. When the IOC refused, they withdrew. In all, twenty-six African countries exited the 1976 Summer Olympics, over one-fourth of the ninety-two countries that participated.[54] Missing were Filbert Bayi of Tanzania, the world record–holder in the 1,500 meters, and John Akii-Bua of Uganda, a 400-meter hurdler who won a gold medal in 1972. "Black Africa is gone," one editorialist wrote. "At the Montreal airport instead of in the starting blocks. . . . Gone for what seems an unreasonable reason. . . . [But it was] their decision. . . . For those who remain, the Montreal Olympics just might become rewarding . . . when the athletes, at last, become the show."[55]

The "show" was the gymnast Nadia Comaneci, the five-foot, eighty-eight-pound Romanian phenom who scored a perfect 10 in seven different exercises to become, at the age of fourteen, the youngest all-around Olympic gold medalist in history. Olympic judges had never given a 10 before, and the scoreboard, set for a maximum score of 9.9, couldn't register it. In addition to Comaneci were the Soviet Viktor Saneyev, who finished first in the triple jump for his third consecutive Olympics; the American Bruce Jenner, who set a world record in the decathlon; and the Cuban Alberto Juantorena, who became the first and only athlete to date ever to win gold in both the 400 and 800 meters at the same Olympics. The Finn Lasse Viren won the 5,000- and 10,000-meter track events for the second time; Sugar Ray Leonard and the brothers Leon and Michael Spinks took gold in boxing; and the U.S. men's swimming team won gold in twelve of thirteen events.

The most dominating performance of the games was by East Germany, the dreaded GDR, whose team of 293 athletes earned 159 medals. Not counting multiple medals for team and relay events, the GDR won an astonishing 90 medals, including 40 gold. "That proves the success of our socialist system and our training methods," gushed Manfred Ewald, president of the East German Olympic Committee.[56] It also proved that massive government subsidies, residential sports schools, and a steroid called Oral-Turinabol really did work: the GDR won more gold medals than the United States. Athletes grumbled. The American swimmer Shirley Babashoff refused to shake hands with the East Germans and said at one point, "I wouldn't want to walk around my neighborhood looking like a guy."[57] The steroid issue haunted Montreal. So did cheating. A Soviet pentathlete by the name of Boris Onishchenko was thrown out of the Olympics for rigging his épée—they called him Boris Dis-Onishchenko—while Soviet officials were accused of trying to trade votes in the diving competition.

These were the embattled games, the $1.6-billion games that ended, fittingly enough, when a bearded twenty-three-year-old redhead named Michael Leduc streaked across the infield during the closing ceremonies. As more than one person wondered, would there be another Olympics? Probably. But Killanin warned he'd "pull the rug, even at the last minute," if the Soviets chose to politicize the games in 1980.[58] "The whole world is absolutely fed up with politicians interfering with sport," he said. "Governments should assist sport . . . but they should never get involved with it."[59] However, by May 1978, at the opening of the IOC's eightieth session in Athens, Killanin's biggest worry wasn't politics; it was cost, because the only city willing to bid for the Olympics, as noted, was Los Angeles, and Los Angeles had very specific demands. The city, under no circumstances, would either pay for or be responsible for the Olympics. Two private organizations, the Los Angeles Olympic Organizing Committee and the U.S. Olympic Committee, would.

Los Angeles "wanted a cast-iron guarantee against financial losses," one journalist wrote, and its mayor and city council loathed the idea of "leaving the tap running until the tub was full."[60] Residents did too. In a poll taken in late 1977 only 35 percent of Angelinos supported the use of city or county funds for the Olympics. They wanted the Olympics, to be sure—a full 70 percent did—they just didn't want to pay for them.[61] The solution, then, was a privately run, privately financed games with virtually no links to the city—in short, a corporate Olympics. It's "a new style of Olympics," said a city councilman, an Olympics "within resources and reason."[62] The IOC was appalled: a corporate Olympics? The Olympics were corporate enough already. Just two years earlier, at Innsbruck, the IOC had warned the athletes that "the display of any clothing or equipment . . . marked conspicuously for advertising" would result in disqualification.[63] Now the Olympics themselves were marked for advertising. (Cases in point: the McDonald's Olympic Swim Stadium and the 7-Eleven Olympic Velodrome both made appearances in Los Angeles.)

Commercialization was one thing. But what really angered the IOC was the "truculent attitude" adopted by the officials of Los Angeles.[64] By privatizing the games and absolving the city of responsibility, Los Angeles was asking the IOC to ignore the Olympic Charter, the *Bhagavad Gita* of sport. Rule 4 of the charter specifically stated that host cities were financially responsible for the games and that any organization that played "any part whatsoever" in the Olympics accepted "the supreme authority of the IOC." Los Angeles said no. "We're the only game in town," one councilman chirped. "We have to recognize that we hold the trump card and the IOC should recognize that too. We're the last hope for them."[65] It was "take it or leave it, Killanin," an approach that IOC officials found to be "rude," "belligerent," "arrogant, even insulting." The two sides girded for a fight. "The environment [in Athens] was worse than cool," wrote William Oscar Johnson of *Sports Illustrated,* it "was heavy with anger." One Los Angeles official remembered "conflict, constant conflict," in a "polarized" situation.[66]

Lost in the huff and unbeknownst to many journalists was the IOC's other Olympic business: the selection of a host city for the 1984 Winter Olympics. The surprise winner, in two rounds of voting, was Sarajevo, Yugoslavia, the city singularly known for its connection to World War I. Sarajevo was an odd choice. The city was distant, polluted, and almost completely devoid of a tourist trade. What is more, Yugoslavia had "never hosted the Olympics, summer or winter, and Sarajevo [wasn't] even a fashionable ski resort" where competitions were held.[67] "An Olympics in Sarajevo?" one journalist exclaimed skeptically. When the IOC announced its decision, some journalists couldn't even spell *Sarajevo.*

Others were hostile. "They are Balkan," one Austrian reporter spat. "They will never put it together. They can organize nothing. Their greatest moment in history came about only through the acts of fops and fools."[68] That wasn't true. But was it possible the IOC had made a mistake with Sarajevo? Under the circumstances, an untested city in an impoverished communist country was a terrible choice, especially since officials from Los Angeles had left the meeting in Athens without a contract. Even scarier was the very real possibility that the United States would boycott the 1980 Summer Olympics in Moscow. If it did, and if Los Angeles refused to host the 1984 Summer Olympics, the IOC was dead. There was "no doubt that Sarajevo [would put] its best foot forward for the Games," one observer wrote. "The problem [was] whether Sarajevo's best foot [was] good enough."[69]

2

The Swedish Prince

IN 1978 Sarajevo was the capital city of the Republic of Bosnia-Herzegovina, one of six republics within the Socialist Federal Republic of Yugoslavia. The country was led by an aging dictator named Josip Broz Tito, a communist war hero who in 1948 had taken Yugoslavia out of the Soviet Bloc. Under Tito, Yugoslavia was "socialist but not Soviet."[1] It was also neutral politically and divided its trade almost equally between East and West. Although not an ally of the United States, Yugoslavia enjoyed good relations with Washington and funded much of its development through American loans. As a result, by the 1960s Yugoslavia had one of the highest growth rates in the world, and its per capita gross domestic product in 1978 was roughly the equivalent of Portugal's.[2] However, the availability of cheap Western credit led to a culture of overborrowing. By 1976 Yugoslavia was $8 billion in debt, by 1982 it was $20 billion in debt, and by the mid-1980s it was one of the ten most deeply indebted nations in the world.[3] To pay down the debt, Yugoslavia attempted to earn hard currency by allowing its citizens to work temporarily in Western Europe as guest workers and by developing a thriving tourist industry on the Adriatic coast of Croatia.

Not to be outdone by its sister republic, Bosnia pitched skiing. The mountainous republic had several small resorts, including one on Mount Jahorina that had played host to the International Students' Winter Week, a kind of World University Games, in 1955. Near Jahorina and within a thirty-kilometer radius of Sarajevo were Mounts Igman and Bjelašnica, both potential ski sites, while Sarajevo itself had a sports hall, perhaps a dozen hotels, and a skating rink. But all of this meant potential tourism, not tourism in fact. Few foreigners ever ventured to Bosnia, and no winter sports enthusiast would have chosen Mount Jahorina over Innsbruck, for example, as a place to ski. Even within Yugoslavia, Bosnia was a distant second or perhaps third as a skiing location. Slovenia, Yugoslavia's northernmost republic bordering Austria, was first, with at least half a dozen ski centers, including one at Kranjska Gora which had held the Men's Alpine World Cup in 1969. To compete with Slovenia, Bosnia needed to make winter tourism a central aspect of its long-term developmental goals. But how? In socialist Yugoslavia, all business decisions, all matters of finance and investment, were made from the top down. That meant that the Central Committee of the Bosnian Communist Party, its officials, and especially its leader were, by necessity, on board. In the late 1960s the leader was Branko Mikulić, an ambitious young Croat who mixed hardline political repression with economic development. Mikulić inherited "a land in which the basic form of transport was the horse and cart," wrote the journalist Mile Stojić, and he and his compatriots "sought to make Bosnia equal" to other Yugoslav republics "by offering a developmental program that included thousands of schools and libraries, an asphalted road to every village," and "culture and education as . . . [a solution to] poverty."[4]

It helped, too, that in 1965 the Yugoslav government finally completed what tourist officials called "the watermill and trout route," a short but important highway connecting the Croatian capital of Zagreb with Sarajevo. It also finished a road from Sarajevo to Mostar, a town in western Bosnia, and one from Mostar to the village of Ploče on the Adriatic coast.[5] These routes opened Bosnia to tourists, but because the republic lacked hotels, tourist agencies, tourist information bureaus, and other key amenities, tourists didn't come. David Binder, a longtime Balkan correspondent for the *New York Times*, commented, "The further out from Belgrade [and further into Bosnia] a traveler goes, the deeper his impression [is] that [in Yugoslavia] haphazardness is a way of life."[6] However, Bosnia was beautiful. In size and topography, it was the Balkan equivalent of West Virginia. It had two national parks—including one, Sutjeska, that featured a primeval forest, one of only two in Europe—several Ottoman-era cities and bridges, and, of course, Sarajevo.

Founded in 1461 by the Ottoman general Isa-Beg Ishaković, Sarajevo took its name from the Turkish words *saray ovasi*, which meant "field around the saray" (*saray* was a Turkic word of Persian derivation meaning "home" or "palace"). Ishaković, a Slav, eventually conquered all of Christian Bosnia as a loyal servant of Sultan Mehmed II, the Ottoman leader who displaced the last Byzantine Greek emperor in 1453. Tiny at first, consisting of no more than a palace, a mosque, and a marketplace in a wide valley on the banks of the Miljačka River, by 1600 Sarajevo was the third largest Ottoman city in Europe, with a population of 23,500.[7] Sarajevo sat in a bowl, surrounded by five heavily wooded mountains: Treskavica (6,850 feet), Bjelašnica (6,781), Jahorina (6,276), Trebević (5,338), and Igman (4,928). The residents of Sarajevo were for the most part Muslims who, like Ishaković, were Bosnian Slavs who converted to Islam before moving to the city. They were joined in time by a small, though not insignificant, number of Orthodox and Catholic Christians as well as Sephardic and even Ashkenazic Jews. Each community lived according to its religion in a defined residential neighborhood called a *mahala*. In 1600 there were over one hundred Muslim mahalas in Sarajevo, each with a minaret, and perhaps three or four non-Muslim mahalas anchored by a church or synagogue.

The very heart of Sarajevo was Baščaršija, the marketplace, a warren of stores, workshops, bazaars, coffeehouses, mosques, and storerooms along the Miljačka River. Baščaršija, the Bosnian expert Robert J. Donia has written, "was the focal point of the city's common life in Ottoman times, where those of all faiths and classes mingled in front of shops and on the streets. Neither the activities conducted in the city's market area nor its appearance . . . changed very much from the city's founding until after the Second World War."[8] When, in 1878, Austria-Hungary occupied Bosnia and displaced the Ottoman Turks, it built scores of neo-Renaissance, neoclassical, neo-Gothic, and secession-style buildings to the west of Baščaršija but otherwise left the market alone. One Austrian-era building was the Gradska Vijećnica, or City Hall, made famous by a photograph from June 1914 of Archduke Ferdinand and his wife, Sophie, descending the building's steps toward a Gräf & Stift convertible car. Just minutes later the pair was shot and killed point-blank at the Latin Bridge on the edge of Baščaršija by a Bosnian Serb terrorist named Gavrilo Princip, a nineteen-year-old student who had been supplied and trained by Serbia and whose organization, Young Bosnia, wished to push Austria out of the Balkans.

The plan worked. In July 1914 Austria declared war on Serbia, Russia declared war on Austria, Germany backed Austria, France and Britain backed Russia, and soon much of the world was at war. Having suffered over five million dead and wounded and with its economy in tatters, in 1918 Austria-Hungary sued for peace. The terms of its treaties were severe: first, it divided itself into two countries, Austria and Hungary. Then Bosnia, Croatia, and Slovenia were combined with Serbia, whose king, a Serb by the name of Alexander Karađorđević, renamed the country Yugoslavia, or "Land of the Southern Slavs."[9] By this point the residents of Sarajevo had lived in three states within fifty years. In just two generations they'd seen Sarajevo westernize, modernize, and industrialize; they'd seen the arrival of railroads, apartments, streetcars, and light bulbs; and of public parks and city grids. Sarajevo had also changed demographically. Its population in 1921 was 78,173, of whom 37.9 percent were Muslims, 27.3 percent were Croats, and 23.8 percent were Serbs.[10] They all spoke a common dialect of Serbo-Croatian and shared a civic identity as residents of Sarajevo and a regional identity as Bosnians.

But whereas Bosnia's Muslims were a separate ethno-religious group unique to Bosnia, Bosnia's Serbs and Croats had clearly defined homelands of their own. Most Serbs, for example, wished to unify Bosnia with Serbia; some even denied nationhood to Bosnia's Muslims by insisting they were Muslim Serbs. Likewise, many Croats wished to unify Bosnia with Croatia and therefore described Bosnia's Muslims as "Croats of Muslim Faith."[11] Caught between two competing ideologies—a greater Serb ideology on the one hand and a greater Croat ideology on the other—the Muslims of Bosnia chose the one option open to them, that is, a multiethnic Yugoslavia. The Bosnian scholars Steven L. Burg and Paul S. Shoup write, "Because the new South Slav state included virtually all Serbs, Croats, and Muslim Slavs within its borders, the preservation of that state . . . became the *sine qua non* of Bosnian Muslim policy. This remained true through all the changes in regime that followed, until the collapse of Yugoslavia in 1991."[12] During the Second World War, for example, when Nazi Germany dismembered Yugoslavia and handed Bosnia to Croatia, Bosnia's Muslims joined Tito's Partisans "in droves."[13] They belonged to the Sixteenth Muslim Brigade, among other formations, and helped liberate Sarajevo on 6 April 1945.

What followed was a rapid period of postwar economic development. The new Yugoslavia was a socialist people's republic ruled by Tito, who decided, rather wisely, to "locate armaments factories and other strategically important industries" in remote regions of Bosnia.[14] Bosnia produced coal, iron ore, lead, zinc, manganese, and bauxite, while its steel and iron works at Zenica, a city thirty-five miles from Sarajevo, were the largest in the Balkans. Nevertheless, by 1971 the per capita income of Bosnia was just 66 percent of the national average. By contrast, Yugoslavia's two richest republics, Slovenia and Croatia, stood at 191 percent and 125 percent, respectively.[15] From 1952 to 1968 Bosnia also had the lowest growth rate of all the Yugoslav republics, and its illiteracy and infant mortality rates were high.[16] "Although Bosnia did make progress," one historian wrote, "its economic position [within] Yugoslavia remained precarious," and the republic "continued to be an 'underdeveloped' region that depended on federal funds for capital investments."[17]

When, in the 1960s, the Yugoslav government began to invest in tourism, Bosnian officials sought to entice federal funds by investing in tourism too. They also read and commissioned reports by the Organization for Economic Cooperation and Development (OECD), a Paris-based entity that had once administered the Marshall Plan but now worked to strengthen European economies by promoting better business practices as well as trade and tax policies to stimulate economic growth. In 1968 the OECD published a paper titled "Analysis of the Possibilities and Problems of Developing Winter Tourism in Yugoslavia" in which it claimed that Bosnia "had all the necessary conditions" to become a winter tourist center and that Sarajevo should consider an Olympic bid.[18] The report sat for a time, but in 1971 a Bosnian Serb professor by the name of Ljubiša Zečević visited the IOC headquarters in Lausanne, Switzerland. Zečević taught physical fitness and sport at the University of Sarajevo and advised a republican agency known as the Commission for Physical Culture. Zečević was connected politically and traveled to Switzerland to meet with the technical director of the IOC, Artur Takač, a fellow Yugoslav.[19]

Zečević had "an abundance of enthusiasm," Takač wrote. But Takač "dissuade[d] [him] on several counts, the most important being that it was too late to bid for the Games of 1976" and that "Sarajevo had no international reputation in winter sports." However, Takač "could see that my action was merely a delaying one and that [Zečević] . . . was determined to bring the Games to his city."[20] Certainly, Zečević was determined, as were the Commission for Physical Culture and its president, Ahmed Karabegović. Then in his thirties, Karabegović, an up-and-coming official, had been secretary general of the Central Committee of the Youth Organizations of Bosnia-Herzegovina, an important position, and in 1973 he had organized the World Table Tennis Championships in Sarajevo. It was Karabegović who asked Zečević to write a report on Sarajevo's chances of landing the Olympics, a report Zečević submitted to several key politicians, including Dragutin Kosovac and Rato Dugonjić, both leaders of the Bosnian government and avid skiers. Zečević also reported to Boris Bakrač, a high-ranking federal politician and a former mayor of Zagreb who was the lone Yugoslav member of the IOC. Bakrač "felt that we definitely needed to apply," Zečević recalled, but he said that organizing the games was very complicated. He even joked that Sarajevo should "go ahead and submit the bid, but pray to God we didn't get it!"[21]

In the meantime, independently of the commission's activities, city officials began a massive $72-million public works initiative funded by the International Bank for Reconstruction and Development, a division of the World Bank.[22] Called the Project for the Protection of [Sarajevo's] Human Environment, the undertaking received "voluntary financial contribution[s]" from the citizens of Sarajevo, who gave between 1.19 and 2.5 percent of their paychecks in four separate increments between 1962 and 1985.[23] Without a doubt this was the largest civic enterprise in the history of Sarajevo. It ultimately cleaned up the city's polluted infrastructure by installing completely new water and sewer systems, a solid waste disposal system, several coal plants, a citywide thermal plant, and a 117-kilometer-long natural gas pipeline from Zvornik to Sarajevo. The Project for the Protection of [Sarajevo's] Human Environment was a twenty-year undertaking in which every major street in Sarajevo was dug up and a new street with proper drainage and sewage put down. There was a new health center, a new maternity hospital, a bevy of schools, a park and sports hall, a sizable addition to the city's National Theatre, and a refurbished Academy of Arts.

With millions of dollars in play and a Bosnian government bent on using foreign credits to bankroll urban development, Sarajevo's officials began considering a bid for the 1984 Winter Olympic Games. Sarajevo's urban renewal project, the eventual information director of the Sarajevo games, Pavle Lukač, wrote, "seemed to aid the efforts of Olympic enthusiasts" and "is why the idea of organizing the Games . . . found greater support than it [otherwise would have]."[24] However, bids were submitted in four-year cycles, with six years between the selection of the host city and the actual hosting of the games. Thus bids for 1976 were submitted in 1970, bids for 1980 in 1974, and so forth. The one glaring exception was Innsbruck, which was awarded the 1976 games in 1973 after voters in Denver, as noted, refused to use state funds to pay for them. "When Denver backed out," Karabegović said, "the IOC was in a bind. We thought maybe, just maybe, we could host the Olympics. And that's when Zeko [Zečević] said to me, 'What do you think? Why don't we submit a bid?' So we went back to Dragutin Kosovac, who at the time was president of the Bosnian government, and Kosovac said he liked the idea, but that it was too soon. 'We still have this big project to finish,' he told us, 'but once we're further along we can think about the Olympics.' "[25]

Kosovac was right. In 1973 Sarajevo was a mess. According to its own internal figures, a full 30 percent of residents got their water not from city pipelines but from backyard wells. Outhouses were common; the city dump frequently burned trash in open pits. Waste from Sarajevo's sewer system flowed directly into the Miljačka, and air pollution emanating from sixty-five thousand stoves, four hundred large furnaces, and dozens of factories was "several times greater" than prescribed limits.[26] Winter was the worst, a time, in the words of one report, when smog "simply 'captured' the city, covering it . . . to the tops of the surrounding hills. While Mount Trebević was sunlit," it continued, "the temperature in the town was minus five degrees Celsius. . . . In the very center of the city, especially around big coal-consuming furnaces, soot covered everything."[27] "That's why we waited," Karabegović recalled. "The city had several key projects to complete. In fact, it had many projects to complete, and once those were done, sometime in the mid-1970s, a bid committee was formed."[28]

Called the Preparation Committee, Sarajevo's bid committee came into being in May 1977 and was appointed by the city's assembly. Its president was Dane Maljković, a recent mayor of Sarajevo who was assisted by sixteen other members whose main activity was to answer three IOC questionnaires.[29] Among the questions: Could Sarajevo "demonstrate that it had comprehensive air and rail transportation facilities?" "What sort of Olympic villages would it provide and where would they be located?" "How would the Games be financed?" In all, the IOC required the Preparation Committee to respond to a general questionnaire, a technical questionnaire, and a television and radio questionnaire and to provide letters of support from the Yugoslav Olympic Committee, the Sarajevo city government, and the Yugoslav federal government plus a refundable deposit of one hundred thousand Swiss francs.[30] The committee prepared and submitted the questionnaires in both English and French in October 1977. At this point several cities and regions had expressed interest in holding the games, including Chamonix and Sapporo; the cross-border Cerdagne region of Spain and France; the Three Valley region of France; the High Tatra region of Czechoslovakia; and Gothenburg, Sweden, which proposed to hold its events in sports facilities that were hundreds of kilometers apart. In the end three cities applied: Sarajevo, Gothenburg, and Sapporo.

Few people thought Sarajevo had a chance. In the world of winter sports the city quite literally was a nonentity, a nobody. It had no bobsled run, no luge run, no ski jumps, and no speed-skating rink; it had one small venue with artificial ice and a single functioning ski slope.[31] To tourists, Sarajevo was terra incognita, a place that was, according to the *Boston Globe,* "a long way from Dorchester."[32] It "doesn't quite have the ring of a weekend in Chamonix, a getaway to St. Moritz or even a few days in Aspen," the *Washington Post* opined. "There are no postcard-pretty shops offering the latest designer thermal underwear, no local yodeling, no horse-drawn sleighs with bells a-chiming, no cozy condos with blazing fires and HBO."[33] "[If you've] been to Harrisburg," the *Philadelphia Daily News* reported, "[then] you've seen Sarajevo."[34]

Sports Illustrated compared it to Fort Wayne, Indiana, while the *San Diego Union* called it "the Pittsburgh of Yugoslavia."[35] In reality, the only thing anyone knew about Sarajevo was that Franz Ferdinand had been killed there in 1914 and that Sarajevo had been a "code word for catastrophe ever since."[36] It's "somewhere in the central boondocks of Yugoslavia," wrote the *Calgary Herald,* and "no doubt you've dispensed with Sarajevo for [any number of] reasons, not the least of which are the hassle and cost of getting there."[37]

Yet Sarajevo did have an ace in the hole: Technical Director Artur Takač. A Yugoslav of Jewish descent from Varaždin, Croatia, Takač was "the technical right hand man" of the IOC presidents Brundage and Killanin and one of the top three people in Lausanne.[38] His career in sports spanned at least forty years: from his participation in the Yugoslavian junior track and field team at the Olympic youth camp of the 1936 Berlin games, to his membership in the leadership bodies of the International Amateur Athletic Federation (IAAF) and the European Athletic Association, to his role as technical director of the IOC. He'd been secretary general of the Yugoslav Track and Field Federation (1945–58), cofounder and president of the Belgrade sports club Partizan (1945), and a member of Yugoslavia's Olympic delegations to London (1948), Helsinki (1952), Rome (1960), and Tokyo (1964). Takač headed the Balkan Games (1958–61), managed the European team in the Europe versus America track and field championships in 1967, and served as an official at every European Athletic Championship between 1950 and 1974.

In 1968 he was the IAAF's technical advisor to the Olympic Games in Mexico City and served as a go-between between Brundage and the Mexican government after Mexican authorities gunned down hundreds of student protesters in a neighborhood of the city named Tlatelolco just days before the games. In 1969 Takač joined the IOC full-time and became "the guy every [Olympic] pooh-bah checked with before doing anything of a technical nature."[39] He supervised the 1972 games in Munich, where he assisted Brundage during the Israeli hostage crisis, the 1972 Winter Games in Sapporo, the 1973 African Games in Lagos, and the 1974 Asian Games in Tehran. He was the only foreign member of the organizing committee of the 1976 games in Montreal. Fluent in eight languages and friends with everyone he came into contact with, Takač had clout. "There wasn't anyone in the world of sport who didn't know Artur," Karabegović said. "If you applied for the Games or you hosted the Games, he was the person you called. Artur knew the Scandinavians, the Africans, the Soviets, the Americans. . . . He knew each IOC president personally, and was close friends with Juan Antonio Samaranch," the man who succeeded Killanin in 1980. "We knew at the very start of the process that we had to have Takač."[40]

At the time, Takač was vice president of the organizing committee of the 1979 Mediterranean Games, which were being held in Split, Croatia. He was also adviser to the 1978 European Indoor Athletic Championships in Milan, which is where Zečević found him in March 1977. "I [received] a phone call from the ubiquitous Zečević," Takač wrote, "[and he said,] 'We want the Winter Olympics' and '[we want you, Artur,] to help.' "[41] This time Takač said yes. Although not technically a member of Sarajevo's bid committee, over the next year Takač was instrumental in helping Sarajevo secure its Olympic bid. "My colleagues relied heavily upon my Olympic knowledge and contacts," he wrote. "I was acquainted with every IOC member and also the presidents and secretaries of the international winter sports federations."[42] These were the crucial contacts to have. In late 1977, for example, Takač paid a personal visit to Marc Hodler, a Swiss lawyer from Bern who was president of the International Ski Federation (FIS) and a voting member of the IOC. "Here I was in the role of salesman," wrote Takač, promoting Sarajevo over Sapporo and Gothenburg as the next Olympic site. Hodler was cautious and told Takač that Sarajevo was "an unknown quantity." He personally favored Sapporo, a convenient destination which had hosted the 1972 Winter Olympics and which he felt could "do the job again."[43]

Nevertheless, Hodler knew that what was convenient for the Olympics wasn't always convenient for winter sports. Since joining the IOC in 1963 he had clashed with Brundage over issues of amateurism and had long promoted the expansion of winter sports to new and exotic locales. In 1965, for example, Hodler's FIS held its Alpine World Championships in Portillo, Chile, still the only Alpine World Championships ever held in the southern hemisphere.[44] Takač knew this and asked Hodler point-blank, "[Isn't it] part of the philosophy . . . of the Olympic Movement to spread the celebration of the Games to new countries, [and] new sites?" The answer, of course, was yes. However, Takač then warned Hodler that if the IOC held the games twice in Innsbruck and twice in Sapporo, it would be giving "the impression that there [was] something of a crisis in winter sports."[45] Too late: there already was a crisis, for at that moment Hodler was at his wit's end with organizers of the 1980 Lake Placid Olympics, whose preparations were "practically zero."[46] The IOC made emergency plans to move the games to either Innsbruck or Grenoble, but since both cities had recently hosted the Olympics, awarding them the games again was opposed in principle. The same was true with regard to Sapporo and its bid for the 1984 Winter Games. But Sapporo had spent a whopping $500 million on the 1972 Olympics and had given "every indication that [its] push, though quiet and diplomatic," was real.[47] Sapporo's city council had voted unanimously to bid for the 1984 games, while its mayor, Takeshi Itagaki, insisted that because the city had already built its Olympic venues, the second Sapporo Olympics would not only reduce costs but also "take place without occasioning the destruction of . . . the environment."[48] Assisting Itagaki were Japan's two IOC members, Prince Tsuneyoshi Takeda, a relative of Emperor Hirohito and Japan's so-called Prince of Sport, and Masaji Kiyokawa, a member of the IOC executive board and the chief executive officer of Kanematsu-Gosho Ltd., one of the largest trading companies in Japan.

Sarajevo's other competitor was Gothenburg, a bustling port city in western Sweden that was home to Volvo motors. The city had hosted the World Figure Skating Championships in 1976 and had two of the best-equipped venues in Europe: the fifty-three-thousand-seat Ullevi Stadium, site of the 1958 World Cup soccer championships, and the twelve-thousand-seat Scandinavium arena. The problem, however, was that Gothenburg's nonstadium events were scheduled to take place in the distant cities of Åre, Hammarstrand, and Falun. Although possible in theory and permitted by the Olympic Charter, a regional Olympics had never been held before. In 1976 the organizers in Montreal had held yachting events in Kingston, Ontario, a distance of 180 miles. But that was yachting, a specialized sport. The Swedes were proposing a different animal altogether: a decentralized Olympics on a wide geographic scale. Åre, for example, where the men's and women's alpine events were located, was 570 miles from Gothenburg, while Hammarstrand, the venue of the luge events, was an equally distant 550 miles. But Swedish officials said not to worry: "All competitors . . . [would] be given the opportunity to attend the opening and closing ceremonies," and each site would have a fully equipped Olympic village. Swedish officials also said that IOC members, federation representatives, and heads of delegation would have "small, comfortable jet aircrafts and helicopters" at their disposal that would run continuously.[49]

To some, including Killanin, the Swedish bid was radical—indeed, too radical. In early 1978 Killanin said he had no desire "to prejudge" Gothenburg, but in his opinion a Swedish Olympics "would be more like a series of world championships than an Olympic Games."[50] The AP journalist Geoffrey Miller averred that most IOC members were horrified by the Swedish bid and believed that a single competition site "was firmly rooted in [de] Coubertin's original design."[51] Either way, the Swedes faced stiff opposition at the IOC's eightieth session in Athens, although the Olympic expert Doug Gilbert believed they'd finish ahead of the Yugoslavs. In fact, in a February 1978 article in the *Montreal Gazette,* Gilbert made no mention of Sarajevo and described the competition as Gothenburg versus Sapporo, a "new idea" versus a "heavy hitter from the past."[52] What Gilbert didn't know was that Takač had been working tirelessly behind the scenes and had contacted every IOC member personally. In addition, Zečević and Djordje Peklić, the head of the Yugoslav Olympic Committee, had been lobbying members from India, Cuba, France, Egypt, Algeria, Eastern Europe, and the USSR. "We were [just] seven votes short of victory," Takač wrote, but as the IOC convened in Athens in May 1978, "I could not see how we could get them."[53]

"I was mulling over these thoughts . . . [when] I saw Prince Bertil, the president of the Swedish Olympic Committee," Takač continued. "[On] an impulse I greeted His Highness." Over drinks and a bit of horse-trading the two men struck a deal: if Gothenburg and Sapporo survived the first round of voting and Sarajevo was out, Sarajevo would throw its votes to Gothenburg. Likewise, if Gothenburg was out, Bertil promised that all six Scandinavian members would vote, in a block, for Sarajevo.[54] The next day, on 18 May 1978, after presentations from all three bid committees and a brief question-and-answer session, the ballots were cast. In the first elimination round Sapporo received thirty-three votes, Sarajevo thirty-one votes, and Gothenburg ten. However, in round two Sarajevo picked up eight additional votes, including six, presumably, from Scandinavia, and defeated Sapporo thirty-nine to thirty-six.[55] Sarajevo was now the official host of the 1984 Winter Olympics. "We couldn't believe it," Karabegović said. "We knew we had a chance, but still, we couldn't believe it. We were thrilled, of course. Everybody was. The IOC had stuck to its principles and had given the Games to a new locale. But then it hit us. We'd won the Olympics. We'd actually won the Olympics. Six years seems like a long time, but we had lots to do."[56]

3

Nobody Changes Light Bulbs

IN FEBRUARY 1983 the journalist William Oscar Johnson and photographer Jerry Cooke drove the length of Yugoslavia, from Slovenia in the north to Macedonia in the south, to produce an itinerary of sorts for people traveling to the 1984 Winter Olympic Games. "[We left Vienna on] a snowy, pewter-colored day," Johnson wrote, "[but weren't] particularly festive. We were, after all, leaving the enormously civilized environs of Vienna—birthplace of the Sacher torte, the waltz and much of the best of Mozart—to spend the next three weeks in Yugoslavia."[1] The two men crossed at Maribor, Slovenia ("a bustling place full of fair Teutonic types"), then stopped at Lake Bled, a resort village high in the Julian Alps. In the luxurious Grand Hotel Toplice, where in 1961 the American chess master Bobby Fischer defeated the Soviet Mikhail Tal, they met with a man from the Lake Bled Tourist Association. "We asked him if he thought the Olympics in Sarajevo would be well run," Johnson wrote. "He frowned and said, 'Tourism is not traditional in Bosnia. There will be problems. . . . The big things, the competitions, will be very good. . . . [But] the problem is the small things. Nobody changes light bulbs. The running water stops and no one fixes it. These are small things. . . . But the small things . . . make [a] big mosaic everyone remembers after the Olympics."[2]

Johnson called it "provincial prejudice," for Slovenes typically viewed Bosnians as peasants and yokels and resented the fact that smoggy Sarajevo and not, say, Ljubljana, the Slovene capital, had landed the games. An Olympics in Bosnia? People told jokes about Bosnia, for everyone knew Mujo and Haso, the two Muslim ne'er-do-wells who were the Laurel and Hardy of Yugoslav jokes. The stereotype was that Bosnians were dumb. In one joke Mujo finished a puzzle. "Look, Haso!" he said. "It took me only a month, but the box here says three to five years." In another Mujo declared, "I think, therefore I am," then poof, he disappeared. Although crude and stupid, Bosnian jokes were common in Yugoslavia, as was the general belief that Muslims were lazy.[3] "The difference between Slovenia and Bosnia is plain," the tourist official said. "[The Muslims there] have [always] looked to Allah to produce for them and patiently wait until tomorrow if Allah does not do it today. . . . Do you know this word 'phlegmatically'? This is what may prevail in Sarajevo."[4]

Another belief, held mostly by elites in Slovenia, was that even a successful Olympics would be an economic boondoggle that cash-strapped Yugoslavia could ill afford. According to one estimate, the games would cost $103 million, paid for by the Yugoslav federal government, the Republic of Bosnia, and the city of Sarajevo.[5] This at a time when Yugoslavia's annual inflation rate topped 23 percent and its trade deficit was $4.3 billion.[6] Led by the conservative politician France Popit, Slovenian officials argued that Sarajevo had no business hosting the Olympics because Bosnia was an underdeveloped region and the recipient of federal aid. In fact, Bosnia, Macedonia, Montenegro, and Kosovo each received money from a federal development fund paid for by Slovenia, Serbia, and Croatia. The fund was enormous, amounting to an annual contribution of 1.85 percent of the donor republics' gross social product.[7] The recipient republics then used the money in whatever way they saw fit. "Much of it was wasted," wrote the scholar Mihailo Crnobrnja, mostly "on prestigious projects or conspicuous consumption. . . . [Therefore,] the Slovenes insisted on having more say over how the money was spent."[8]

According to the Bosnian politician Raif Dizdarević, the Slovenes were so opposed to the Olympics that in spring 1979 they petitioned Tito directly, as the eighty-seven-year-old president was the undisputed leader and arbiter of Yugoslav affairs. The Slovenes "set out the dismissive view that the Olympics would be a major expenditure at a time of economic difficulties," Dizdarević wrote, and actually told Tito "the Games should not be hosted. . . . [We] regarded [this] as extremely improper."[9] If Tito said no to the Olympics there would be no Olympics. Panicked, in June 1979 Dizdarević and his fellow politician Nikola Stojanović visited Tito at Brioni, a secluded island off the coast of Croatia where the president conducted business. Winston Churchill, Nikita Khrushchev, Gamal Nasser, Fidel Castro, Muammar Kaddafi—they'd all visited Brioni, and Dizdarević, the chairman of Bosnia's federal presidency, was next. "[We] informed President Tito . . . of the multi-faceted international importance of and the benefits to be gained from being chosen as the host city. . . . [We also told him] of our firm resolve to treat [the Olympics] as a development project with lasting benefits." The Slovenes, they argued, had "failed to understand the significance of the Games" and wanted the Bosnians to "give them up." Tito responded, "Yes, I heard that too," but he commended Sarajevo's efforts and refused, ultimately, to interfere. "Just go on as you've begun," he said.[10]

The bigger issue was Tito himself—he was dying. The aging dictator suffered from arteriosclerosis, an illness that, as one observer wrote, "could not have come at a more unsettling time."[11] Tito, when he died in May 1980, had no clear successor; his chief aide and confidant, Edvard Kardelj, had died in February 1979, and no leader was strong enough or popular enough to replace him. The solution was the formation of a nine-man collective presidency, whose membership included one representative from each of Yugoslavia's six republics and two autonomous regions as well as the president of the League of Communists of Yugoslavia. The new presidency had a rotating chair. The person who held the chair was Yugoslavia's head of state and president for a period of one year. Therefore, the first president was a Macedonian, the second a Bosnian, the third a Slovenian, and so on. It's a "complex system," one reporter wrote, "intended to prevent anyone from rising to a dictatorial level and to give each" of Yugoslavia's constituencies "an equal say."[12] The presidency looked good on paper, but the question was, would it work? "Collective leadership is not normal," said Milovan Djilas, Yugoslavia's famed dissident. "It is not natural for the politics of our system."[13] Experts feared the country might fall victim to internal unrest, mainly in the form of Croatian or Albanian independence movements or perhaps a foreign invasion.

Belgrade had been free of Moscow since 1948, but observers believed a leaderless Yugoslavia "could invite Soviet meddling—perhaps even a bid by the Kremlin to re-impose Russian control."[14] But the chances were slim. Yugoslavia had a standing army of 250,000 men and women plus reservists and partisans numbering 1 to 2 million. In the case of an invasion, Tito's plan was to meet the Soviets in the open country north of Belgrade. There, army units would stall the invader momentarily while irregular forces took up arms and fled to the mountains. Tito called it his Total People Defense Force and guaranteed that "every citizen, irrespective of sex, age, or occupation," would resist.[15] At one point Yugoslavia staged "Nothing Will Surprise Us" drills and tested its workers by sending supposed agents provocateurs to its factories.

"The Russians can come any time," said one official, but "there'll be war."[16] In response, the Soviets scoffed. Moscow had no plans to invade Yugoslavia and denied what it called an "absurd fabrication" dreamed up by the West. "The Soviet Union firmly abides by and endeavors to develop . . . friendly relations" with Yugoslavia, Premier Leonid Brezhnev stated. These relations were based on "internationalist comradely voluntary cooperation," he said, and "absolute non-interference in [Yugoslav] affairs."[17]

Brezhnev was the man who in 1968 had sent two hundred thousand troops into Czechoslovakia and whose Brezhnev Doctrine declared that if a socialist country was threatened it was Moscow's duty to intervene. The Soviets used the doctrine to justify their invasion of Afghanistan in December 1979, when the socialist government of Nur Muhammad Taraki was overthrown by Hafizullah Amin. The invasion led to a 104–18 vote in the UN General Assembly calling for the "immediate, unconditional, and total withdrawal" of all Soviet troops from Afghanistan.[18] In addition, the United States halted technology shipments to Russia, embargoed grain sales, and started a clandestine program to arm the mujahedeen. In January President Jimmy Carter issued an ultimatum: if the Soviets failed to leave Afghanistan within one month, America would boycott the 1980 Summer Olympics in Moscow.

"That was a nervous time for us," said Karabegović, who in 1978 was named secretary general of the Sarajevo Olympic Organizing Committee (SOOC). "Tito had just had his leg amputated, and people thought that without Tito, Yugoslavia was doomed. There were some who also thought that if the Americans boycotted the Moscow games, the Olympics were doomed, too."[19] Karabegović remembers that when Carter issued the ultimatum, he and a team of SOOC officials were in Sarajevo at the Hotel Europa listening to bid proposals from American television companies wishing to broadcast the games. The Sarajevans expected to be paid tens of millions of dollars, for ABC had paid $21 million for the Lake Placid games in 1976 and $10 million for the Innsbruck games in 1973. This was a 110 percent increase in three years, the result largely of the efforts of Roone Arledge, the innovative president of ABC Sports. Arledge had been with the network since 1960 and had what the sports announcer Howard Cosell called that "intuitive genius, that sixth sense . . . [of] what would or wouldn't play on television."[20] Arledge wanted drama—lots and lots of drama. In a memo to ABC written soon after he arrived at the network, Arledge outlined how he'd televise a football game: "[I'd use] cameras mounted in jeeps, on mike booms, or . . . [on] helicopters," he wrote, to get shots that "we cannot get from a fixed camera—a coach's face as a man drops a pass in the clear . . . a pretty cheerleader just after her hero has scored a touchdown . . . a student hawking programs in the stands." More than a football game, what Arledge wanted was a human interest story of "excitement, wonder, jubilation and despair."[21]

"The basic concept of everything we [did]," Arledge said, was that "people [were] interested in people."[22] This was the leitmotif of ABC's program *Wide World of Sports,* which Arledge created, and of six Olympic broadcasts he produced between 1964 and 1976. Viewers loved it. "It didn't matter [if] the United States won only one gold medal to the Soviet's eleven," Arledge remembered, "or [if] ABC ran the programs in the worst possible time slots: the more they aired, the bigger the audience grew."[23] By the summer of 1972, for example, ABC's Olympic broadcast reached a nightly audience of 16.2 million homes. Four years later, it reached 16.8 million homes, a 47 percent market share that made the Olympics America's number one television program for seven nights in a row.[24] Although the Winter Olympics attracted fewer viewers than the Summer Olympics, the 1976 games at Innsbruck attracted more viewers, by segment, than either CBS or NBC. "What nobody seems to understand in this country," a network spokesman said "is that the Olympics transcend . . . everything. Look, in U.S. rating circles any show that hits 30 percent" is considered "a hit." For "two weeks in Innsbruck we averaged 34 percent overall and had a high of 40 percent."[25]

In fact, ABC's Innsbruck coverage was so successful that its unusually high ratings carried over into other network shows. *Happy Days, The Six Million Dollar Man,* and *Laverne & Shirley* all experienced what critics called the Olympic bump. ABC's ratings "bonanza," the *New York Times* reported, "came not from entertainment, but from sports," in particular "its extraordinary coverage of the Winter and Summer Olympics."[26] NBC and CBS took note. Both networks wanted the Olympics badly, especially NBC, which had just had the worst year, ratings-wise, in its thirty-seven-year history. Therefore, in February 1977 NBC aggressively pursued the 1980 Moscow games, which it won with an $87-million bid. Then, in September 1979, ABC won back the Olympics at Los Angeles with a whopping $225-million bid. "Perhaps we did pay a bit more than we had to for the Olympics," Arledge said. "[But] look, if we're going to blow money, let's do it on the Olympics, not some bush-league thing."[27] Representatives from all three networks were in Sarajevo in January 1980. "The men from NBC were nervous," Karabegović said. They'd asked for a thirty- to sixty-day moratorium on bid negotiations while Carter's boycott threat was sorted out.[28] As it stood, NBC had already paid the Soviets $61 million. The network had insured its investment through Lloyd's of London but faced programming and profit losses of at least $45 million.

In a statement to the press, NBC explained that owing to "unresolved questions about the 1980 [Summer] Olympics" it couldn't negotiate in Sarajevo because this was "an inappropriate time."[29] However, as Karabegović explains, the Bosnians couldn't wait. Since winning the bid in May 1978, they'd formed an interim organizing committee with the mayor of Sarajevo, Anto Sučić, as its head and Karabegović as its secretary general, but they'd yet to build any buildings. They'd set up boards that had planned all construction, accommodation, sport, information, and finance, but, as Karabegović told the IOC, "funds were lacking."[30] Sarajevo "needed the money 'up front,'" wrote one scholar, "which it was likely to get only if it concluded a television deal quickly. Delay was anathema."[31] Thus, when NBC's representatives asked for an extension, Karabegović said no. "I remember being absolutely, totally disheartened by the news," said Geoff Mason, an NBC negotiator at Sarajevo and vice president of NBC Sports. "Neal Pilson from CBS came down to my room and said, 'Mase, give us a break! You've got to submit a competitive number. If you don't, this whole thing could fall apart.'"[32]

What Pilson didn't know, however, was that Sarajevo was desperate for money and that ABC had told Karabegović that the network "was so eager to obtain the Games that [it] would . . . agree to any figure put forward." In addition, ABC's two representatives, John Martin and Georges Croses, had asked Karabegović to keep them "informed of CBS's offer."[33] However, the IOC had told the SOOC on several occasions that bids were confidential and that it should "not exchange . . . information from one bidder to the other." It also insisted that negotiations in Sarajevo were preliminary and that a second, final meeting would take place in Lausanne. Why? Because the IOC owned the Olympics "lock, stock, and barrel."[34] It derived almost all of its income from the sale of television rights and claimed, by contract, one-third of any amount paid to the SOOC. This was the so-called Rome formula, which the IOC, its one hundred or so National Olympic Committees (NOCs), and the International Sport Federations (ISFs) had agreed to in 1966. Under its terms, the host city kept two-thirds of all television monies, while the IOC kept one-third, which it shared equally with the ISFs and the NOCs.[35] The formula seemed fair, but while the IOC, the NOCs, and the ISFs made tens of millions of dollars, they paid nothing to Sarajevo, which was assuming all the risk.

In 1969 the organizers in Munich sidestepped the Rome formula by insisting that its $13.5-million contract with ABC had two parts: a $7.5-million television rights fee and a $6-million technical services fee. The rights fee was subject to the formula, but the technical services fee was not.[36] The next four Olympics—Innsbruck, Montreal, Lake Placid, and Moscow—all used similar tactics to maximize television rights while limiting the amount they sent to the IOC. In one instance, Montreal's organizers sold the games' Canadian rights to the Canadian Broadcasting Company (CBC) for $1. The CBC had given the organizers perhaps $25 million in goods and services, hence the $1 token payment.[37] Naturally, the IOC was apoplectic. Television rights paid for its Lausanne operation, which included a staff of twenty in an eighteenth-century mansion called the Château de Vidy that it used as its headquarters. Lord Killanin lived in Ireland, and affairs in Lausanne were handled by Monique Berlioux, a former French Olympian who was the day-to-day administrative head of the IOC. Tough, imperious, and rigid, Berlioux was to many the real IOC president. She ran the organization "like [a] headmistress at a Swiss finishing school."[38] "I hate being disappointed," she once said. "Those who disappoint me, I prefer not to see them anymore. I wash them from my memory."[39]

Known simply as Madame, Berlioux could veto, directly or indirectly, any contract associated with the IOC. "Her blessing [was] the Olympic seal of approval," wrote Peter Ueberroth, who dealt with Berlioux as head of the LA'84 organizing committee. "If she was on your side, you had clear sailing." But if "she sensed any Olympic Charter violations or potential damage to the movement, there was no more formidable foe." In September 1979 Berlioux approved a contract for Los Angeles that had a $100-million rights fee and a $125-million technical services fee. Thus Lausanne's cut was $33.3 million, more money, wrote Ueberroth, than it had ever had.[40] In fact, the Los Angeles money emboldened Berlioux, for instead of allowing Sarajevo to subtract a technical services fee, which other Olympics had done, she demanded one-third of its *entire* television contract. Madame was miffed, it seems, at Karabegović, who had ignored IOC instructions by soliciting final bids in Sarajevo without advising or getting input from Lausanne. The two IOC observers in Sarajevo, Daniel Montureux and Alain Coupat, both told Karabegović "endlessly" that "contracts concerning radio and television [could] only be negotiated and concluded jointly . . . and to the IOC's benefit."[41] They also told him that final negotiations should take place in Lausanne.

Nevertheless, Karabegović ignored the two men, then went back and forth between networks to solicit the highest bid. CBS offered $90 million, which ABC countered with a winning bid of $91.5 million. This was more money than any network had ever paid for broadcast rights to the Winter Olympics, and the second-highest amount for any Olympics ever. "Prestige, primetime promotion, and profit," wrote the AP, "[are what] motivated ABC."[42] Karabegović and the SOOC expected that at least $45 million of the $91.5-million contract would be given to Sarajevo as a technical services fee. That meant the remainder, $46.5 million, would be split, according to the Rome formula, between the SOOC and the IOC. But Berlioux held firm. She demanded one-third not of $46.5 million but of $91.5 million and prolonged the negotiations through the summer of 1980. The longer she waited, the more desperate Karabegović became. In May he informed Berlioux in Lausanne that he couldn't comprehend "why the IOC did not understand who was going to pay [for Sarajevo's] costs," to which Berlioux retorted, "It was not [the IOC's place] to bow to the rules" of Sarajevo.[43]

Eventually, in June 1980, Berlioux accepted a small decrease, from 33 percent to 27.5 percent, which gave the IOC a $25-million share. Sarajevo's cut was $66.5 million. The problem, however, was that Sarajevo's contract with ABC was "back loaded," that is, three of its five payments, or $46.5 million, came just before the Olympics or even after the Olympics were over.[44] The first check, for $10 million, was due within thirty days of the signing of the contract. A second check for $10 million was due on 1 November 1982. The rest of the money, in sums of $11 million, $15 million, and $20.5 million, was due in January, February, and March 1984. There were other foreign incomes, including $11.2 million from the sale of broadcast rights to non-American networks, of which the IOC took a third, $11.6 million in sponsorships and licensing fees from companies such as Coke, Pan Am, Mattel, and Mitsubishi, and approximately $8.5 million from tickets, advertising, taxes on foreign visitors, duty-free sales, and the like.[45] However, the earliest anyone paid anything to Sarajevo was 1981. Mizuno, for example, the official designer of the Torch Relay Shoe, paid $300,000 in four installments between November 1981 and February 1984.[46]

Although the Yugoslav federal government, the Bosnian republican government, and the city of Sarajevo had all pledged to support the Olympics, in the summer of 1980 the SOOC was broke. It was so broke that in September, Karabegović actually asked the IOC for a $10-million loan, on top of the $10 million he'd already received from ABC. The SOOC had hoped that all three constituents—the federal government, the Bosnian government, and the city—would split the cost of the Olympics three ways. It had even told the IOC in a report in January 1979 that a "financing agreement . . . [of] 1/3 each [was] almost approved."[47] It wasn't. Tito died in May 1980, and in June federal authorities announced an economic stabilization plan in which they devalued the dinar by 30 percent. They had hoped that by devaluing the currency they could curb the country's huge trade imbalance by making Yugoslav goods cheaper to buy abroad. In addition, they fixed prices on food, gas, and other commodities and limited the use of bank credits to combat inflation. As it stood, Yugoslavia had the highest inflation rate in Europe at 27 percent and the highest unemployment rate in Europe, 12 percent, as well as a trade deficit of $6 billion. It owed $13 billion to foreign banks.[48]

"The situation demands that we learn to live for a time with reduced supplies of energy and raw materials," insisted one official, with "limited amounts of foreign currency for imports, [and] smaller consumption. We can only spend so much as we produce."[49] Although utterly essential, Yugoslavia's economic stabilization plan hit people where it hurt. Gasoline, coffee, cooking oil, laundry detergent, and other essential imports were rationed. In Belgrade, for example, residents used coupons to buy 5.3 grams of coffee per month. They received two pints of cooking oil, two pounds of detergent, and ten gallons of gasoline per month.[50] For the first time since the 1950s Yugoslavs stood in line. In Titograd, the capital of Montenegro, a riot erupted when a local radio station announced that laundry detergent was on sale. Rioters looted, smashed windows, and fought battles with police in which twenty people were injured. Somehow residents still managed to buy (or hoard) sixty-five tons of laundry detergent in five hours.[51] In October 1981 the Yugoslav national airline, JAT, announced it was canceling its Paris and Munich flights and scores of domestic flights for lack of kerosene.[52] Mining, oil refining, and steel and iron production all suffered shortages in petroleum, while several large power plants, including a nuclear plant, were idle.[53]

"The system is in economic collapse," one observer claimed, anonymously. "But we can't change the system without changing the structure. In economics, we need more of a free market. In politics, we need more pluralism. In government, we need more central authority. For forty years, we were not supposed to discuss such matters, but now we can and do."[54] In late 1980, for example, a Croatian politician told Stana Tomašević-Arnesen, the president of the Federal Chamber of Yugoslavia, that Sarajevo's Olympic program "would be a financial fiasco" and requested, as part of the spending cuts required by Yugoslavia's stabilization program, that the Olympics be canceled.[55] In response, Mayor Sučić affirmed that any investment in the games would "prove to be manifoldly remunerative" and that, contrary to rumors, revenues from foreign firms interested in organizing the games "had exceeded expectations."[56] Nevertheless, by fall 1980 the press regularly described Sarajevo as being "financially troubled," and one newspaper, the *Kärntner Tageszeitung* of Austria, ran a headline that read, "Yugoslavs Do Not Have Money—Innsbruck Instead of Sarajevo?"[57]

Adding pressure to Sarajevo and its efforts to organize the Olympics was Lake Placid. From day one, the Olympics held there in 1980 had been a financial and organizational disaster. Back in 1974 the Lake Placid candidature committee had claimed that preparations for the 1980 Winter Olympics would cost just $22 million.[58] However, inflation, cost overruns, price gouging, and several well-publicized scandals pushed the final bill to over $150 million. A sleepy village in the remote Adirondack region of New York, Lake Placid had a population of 2,700. It had one stoplight and one high school, and it was thirty miles from the interstate highway via a desolate two-lane road. Fearing gridlock, officials limited access to 51,000 spectators per day and diverted traffic to one of three parking lots ten or so miles from Lake Placid, where they shuttled passengers by bus. At least, that was the plan. But after a bitter dispute arose between the Teamsters Union and a Canadian company tasked with handling the games, only 117 buses were in use on opening day.[59] Spectators stood and stood and stood. At one point 12,000 people were stranded in nine-inch snow in wind-chill temperatures of minus ten degrees, some, oddly enough, in tennis shoes and sandals. What started as a logistical nightmare turned into a health hazard. Governor Hugh Carey declared a limited state of emergency and ordered state police to form a thirty-mile perimeter around Lake Placid that only residents and ticketed spectators could enter.[60]

Carey sent in several dozen public school buses and asked Greyhound, the intercity bus company, to intervene. In the meantime over a thousand people who had tickets to the opening ceremonies missed the event because they were stranded at another venue seven miles away.[61] The five-member Horack

family of California had tickets to the speed-skating events but arrived at
Lake Placid just as they concluded. "We got here for the tail-end of the wom-
en's 1,000," huffed an angry Mrs. Horack. "With airfare, using up our vacation
time and everything else, we're out about $1,500. I don't know who or what,
but if there is any way, we're going to sue."[62] The Horacks were lucky. They
at least saw the event. Others had tickets but sat in buses or in parking lots
and never did arrive. According to one report, on day three of the Olympics,
44,795 people had tickets to events but only 29,500 attended. Perhaps most
revealing was the USA–Norway hockey match, which the American team
won in front of just 1,100 fans.[63] The press, both foreign and domestic, jeered.
"This is the second worst thing I've ever been involved in," an Italian journalist said. "The first is World War II."[64] United Press International described
Lake Placid as "disorganized chaos," while a dismayed British reporter called
it "Apocolympics Now."[65]

"Lake Placid was just too small," Karabegović asserted. "There were only a
few roads in or out, and the press center was a high school. I don't know why
the bus system didn't work, but I can tell you it was a catastrophe—a complete
and total catastrophe. I think, too, that [Cyrus] Vance's speech tainted the
Games from the start."[66] Vance, the U.S. secretary of state, addressed the IOC
in Lake Placid. Sent to New York by Jimmy Carter, he told the committee that
since the Soviets had no plans to leave Afghanistan, the Moscow Summer
Olympics should be canceled or moved. "The ancient games were held in the
city-state of Elis," Vance intoned. "They marked a 'truce of the gods.' During this truce, open warfare against or by the host city-state was forbidden.
In the view of my government, it would be a violation of this fundamental
Olympic principle to conduct or attend Olympic Games in a nation which is
currently engaging in an aggressive war."[67] Killanin was appalled. Opening
speeches at IOC sessions were "purely ceremonial," he explained, but Vance
was "trying to torpedo the Games."[68] It didn't work. The seventy-three IOC
members present, including two Americans, voted against Vance's plan. "I
don't want to be provocative," claimed Killanin, "but the United States was
fighting in Cambodia at the time the current Winter Games were allocated.
. . . I think it's the same thing with the Olympics in Moscow. . . . What the
Soviets have done in Afghanistan doesn't change the circumstances under
which the Games were awarded."[69]

Carter was not deterred. On 20 February his one-month withdrawal dead-
line came and went. It was official: America would boycott the games. The

problem, however, was that it was not the U.S. government that sent athletes to the Olympics; the nonprofit USOC did. Carter could have issued an executive order banning all travel to Russia, but what he needed was a show of support from the USOC. The USOC president, Robert Kane, had said publicly that he'd accept any decision the president made, but that for him to call a boycott of the games he required a yes vote in the USOC's House of Delegates. The vote was scheduled for April. But rather than wait for the vote, Carter played hardball. With help from Lloyd Cutler, his White House counsel and Olympics expert, he pressured the USOC by threatening, first, to revoke its status as a nonprofit organization, meaning it would have to pay taxes, and then to renegotiate the lease on its training facility in Colorado Springs. Carter also leaned on fifty corporate sponsors, the organization's lifeblood, and promised to obstruct legislation calling for a one-dollar check-off box in which people could donate to the USOC through their tax returns.[70] Kane called Carter's tactics repugnant. They were unproductive, he said, not to mention needless because "we said right from the start that . . . [we would] follow the President's advice. . . . We never departed from that."[71]

The House of Delegates voted 1,604 to 797 to boycott the games. They'd been strong-armed, true, but a Roper Poll conducted in March 1980 found that USOC delegates favored a boycott more than the average American did—69 percent to 58 percent.[72] As one delegate put it, "You have to put the interests of your country first. Heaven help us if we don't do that."[73] But what were Yugoslavia's interests? Some sixty countries, including Israel and Iran, joined Carter's boycott, but if Yugoslavia boycotted the Moscow games, the Soviets would retaliate by boycotting the Sarajevo games. Besides, the Yugoslavs were angry at Carter. When Tito died in May 1980, those attending the funeral included Leonid Brezhnev, Margaret Thatcher, Erich Honecker, Helmut Schmidt, Indira Gandhi, Robert Mugabe, Nicolae Ceausescu, Kurt Waldheim, Hua Guofeng, and Hafez al-Assad, among others. There were twenty-nine heads of state, twenty-seven prime ministers, forty-seven foreign ministers, four kings, five princes, and two sheiks—but no Carter.[74] Instead, Washington sent Vice President Walter Mondale, Deputy Secretary of State Warren Christopher, and Carter's mother. One U.S. diplomat said, defensively, "We have nothing to apologize for. Mondale is a major figure."[75] Carter blamed the Iranian hostage crisis—"a trip under these circumstances [is] not appropriate," explained one staffer—but in reality he refused to meet or even be seen with Brezhnev.[76]

The Soviet premier had flown to Belgrade for the funeral just hours after meeting with Killanin. The two men spoke in the Kremlin, where Killanin pleaded with Brezhnev to do something—anything—"to avoid the . . . destruction of the Games."[77] A week later in Washington he made a similar plea to Carter. "The President asked me what he could do to help the Olympic Movement. . . . I replied that the most helpful thing he could do was [to allow his athletes] . . . to go to Moscow. . . . [His] smile vanished for a second, and he replied that of course this was not possible."[78] Boycott notwithstanding, the Olympics began in Moscow in July 1980. Eighty-one countries participated, the lowest number since 1956. Estimates vary, but it's possible the Soviet Union spent $9 billion on the games, a staggering amount considering that perhaps one hundred thousand foreigners attended.[79] Some Olympic squads, most notably Britain's, participated in the games without their government's support. Nevertheless, so few athletes participated, the journalist Christopher Booker noted, that when teams lined the infield during the opening ceremonies you could see the grass.[80] Missing, too, were nineteen members of the Afghan field hockey team, killed in a mujahedeen ambush near Kunduz. In a statement issued by Tass, the Soviet news agency, the three surviving members blamed not the insurgents but the boycott mandated by Carter.[81]

In retrospect, the effects of the boycott are unclear. The UK *Guardian* called it "a mess, a stand-off, a no-score draw."[82] On the field, the Soviets won more medals, an astounding 195, than any country has ever won in a single Olympics. The East Germans won 126, and together they won more medals than all other participating countries combined. Yet the Soviets had spent billions on the games, much of it hard currency they simply didn't have. Like the Yugoslav dinar, the ruble wasn't convertible, and the USSR had hard currency debts of $21 billion dollars. It owed $58.5 billion by 1989.[83] Like most cities, Moscow had hosted the games as a public relations move, but with sixty-one countries missing, the showcase was a bust. For America, on the other hand, the boycott was only moderately successful. Although sixty-one absentee countries may seem like a lot, only five were members of NATO. France, Italy, Britain, the Netherlands, Belgium, Greece, Luxembourg, Portugal, Denmark, and Iceland all had teams in Moscow, as did Australia, New Zealand, Sweden, Ireland, and America's "territory appurtenant," Puerto Rico. Carter himself suffered, for the same Americans who supported the boycott refused to support him at the polls in the 1980 election. The boycott wasn't the reason he lost, but it was "politically damaging," he wrote, and athletes blamed Carter for dashing their Olympic dreams.[84] "Carter said 'we' [were] going to boycott the Olympics," the rower Anita DeFrantz charged. "I [didn't] understand the 'we.'"[85]

The bigger question in 1980 was, would the Olympics survive? In October 1978 the Los Angeles Olympics Organizing Committee (LAOOC) finally got a contract. It would host the Summer Olympics, but the city of Los Angeles would not be liable. Instead, the games would be financed privately, and the LAOOC and the USOC would assume the risk. The money was there—in September 1979 ABC agreed to pay $225 million for the games' broadcast rights—but what if the Soviets bowed out? Could a "for-profit" games with tight margins handle a communist boycott? What would Arledge do with two hundred hours of coverage when half of the world's world champions were absent?[86] It was within this maelstrom that Sarajevo began organizing its games. Tito was dead. The country was broke. Ethnic and political tensions were rising. And there were riots in Kosovo. Observers took note. "In Sarajevo, the IOC has picked another potential . . . hot spot," wrote the CIA analyst David Kanin. "Yugoslavia is rent with ethnic ferment and, with Tito's death, could conceivably face political ferment [as well]. . . . It is to be hoped that the Balkans will be quieter during the 1984 Winter Olympics than when the Archduke of Austria-Hungary paid a visit to Sarajevo seventy years before."[87] The columnist George Will had a smarmier take. Sarajevo "will be the site of the 1984 Winter Olympics," he wrote, "if there is an Olympics, and a Yugoslavia, and a 1984."[88]

4

No Amount of Slivovitz

Vučko was a wolf, a skinny cartoon wolf with big eyes, a long, pointy snout, and a bulbous nose. Designed by the painter Jože Trobec of Slovenia, Vučko had beaten out Snowball, Weasel, and Lamb to become the official mascot of the 1984 Winter Olympics. He was cute, clearly, but for some reason his fingers were crossed. When asked why, Pavle Lukač, the games' press director, replied, "[So] nothing can go wrong."[1] Lukač was joking—sort of. Planning the games was a huge undertaking. In fact, it took two full years, from May 1978 to May 1980, for the SOOC to simply assess its needs.

They were, in a word, vast. Sarajevo had one sports hall with artificial ice, trails for cross-country and biathlon on Mount Igman, and a single ski facility on Mount Jahorina. That was it: a skating rink, a so-so collection of mountain trails, and a ski slope. Virtually every town in New Hampshire had more facilities than that. To host the games, Sarajevo needed a second ski resort, two new ice rinks, a speed-skating oval, a luge run, a bobsled run, 70- and 90-meter ski jumps, and a shooting range. But those were just the sports facilities. Now add roads—100 miles of roads—sewer lines, power lines, telephone lines, parking lots, ski lifts, bathrooms, locker rooms, restaurants, a state-of-the-art radio and television facility, a press facility, an expanded airport and railroad station, a renovated theater, 9 new hotels, 5 refurbished hotels, 2 Olympic villages, and a press village. In all, the city was faced with constructing 163 major projects involving tens of thousands of workers.

Construction began in earnest in April 1980 with the clearing of seven separate runs and men's alpine facilities on Mount Bjelašnica. At 6,781 feet, Bjelašnica was the second tallest of Sarajevo's five surrounding mountains and was twenty-one miles from the city. Although the mountain was largely uninhabited, there were ten small villages on Bjelašnica, including Lukomir and Umoljani, where locals practiced a seminomadic lifestyle as herders. According to one SOOC publication, life here was so remote that locals called themselves Planinštaci, an archaic word meaning "mountain folk," and divided the world into two groups: those down the mountain to the south and west were Humljaci (a very old name for Herzegovinians), while those to the north and east were Bošnjaci (Bosnians).[2] Bjelašnica was thickly wooded. To inspect the site and all of its courses, in April 1980 Peter Baumgartner, a technical delegate from the International Ski Federation (ISF), hiked each run, a total of eight thousand feet in two days.[3] Baumgartner was impressed. Workers had clear-cut trees for a downhill course, five supplementary courses, and a combined course for the slalom and giant slalom. Now they were blasting rocks and building a road to Sarajevo. Assisting them were several thousand students, members of communist youth brigades from Yugoslavia and elsewhere around the world who'd come to Sarajevo to help out.

These Youth Labor Actions (*Omladinske radne akcije*), as they were known, were state-supported building projects in which college-aged kids volunteered to dig ditches for the summer as a very small step toward building a socialist society. The kids' reasoning, however, was only partly ideological. In the mountains of Bosnia they were away from their parents and in close proximity to the opposite sex. They were seeing the world. For Africans and Asians and youth from more oppressive countries like the USSR, a summer in Yugoslavia wasn't work; it was a vacation.[4] Westerners came too. One rumored alum of earlier actions in the fifties was the future Canadian premier Pierre Trudeau; another was Saloth Sar, a Cambodian student later known to the world as Pol Pot. Notable projects included the Highway of Brotherhood and Unity between Zagreb and Belgrade, the Brčko–Banovići and Šamac–Sarajevo railways, and the urban development New Belgrade.[5] In 1980 the project on Bjelašnica included the children of Yugoslav guest workers from Germany, known as *gastarbeiter,* and a group of French scouts. In all, fifty work groups and over thirty-two hundred students came to Sarajevo. They built roads on Bjelašnica, cleared courses on Mount Jahorina, and excavated a combined bobsled and luge run on Mount Trebević.[6]

The men's downhill at Bjelašnica was extremely fast. According to Olympic rules, the course required a vertical drop of 2,625 feet (800 meters), but Bjelašnica was 25 feet short. Therefore, the course designers added a starting ramp at the very top of a restaurant at the summit, and the problem was solved. "This may be the first Olympics in history," one journalist quipped, "in which a downhiller [can] hand his luncheon tray over to a waitress, buckle on his crash helmet and say, 'Ta ta, dahling, I'm off to the races.' There's only a small matter of a 51-degree drop to negotiate on the way to . . . the racecourse. It's like skiing off the side of the World Trade Center."[7] From there, competitors roared downhill at speeds of 65 miles-per-hour along a 9,823-foot course to the finish line. The ISF delegate Baumgartner predicted an average time of 1 minute 45 seconds. What he didn't say was that the fastest downhill time in Olympic history at the time was 1 minute 45:50 seconds. Speed was one thing, weather was another. Bjelašnica averaged over two hundred days of snow per year. (The name Bjelašnica comes from the South Slavic word *bijel,* meaning "white.") But down the slope toward the finish line, temperatures warmed considerably. On sunny days in February the temperature sometimes reached forty or even fifty degrees Fahrenheit. Bjelašnica "is something like a border," said Serge Lang, the founder of the Alpine World Cup. It has a "continental climate above, but warm weather on the lower part. The snow conditions are good at the top but the finish is like water."[8]

Below Bjelašnica, sixteen miles to the southwest of Sarajevo, was Mount Igman, where the Nordic events were held. At 4,928 feet, Igman was Sarajevo's fifth-highest mountain and was steeped in the history of the Second World War. In January 1942, in a blinding snowstorm and subzero temperatures, Tito's First Proletarian Brigade escaped German encirclement by marching over Igman, a distance of six or seven miles. They were heading to Veliko Polje, or "Large Field," on a plateau toward the base of Igman in Partisan territory. It took them eighteen hours to get there.[9] In the postwar years Veliko Polje hosted the Igman March commemorative ski competition, while its trails were used for cross-country and biathlon competitions, including the 1980 Junior World Biathlon Championships. In preparation for 1984 the organizers refurbished the trails and built a new shooting range, but Veliko Polje was more or less Olympics-ready. Next to Veliko Polje was Malo Polje ("Small Field"), the site of the 70- and 90-meter ski jumps. The jumps were designed by the brothers Janez and Lado Gorišek, famed ski-jump engineers who in 1969 designed the largest ski jump in the world in Planinca, Slovenia. (Known as Mammoth Hill, the 705-foot Planinca jump has since been relegated to second largest.) Between Malo Polje and Veliko Polje was Hotel Igman, a brand-new 164-room structure that doubled as Olympic

Village B. The SOOC had built Village B specifically for Nordic competitors who needed to acclimate to the altitude.

Due east of Igman, seventeen miles southeast of Sarajevo, stood Mount Jahorina, which, at 6,276 feet, was Sarajevo's third-highest mountain. Jahorina, which hosted the women's alpine events, had been a popular ski site since at least the 1930s. Beginning in 1947, it hosted the annual Bosnian championships, and by 1979 had held numerous junior championships at the European level. Yet Jahorina was run-down. It was "out-at-the-elbows," wrote one journalist, and "the least attractive" of all of Sarajevo's venues.[10] It needed, among other things, new ski lifts, a completely new downhill run, reconstructed slalom and giant slalom runs, new start and finish facilities, and a hotel. It wasn't Bjelašnica, a much bigger project with three hotels, but Jahorina was a job.

Below Jahorina, overlooking Sarajevo to the southeast, was Mount Trebević (5,338 feet), a midsized mountain a mere six miles from the city. Connected to Sarajevo by a cable car, the lower portion of Trebević had long been a picnic area where residents came to enjoy the amazing view of the city. Here, luge and bobsled runs were being built, and the organizers combined the two tracks to save money. The problem, explained Jan Steler, the head of the International Luge Federation, was that bobsled courses required wide-radius curves and long straightaways, while luge courses were curvy and tight. Thus the "curves required by bobsleigh [would] be of little interest to lugers," wrote Steler, but elements of the luge course made it "much less interesting for bobsleigh." The solution was speed—more speed. The German company that designed the track increased its gradient from 10 percent to 10.3 percent, which made it, in Steler's estimation, "the fastest track in the world."[11]

Below Trebević in the heart of Sarajevo was Skenderija, an exhibition and sports facility built in 1969. A flat, horizontal structure of unadorned concrete, it opened with a gala performance of *Battle of Neretva*, a $12-million Partisan war film starring Yul Brynner and Orson Welles.[12] Skenderija had a large hall with an ice rink; it hosted Bosnian competitions in hockey and figure skating but needed a second rink for the Olympics. Therefore, the organizers built Skenderija II, a 234,000-square-foot facility next to Skenderija I with an ice rink and, in the basement, a press center. The center had 31 editorial rooms, 750 desks, 96 telephones, 50 telex machines, 15 fax machines (among the first in Yugoslavia), 246 typewriters, and a 58-employee photo lab staffed by Kodak. This was the games' nerve center or, at least, the place where reporters gathered. In front of Skenderija I was the medal stand.

North of Skenderija, in the Koševo section of Sarajevo, was the Zetra Sports Complex, which included Zetra Hall, where ice-skating and hockey events and the closing ceremonies were held, an outdoor speed-skating oval, and Koševo Stadium, a 30,000-seat soccer arena where the games' opening ceremonies were held. The stadium had been built in 1947 and was home to FC Sarajevo, a soccer club, but in 1980–81 it was expanded, slightly for the games. The speed-skating oval was new, as was Zetra Hall, "an ultramodern, angular edifice" which opened in 1982.[13]

To the west of Skenderija was Mojmilo, where Olympic Village A, the main Olympic village, was located. A nondescript, newly built suburban area, Mojmilo included several large housing blocks and 639 apartments. Here, athletes and officials slept three and four to a room; thus, there were 2,250 beds. The village had a disco, a movie theater, a game room, a weight room, a medical center, and a cafeteria which cooked over 100,000 meals.[14] Next to Mojmilo was Dobrinja, an even bigger village of 2,154 flats and 8,500 beds where the press was installed. Bland yet functional, Olympic Village A and the Press Village were finished in 1983. Next was the Holiday Inn, a boxy, yellow, modernist structure in central Sarajevo that housed the so-called Olympic family. The family included President Juan Antonio Samaranch, members of the IOC and various key administrators such as Monique Berlioux, the heads of International Sports Federations and National Olympic Committees, the literal family of the Olympic founder, Pierre de Coubertin, and delegations from organizing committees who had recently hosted or would host the games.[15] Samaranch's personal guests, who also stayed at the Holiday Inn, included King Carl XVI Gustav of Sweden, King Olaf V of Norway, Duke Alfonso de Borbon, the grandson of the Spanish king and pretender to the French throne, Premier Peter Lougheed of Alberta, Canada, the host of the next Winter Olympics in Calgary, and Amadou Mahtar M'Bow, the director general of the United Nations Educational, Scientific and Cultural Organization (UNESCO).[16]

As the SOOC official Sabahudin Seleskovic explained, "We wanted a nicer chain, such as Hilton, but Hilton wanted more money. So we chose Holiday Inn. We knew Holiday Inn was a mid-level hotel in America, a hotel for motorists, but visitors were floored when they saw it. It was really nice."[17] Indeed, the Holiday Inn had 354 rooms, 2 restaurants, several café-bars, a pastry shop, a meeting hall, a bowling alley, and a disco. The Holiday Inn opened in a grand ceremony featuring Samaranch, its first guest, in October 1983.[18] A sixty-three-year-old Spaniard and former politician in the Francisco Franco regime, Samaranch was elected IOC president in July 1980. Ambitious, autocratic, and coolly manipulative, Samaranch was the first IOC president since Coubertin to live in Lausanne. He stayed in what's now known as the Coco Chanel Suite at the überexpensive Palace and Spa Hotel and commuted to work in a limousine.[19] Unlike Lord Killanin, an absentee president who lived in Ireland and who for years had left Berlioux in charge, Samaranch was a hands-on administrator. He clashed with Berlioux frequently, and by late 1983 the determined president wanted the director out.[20] He finally pushed her out in June 1985.[21]

"When we first won the bid," Ahmed Karabegović said, "Monique Berlioux was the alpha and omega of Olympic sports. She was the boss. And she was very reserved in her dealings with us. I'd say too reserved. But that changed with Samaranch. Our Olympics were his first Olympics as president, so he was adamant that they would work." Between April 1981 and October 1983, for example, Samaranch visited Sarajevo at least four times. By contrast, in the four years prior to the 1980 Winter Olympics, Killanin had visited Lake Placid only once. "We had had enough of Berlioux," Karabegović said. "Our first ABC payment was $10 million, but [SOOC Vice President] Anto Sučić said we needed $20 million to get started." So, in 1980, the Sarajevo contingent, as noted earlier, asked Berlioux for a loan. "[When nothing happened,] we asked Mr. Samaranch, and it was Samaranch who helped us."[22] Indeed, the new Olympic president was instrumental in providing Sarajevo with at least $8 million in loans.[23] The SOOC needed the money desperately because the Yugoslav parliament, or Skupština, had yet to pony up. As of June 1982, Bosnia, Montenegro, Croatia, and Macedonia had all agreed to finance the games, but Slovenia, Serbia, and the provinces of Vojvodina and Kosovo refused. Slovenia took the hardest line: a cost-sharing arrangement, it argued, should have been worked out in advance. Serbia wanted "further coordination" and Kosovo an Olympic lottery, while Vojvodina would pay for the games only if the Skupština paid, retroactively, for the World Table Tennis Championships it had held in 1981.[24]

In July a deal was struck. The Yugoslav federal government and the other non-Bosnian republics and provinces would pay 32.3 percent of any costs above and beyond revenues for a "planned contribution" of 783.9 million dinars.[25] In 1982 the dinar-to-dollar exchange rate averaged 50 to 1, meaning the total contribution was $15.3 million dollars. Owing to inflation, however, the dinar fell to 92 to 1 in 1983, and 127 to 1 in January 1984.[26] The result? The contribution wasn't much. In exchange, the Balkan historian John R. Lampe asserts, Bosnian officials promised to negotiate a larger payment from ABC and from other world networks, though ABC's $91.5-million contract and Sarajevo's $66.5-million share remained unchanged.[27] (Eleven other networks paid $11.2 million total, from the European Broadcasting Union at $4.1 million and NHK Tokyo at $2.5 million to the tiny Bermuda Broadcasting Company at $6,750. Sarajevo's cut, calculated by the Rome formula, was $7.5 million.)[28] The scholar Kate Meehan Pedrotty claims that the Skupština's intransigence in paying for the games showed that Yugoslavia's republics—self-absorbed and motivated by self-interest—were willing to let the Olympics fail. What was missing was "a communal 'Yugoslav' ethos," she wrote, and it's this "calculus," self-interest versus unity, which "boded . . . ill for [Yugoslavia's] future as a unified country."[29]

Yet Branko Mikulić, who in 1982 became Bosnia's republican president, insisted that hosting the games would be beneficial to all Yugoslavs, not just Bosnians. "For us the Olympic Games represent . . . an impetus for a fast development of . . . [a] tourist economy," he said. By holding the games, "[we] speed up . . . [the] process—not only in the area in which the Games . . . take place, but in the entire republic and, without a doubt, in all Yugoslavia."[30] Mikulić had been dogged by rumors. One held that SOOC officials were squandering money; another, that Mikulić was hiding costs and that Olympic expenses were higher than expected. The SOOC's first estimate, in January 1979, was $103 million dollars. Later, it upped the estimate to $163 million, but in January 1981 the Serbian magazine *NIN* claimed that the real cost was $174 million, a difference of $11 million.[31] Mikulić struck back, insisting that the games would make at least $30 million in profit; to say otherwise, he said, was to "disseminate . . . falsehoods." At a meeting of the City Committee of the Sarajevo League of Communists in January 1983, Mikulić charged that nationalists, anticommunists, and fascist Croatian émigrés were hoping to turn the Olympics into "a Bosnian graveyard." "We did not [think] . . . that this big and important project could be realized without . . . intrigues and speculation," he said. But "a lie repeated ten times, if not unmasked, [will] be accepted as truth."[32]

The truth was that the Sarajevo Olympics proved cheaper than expected, not because SOOC officials were frugal necessarily but because most of their contracts were fixed-price contracts with domestic suppliers.[33] Under a fixed-price contract suppliers provide goods and services at a settled, predetermined price. Should costs rise or, in Yugoslavia's case, inflation strike, the seller is bound by the terms of the contract. The SOOC signed its contracts between 1979 and 1981, when the dinar-to-dollar exchange rate was between 18 and 35 to 1. However, since most facilities took over a year to build, when they were finished the dinar-to-dollar exchange rate was at least 50 to 1. That meant, for example, that a contract for a 400-million-dinar speed-skating rink was worth $11.4 million in 1981 but just $8 million in 1982. For the cash-strapped SOOC, that was a savings of 31 percent. The SOOC enjoyed similar savings on Zetra Hall, which cost a billion dinars, and on everything else it built. The one caveat was that it used domestic suppliers, whom it paid in dinars, while foreign suppliers received foreign currency. Luckily, the SOOC's main source of currency, foreign or domestic, was its contract with ABC. It was one of 459 contracts with foreign suppliers and sponsors that brought in perhaps $80 to $85 million.[34] Television brought in $74 million, while the largest nontelevision deal was a $2.9-million contract with Coca-Cola.[35] Mitsubishi was the games' "sole official supplier of four-wheel drive and VIP cars," Kodak was the games' film developer, and Diners Club its credit card company. Adidas provided bobsled and cross-country apparel, TDK the video and audio tapes, and Mizuno the torch.

There were Yugoslav partners, too, 218 of them. Domestic sponsorships and licensing agreements brought in 1.4 billion dinars, advertising 110 million, coins and stamps 213.5 million, and the Olympic lottery 150.7 million.[36] Then, there were donors—lots and lots of donors. Sarajevo's twenty-year urban renewal project, the "Project for the Protection of [Sarajevo's] Human Environment," included a supposedly voluntary income tax of 2.5 percent on all residents for the period 1981–85. The tax brought in three billion dinars, which the City of Sarajevo used, in part, for the Olympics.[37] The tax revenue was in addition to thousands of donations by ordinary Yugoslavs as well as cash and gifts-in-kind contributions from over three thousand labor organizations.[38] The most famous donation perhaps was a kilogram of gold given by a Sarajevo goldsmith named Fuad Kasumagić. For over two decades Kasumagić had collected gold dust by sweeping his floor and cleaning his filters, then burning the refuse into ash. By 1982 he'd collected over six hundred kilos of ash, which he burned down using even higher temperatures to extract the gold. At 24 karats, the gold was worth over $14,000, nearly five times what the average Yugoslav made in a year. Yet Kasumagić called it a "modest contribution." "I wanted to do something to help the Games," he said. "[I wanted] to contribute . . . to their success."[39] A pensioner from Zrenjanin in Vojvodina donated a tapestry, an émigré Bosnian from America donated a coin collection, and Yugoslav guest workers in France hosted dinner programs and held bingo games to raise money. A group from Malmö, Sweden, contributed an arthroscope.[40]

"The important thing is that there was absolutely no political pressure" applied to elicit "these donations," said Mirko Mladić, chief of the SOOC's marketing office. "They were all spontaneous."[41] Later, the SOOC claimed that over 1.2 million Yugoslavs had donated to the games, either through the voluntary income tax or through personal contributions like that of Kasumagić, the goldsmith. The fact that anyone would donate anything to the games, at least in Bosnia, was amazing. From 1980 to 1983, for example, real personal income in Yugoslavia fell by 30 percent. In 1983 the dinar lost half its value, while the price of gasoline doubled.[42] The country, as noted, faced a $19-billion debt. "Yugoslavia has financial problems," one observer wrote, "really crushing ones. The nation is deeper in debt, proportionally measured, than other countries that are bankrupt."[43] But then, as one donor put it, "We want to help. We want the Olympics to be . . . successful. . . . [They're] good for Sarajevo and good for Yugoslavia. . . . [They're] good for everyone."[44]

What was good for everyone was that Sarajevo finished its sports facilities by the winter of 1982. That was the completion date, the beginning of a fifty-nine-day, ten-event schedule known as the pre-Olympics. In IOC-speak, the pre-Olympics are a dry run, a test of each Olympic venue and of organizers' ability to manage competitions in the venues under international conditions. Host cities typically hold the pre-Olympics a year or two before the regular Olympics are to start. The first event was the World Junior Figure Skating Championships, held from 14 to 19 December 1982 at Zetra Hall. Samaranch intended to open the event, but because of weather conditions he almost didn't make it. This was the second time he almost didn't make it. The first was in December 1981, when he, Berlioux, members of the IOC executive board, and the heads of six International Sport Federations—bar none, the most important people anywhere in the world in the field of winter sports—were stranded in Belgrade because Sarajevo was snowed in. They were promised a train, but the train was late, and the party sat in Belgrade's main train station for four hours. It took them eight more hours, in an overnight trip with nowhere to sleep, to get to Sarajevo.[45]

Samaranch's trip in 1982 was better, though only somewhat. This time he landed in Mostar, a city in Herzegovina, but because of fog had to be driven by car for two and a half hours to reach Sarajevo.[46] "With the opening of this magnificent indoor sports hall," he declared, "all facilities necessary for the successful staging of the Games . . . are now completed and available for practice tests. I wish to emphasize in particular this point, as it is not common to see such a favorable situation so long before the Games."[47] Samaranch's new worry was the weather. If even he had trouble making it, what would happen if twenty thousand tourists had to travel to the Olympics in a snowstorm? Like Vučko, all Samaranch could do was keep his fingers crossed, though, to be fair, the SOOC took several weather-related precautions. It added, for example, brand new "Olympic" and "Bosna Ekspres" trains from Belgrade and Zagreb and brought in snow plows and even snow-plow mechanics from Austria. It also enlisted seven hundred army recruits to shovel snow.[48]

The army was in full force in February 1983, when Sarajevo hosted a Women's Alpine World Cup event on Mount Jahorina in the midst of a snowstorm. Seventy-five-mile-an-hour winds ripped through the course, upsetting ski lifts and burying the poles in snow. Worse yet, a busload of journalists sent to cover the event slid off the road and into a ravine. Luckily, no one was hurt. "Weather is one of our biggest problems," Aziz Hadžihasanović, an official with the SOOC, admitted. "It's one factor we cannot control."[49] One factor? It seemed, at times, the SOOC had no control over anything. For starters, visitors arrived in Sarajevo to find that their reservations had been lost; there weren't enough translators or buses; the press center was closed, inexplicably, each day from eleven to five. "The organizers just don't have a clear idea [of] what jobs they have to do," said one U.S. official. "They're beginning to learn, but it's a little bit late in the calendar."[50]

The very worst event, by far, was the Men's Alpine World Cup competition on Mount Bjelašnica. Held a week prior to the Women's World Cup, which had been canceled, the Men's World Cup was a disaster. This time there wasn't enough snow, and Bjelašnica, being Bjelašnica, was sunny. Soldiers attempted to patch up the course by carting in snow from the forest, then stamping it down with their feet. It didn't work. The snow was soft and in some places mushy. When "you're skiing through holes and garbage on the course and guys are . . . missing gates and hitting rocks with their skis," the Canadian skier Ken Read griped, "it's ridiculous." Bjelašnica "is dangerous."[51] Even more dangerous was the course's design. Toward the bottom of the slope, engineers had built eleven artificial bumps, which added drama to the course but were badly placed and treacherous to skiers. "I can honestly say I was afraid for my life," admitted the Austrian great Franz Klammer, winner of four World Cup downhill titles and a gold at Innsbruck. "I've never said [that] before."

The course was so dangerous that some skiers, including Todd Brooker of Canada, gave up. "I wasn't trying," he said, and "I was angry at myself for being scared . . . [but] I wasn't the only one."[52] The best downhill skier in the world in 1982 was Peter Mueller of Switzerland, and he ended up on a stretcher. Traveling "in excess of 120 kilometers per hour," Mueller flew awkwardly off a bump, lost a ski, and slammed into the ground. One witness described the fall as "a helicopter followed by a head plant." Mueller, who suffered a "serious brain concussion" and facial injuries, was medevaced via helicopter to the hospital.[53] This happened on a Wednesday. On Thursday the organizers postponed the race because of weather and rescheduled it for Friday. The only problem was that the men's tour was supposed to be in Slovenia on Friday—therefore, the SOOC paid $40,000 in expenses to keep the skiers overnight. When they finally made it to the airport, there weren't enough planes; several skiers, including Gerhard Pfaffenbichler, the men's downhill winner, were left behind.[54]

With literally no rest, officials hosted the European two-man and four-man bobsled championships the next day. Things went as planned, thankfully, but the Fédération Internationale de Bobsleigh et de Tobogganing, the sport's governing body, decided that several turns were dangerous and ordered a reconstruction. (Still, the SOOC was proud to note that in over twelve hundred heats, "only one serious injury was reported.")[55] The rest of the events were a mixed bag. Bad weather struck again during the Nordic events, held in February 1983 on Mount Igman, when a mixture of rain and snow as well as sideways winds and dangerous updrafts affected the ski jumps. As the American jumper Jeff Hastings recalled, the locals "had no idea what was going on. The wind was coming and going and it . . . seemed like it [wasn't] a fair competition. I think one of the Norwegian papers ran a headline that said 'Sorry-evo' instead of Sarajevo. That's what many people thought . . . that there was no way an Olympics could be held there."[56] That list of skeptics included Hastings. Back in 1983 he told one reporter, "The thing about Yugoslavia is that I hover between elation and despair at the organization. But the people are so nice."[57]

The press was brutal. "There will be at least one group of amateurs at the Winter Olympics in February," wrote the *Baltimore Sun,* "the Yugoslav hosts."[58] *Sports Illustrated* questioned whether Sarajevo could "actually succeed at the . . . task of staging the . . . Winter Games." "The Sarajevo Olympics will be [an expensive] production," it wrote, "in a nation that is far from rich, that has a $20 billion foreign debt" and that "is wracked by 30 percent inflation. But it is, of course, too late to turn back. . . . A country's pride hangs in the balance, and if the Games aren't a success, some say, no amount of slivovitz [the country's plum brandy] will . . . soften the sense of shame."[59] Yet officials claimed in signs and posters and even in a promotional film that Sarajevo was ready. It was a message repeated again and again by Branko Mikulić and by Prime Minister Milka Planinc, who visited Sarajevo in May 1983. A Croatian politician and former Partisan, Planinc praised the SOOC for its courage. "It was risky," she said. "[But now construction is] coming to an end" and "[we've] reached the stage [in which] congratulations are in order. . . . [I am] certain that the Olympic Games will be a success."[60] Yet construction was one thing—by this point the SOOC had built 90 percent of its buildings—service was another. Would anyone change the light bulbs? There were perhaps twenty thousand tourists, seven thousand journalists, and thirteen hundred athletes on the way. Could Sarajevo house everyone? What about buses and food? There were eight hundred thousand tickets to distribute, ABC and IOC bigwigs to manage, and security to be made tight. It couldn't just look tight. A *Boston Globe* reporter predicted "a real botch." There'll be "large-scale confusion," he wrote. "Big trouble at customs. . . . The buses won't run on schedule. If Lake Placid was a botch at the last Olympics, then imagine what a botch this place will be."[61]

IOC officials disagreed. "Construction of facilities is up to date and in good progress," the technical director, Walther Troeger, wrote in February 1983. "Problems . . . related to manpower, lack of experience by officials and organizers," and "[a lack] of adequate services have been recognized by the [SOOC], which will do [its] utmost to resolve them."[62] A Swedish delegation sent in October 1983 examined everything from venues and competition schedules to airport terminals, hotel rooms, and ID cards. "We had two extremely busy and intensive days," one official reported, and it "is a pleasure to inform you that the entire delegation was satisfied (even enthusiastic) when returning home." Holding the Olympics here, he wrote, would be "nema problema."[63] That meant "no problem." It was hard to believe. But, after murders in Munich, a boycott in Moscow, and gaudy overruns in Lake Placid and Montreal, there was nothing Sarajevo could do that hadn't been done before. But what it could do, against all odds and contrary to expectations, was hold the Olympics. "It's the chance of a lifetime," the SOOC press director Pavle Lukač boasted. "[For us, it's a] movement, a matter of . . . prestige and honor." By holding the games, he predicted, "we will advance Sarajevo's development by 100 years."[64] All he needed now was the torch.

A practice first observed in the 700s BC, the lighting of the flame was introduced at the 1928 Summer Olympics in Amsterdam, and the torch relay at the 1936 Summer Olympics in Berlin. The Sarajevo torch was lit at Olympia, Greece, where the Temple of Hera used to stand and where all Olympic torches are lit, then taken to the Panathenaic Stadium in Athens on 29 January 1984. From there, an SOOC contingent led by Vice President Anto Sučić carried the flame, via airplane, to Dubrovnik, Croatia, on the Adriatic coast. It then traveled in the form of two torches over two sixteen-hundred-mile routes, an eastern route and a western route, through which it visited every major city as well as several points of historical interest in Yugoslavia. The eastern route went through Titograd (now Podgorica) in Montenegro; Priština in Kosovo; Skopje in Macedonia; the Serbian cities of Niš, Kragujevac, and Belgrade; Novi Sad in Vojvodina; Srebrenica, Bijeljina, and Brčko in eastern Bosnia, before arriving in Sarajevo. The western route led up the Croatian coast through the cities of Mostar, Split, and Rijeka. From there it went through the Slovene capital of Ljubljana, then made a U-turn at Maribor before heading back to Kumrovec, the famed Croatian village where, in 1892, Comrade Tito was born. It then went to Zagreb, on through northern and central Bosnia, and into Sarajevo. The two flames met on 7 February at Skenderija.

The next day the opening ceremonies took place at Koševo Stadium. In front of 45,000 spectators, 800 school kids in bright, futuristic costumes danced in the infield. They were joined by 1,200 folk dancers, 400 flag-bearers, and 3 military bands. When the famed Parade of Nations took place, there were 1,272 athletes from 49 countries in attendance. They marched in alphabetical order according to their names in Serbo-Croatian; the United States, the *Sjedinjene Američke Države,* entered the stadium before the Soviet Union, the *Sovjetski Savez.* The very last team, according to custom, was the host, Yugoslavia. Mikulić spoke, as did Samaranch and Mika Špiljak, the president of Yugoslavia. "We are convinced that once again we shall demonstrate to the entire world the true meaning of sport as an expression of friendship and fraternity," said Samaranch. "*Hvala* Sarajevo. *Hvala* Yugoslavia. Thank you Sarajevo. Thank you Yugoslavia."[65] The mayor of Lake Placid passed the Olympic flag to Uglješa Uzelac, the mayor of Sarajevo, whereupon eight Yugoslav athletes—one from each of the six Yugoslav republics and two autonomous regions—hoisted it up the flagpole. Sandra Dubravčić, a nineteen-year-old figure skater from Croatia, lit the torch. "Plumes of smoke," one journalist wrote, "purple, rose, turquoise, royal blue and yellow, appeared behind the flame, coloring the heavens. And for just a moment, the smog and smoke that [hung] over this city like a shroud were obliterated."[66]

5

Up Close and Personal

AMERICANS knew who he was. He was the "Rainbow Man," the "John 3:16 Man," the skinny, bearded, attention-seeking, Bible-thumping sports fan in the rainbow-colored wig. His real name was Rollen Stewart—"Rock-'n'-Rollen" Stewart—and he appeared, seemingly, at every game, every race, and every golf match on television. Stewart's outfit was simple: jeans, a white T-shirt with the words "Jesus Saves" on the front and "Repent" on the back, and a rainbow-colored wig. It was his trademark. Arriving early at games, he placed banners in strategic places (on fences at the fifty-yard line, for example) so viewers at home could see. They read: "John 3:16," a reference to the New Testament passage "For God so loved the world that he gave his one and only Son, that whoever believes in him shall not perish but have eternal life." "When I first began seeking TV exposure at big sports events," said Stewart, a native of Cle Elum, Washington, "my main purpose was to draw attention [to myself]. . . . But [in 1980] I dropped into a little revival service and was converted. I became a Christian. I set my goal on evangelizing the world."[1] Beginning with the 1977 NBA Finals, Stewart drove thousands of miles a year, from the Preakness to the Rose Bowl, from the World Series and the Masters to the Indianapolis 500 and the Super Bowl.

In February 1984 Stewart was in Sarajevo, where his first stop was the Mount Trebević luge run. He stood near a camera, held up a John 3:16 sign, and was arrested. "[The police] took me to a headquarters and questioned me for about seven hours," Stewart said. "They took away all my shirts with the inscription on them and also all my pamphlets. They'd never heard of John 3:16 and I had a hard time trying to explain [it] to them."[2] The officials released Stewart with a warning: he could stay at the games and keep his wig, but his proselytizing was over. To ensure it was over, the police followed Stewart for the rest of the games; when he showed up at a Canada–Norway hockey match, for example, he had thirty-five policemen in tow. "It is our job to ensure the security of all competitors, officials, and visitors," said the SOOC vice president, Anto Sučić, "[and] we intend to do that."[3] Sučić's fear was that terrorist groups like Black September, the Palestinian organization that had ruined the Munich Olympics, would ruin his Olympics, too. In 1984, for example, the FBI claimed there were "fifteen to twenty-five . . . transnational or international groups" who were a threat to the Olympics. They included, among others, a Croatian separatist organization known as the Croatian Freedom Fighters (CFF).[4]

In 1980 the CFF detonated a bomb in the Story Room of the Statue of Liberty and blew up a Yugoslav bank in Manhattan and a Yugoslav tourist agency in Queens. The group promised "coordinated actions by Croats at home and in emigration until Yugoslavia [was] destroyed." In 1981 a second group, the Croatian Revolutionary Cell, Bruno Bušić Department, blew up a publishing house in Germany.[5] "Croatian separatists have been quoted . . . as saying" that in 1984 they would "stage 'another Munich,'" wrote one journalist, that they would " 'take some bodies out' to dramatize their demands."[6] Joining Croats in opposing Yugoslavia were Albanians. In Serbia's southern province of Kosovo, 1.58 million Albanians, or 77.4 percent of the population, lived in poverty. In 1979, for example, Kosovo's per capita income was $795, only 30 percent of the Yugoslav average and just one-seventh of Slovenia's.[7] Conditions were so bad that in 1981 Albanians in Kosovo staged a province-wide strike, demanding increases in pay, better living conditions, and the elevation of Kosovo to a republic. In several cities, including Priština, the strikes became riots; hundreds were killed and injured, while thirty thousand troops intervened. As the Balkan expert Sabrina P. Ramet explains, the "pacification failed, as local Albanians continued to scrawl anti-Serbian and anti-Yugoslav graffiti" and "arson, sabotage, terrorism, and pamphleteering [became] a way of life."[8] In late 1983, for example, Albanian separatists detonated two bombs and set fire to a factory in Priština, disrupted a folk performance in Stuttgart, and attacked a Yugoslav television reporter in New York.[9]

According to Ashwini Kumar, an IOC member from India and Samaranch's chief security delegate to Sarajevo, Bosnian President Branko Mikulić feared that if Sarajevo were attacked, the attack would come either from "Yugoslav emigrant groups," that is, Croatians or Albanians, or from "West

German terrorists of the Baader Meinhof Groups." At a meeting in Sarajevo in September 1983 Mikulić told Kumar that these were the groups he worried about, not the Palestinians, who he claimed were not a threat. He knew this because federal authorities in Belgrade "had promised to handle terrorism from the Palestinian Group" by contacting Palestinian leaders "at the highest level."[10] Yugoslavia was a founding member of the pro-Arab Non-Aligned Movement and was close, diplomatically, to Egypt. It had supported the Palestinian cause for years.[11] "We really did fear an attack," said Ahmed Karabegović, "from exiles mainly." A Croat group "had blown up a plane over Czechoslovakia, and in Sweden they'd also killed an ambassador, so we knew they were serious. I can tell you this, though. We had plainclothes policemen everywhere, in the streets, at entrances to and from the city, and the airport was locked down."[12]

Observers noticed cops with machine guns, riot-control vehicles with water cannons, metal detectors, X-ray machines, checkpoints, even a tank. "Every key intersection even remotely involved in the Games is guarded," one journalist wrote. "The city is swarming with police and soldiers," and "they are not . . . direct[ing] traffic."[13] Olympic Villages A and B, for example, had twenty-four-hour security, were off-limits to friends and family members, and were surrounded by a seven-foot-high touch-sensitive fence. One coach remembers pulling back the curtain on her window and seeing a guard: "He was five feet away, maybe. I was freaked out at first, but thought, 'Well, at least we're safe.'"[14] The American biathlete Josh Thompson insists that Sarajevo had the tightest security he'd ever seen. "On biathlon courses you usually have a course marshal at central intersections," he said. "But in Sarajevo, the marshals were lined up in sight of each other and had machine guns. I couldn't tell if they were keeping us on the course or somebody else off."[15] In Sarajevo to study the games was Daryl F. Gates, the controversial Los Angeles police chief and founder of SWAT, the city's Special Weapons and Tactics team whose focus was counterterrorism. Gates described the trip in his memoir *Chief: My Life in the LAPD:*

"I flew to . . . [Sarajevo] and asked the minister of police how he dealt with criminals." [The minister was Duško Zgonjanin, the head of Bosnia's Internal Affairs ministry].

"We put the word out that it was time to leave town, that no one was to commit a crime during the Olympics," he said.

"How [did] you get the word out?" I asked, intrigued.

"We have ways."

"What did you do with people who maybe had a disagreement with the government?"

"Oh, we've put them all in jail."

"What—you just took them off the street?"

"All of them. Any criminal who wouldn't listen to reason went to jail."

"Um, I don't think we can."

"You have to. There's no way you can put on the Olympics and be safe unless you do that."[16]

Gates was impressed. So impressed that he returned to Los Angeles and carried out a Sarajevo-like cleanup of his own. In July 1984 the LAPD began rousting the homeless. "We'll be doing this every day between now and the Olympics," said a policeman through a bullhorn on skid row. "Because we want you people out of here."[17] Under Gates's direction the LAPD also nabbed prostitutes at rates "three times the average" and implemented pre-Olympic "gang sweeps" in which "overwhelming numbers of people," mostly black and Latino males, were arrested but never charged.[18] (This was nothing. The Mexico City massacre was, to some extent, a pre-Olympics cleanup effort, as was the forced removal of tens of thousands of "inebriates and habitual troublemakers" from Moscow. In Project Homeward Bound, Atlanta put its undesirables on buses and took them away.)[19] To Gates, Sarajevo had done a good job cleaning its streets, but, as he told Zgonjanin, he didn't have "a place [in Los Angeles] big enough" for "all the agitators, criminals, and sympathizers" that Zgonjanin wanted locked up.[20] Gates could only dream, for in the end Sarajevo's security measures worked. The city saw few arrests, and its one "attack" occurred when the Austrian ski jumper Hans Wallner hit a security guard in the face. Wallner apologized and was released.[21]

The games' biggest crime was the overcharging of the Hollywood star Kirk Douglas by a greedy restaurateur named Fahrudin Sahić. Sahić ran a restaurant downtown named Una and billed Douglas 54,000 dinars for a 5,400-dinar bill, a difference of $400. He also asked Douglas to pay in dollars instead of dinars, an act forbidden by law. Sahić picked the wrong the person to cheat. Douglas was the personal guest of the Yugoslav Olympic Committee, had once shot a film in Yugoslavia, and was a friend of Tito. (The dictator loved Westerns, especially Douglas's film *Gunfight at the O.K. Corral*). When a Yugoslav hostess learned of the bill, she told authorities what had happened, and Sahić was shut down.[22] Although past his prime as an actor, Douglas was a star. He was, in fact, the biggest celebrity in Sarajevo, in a list that included Princess Anne of Great Britain, King Olaf V of Norway, King Gustav XVI of Sweden, Prince Faisal Bin Fahd of Saudi Arabia, Grand Duke Jean of Luxembourg, Prince Tsuneyoshi Takeda of Japan, the Soviet cosmonaut Alexey Leonov, the Soviet chess champion Anatoly Karpov, Kara Kennedy, the daughter of Senator Ted Kennedy, the former Olympian Jack Kelly, the brother of Grace Kelly, the industrialist Armand Hammer, the Los Angeles mayor Tom Bradley, the Los Angeles Olympics organizer and future commissioner of Major League Baseball Peter Ueberroth.

Marylou Whitney was also in Sarajevo. The fourth wife of Cornelius "Sonny" Vanderbilt Whitney, Marylou Whitney was a New York socialite and philanthropist who'd given $100,000 to the Lake Placid Olympic Organizing Committee. Each year Whitney threw the Whitney Gala on the eve of the Whitney Stakes at the Saratoga Race Course in New York. She also held a black-tie ball at the Winter Olympics in Lake Placid and one in 1984 in Sarajevo. "Neither ice nor snow nor blustery winds will keep Mrs. Cornelius Vanderbilt Whitney from giving a razzle-dazzle party in Sarajevo," wrote Aileen Elder Mehle in her "Suzy Says" gossip column. Mehle failed to mention the irony: the wife of "Sonny" Vanderbilt Whitney, the scion of two of the richest families in U.S. history and cofounder of Pan-Am, throwing a $50,000 party in the parliament building of Bosnia, a socialist republic. "No one [has ever been] allowed to give parties there," wrote Mehle, "but in the Whitneys' case they made an exception."[23] The menu said it all: beluga caviar, shrimp and trout bellevue, filet mignon, a Bosnian dish called *ćevapčići,* lobster, and boar. To decorate the parliament, Whitney flew in a design firm from New York whose clients included Edgar Bronfman, the chairman of Seagram's, and President Richard Nixon. As one author put it, "It was the sort of display that [had] doubtless been missing from Sarajevo since the salad days of the Austro-Hungarian Empire."[24]

One of Whitney's guests was John Denver, the famed American folksinger, who had come to Sarajevo through ABC. "An intriguing addition to our ABC team this year is John Denver," said the ABC commentator Jim McKay in his opening broadcast. "Yes, that John Denver, the singing and song-writing one. John is a great singer, of course, but he also has a remarkable ability to communicate with people. He'll be doing that here; visiting the athletes, the people of Yugoslavia, and bringing us back his special reports." In one segment, Denver visited Lipica, Slovenia, the home of the Lipizzaner stud farm.

He then road a bobsled, sang "Take Me Home / Country Roads" with a group of school children, and watched as women in Mokro, a village south of Sarajevo, spun wool into yarn. In his nearly two hours of television time Denver appeared in twenty vignettes and sang at least five songs. "Clearly, ABC [had] more air time than it knew what to do with," wrote the *New York Times*. Denver was "everywhere; sports events were not."[25]

The problem was that ABC had signed on for 63½ hours of coverage. There was a 30-minute hockey preview on 6 February, then, on average, over 5 hours of Olympics coverage in America every day for 12 days. At $91.5 million, ABC had shelled out $24,000 a minute, $400 a second. That was a 510 percent increase over the Lake Placid games in 1980, not including costs. ABC's Olympic coverage makes "a Cecil B. DeMille epic look like a low-budget short," one analyst wrote: "$35 million worth of broadcast equipment, a crew of 865 engineers, production personnel, managers, and other workers housed in 700 rooms in 6 hotels and an apartment building; at least 86 studio and handheld video cameras, 77 videotape recorders, a portable satellite Earth station, and nearly 200 miles of cable."[26] What really boggles the mind is that ABC's coverage was supplemental. As part of each city's IOC contract, the games' main feed was handled by the host, in this case the *Jugoslovenska radio-televizija* network (JRT). JRT provided ABC with over 200 hours of film. Broadcast live, it covered every event from every venue without commentary but with ambient sound. In TV-speak, this was the neutral feed.

ABC used the feed, but its 86 cameras, its 28 on-air analysts, and its endless supply of interviews, travelogues, and "Up Close and Personal" vignettes created what one critic called the "Sarajevo Soufflé."[27] "The Olympics are only good on television when an event is taking place," wrote Andy Rooney, the well-known *60 Minutes* curmudgeon. "Unfortunately, there's a lot of filler. Television has to pad events to make them last longer . . . [but] I'm not interested in what [a skier's] life was like when he was a boy in Spitzbergen."[28] What Rooney was referring to in particular was the "Up Close and Personal" vignettes, the three-minute background pieces that had graced ABC broadcasts since 1972. The segment typically went like this:

Al Michaels: "[Here's] Scott Hamilton, seeking the gold medal and the leader coming into the free-skating program. If you didn't recognize him on the street, Olympic champion is about the last thing that would enter your mind when you saw him. But he's an extraordinary man, and with Jim McKay, let's meet Scott Hamilton up close and personal." The graphic showed a spinning globe that stopped at Colorado, where Hamilton trained. The setting: Hamilton drives to practice; Hamilton at practice. The theme: fear. "There's no mold for turning out Scott Hamiltons," said McKay. "You wouldn't make a mold for an athlete who was only 5 feet 3 inches tall and weighed just 110 pounds. You wouldn't create an athlete who almost died as a child yet would take on the job as Olympics favorite at age twenty-five, now would you? It's a prospect that frightens Scotty." The scene cuts to Hamilton: "It's scary because I don't want to disappoint anybody. Three times I won worlds, but now . . . it's the Olympics. Now . . . I'm in the spotlight. It's different, and it's harder." More stories: Hamilton's mother has died; he remembers her by wearing a wristband (shot of wristband); he's filled with ambition; he tells viewers he *is* an athlete and figure skating *is* a sport. The vignette ends. The broadcast returns to Michaels, and Hamilton skates.

"The initial 'Up Close and Personal' concept was to give people a feel of where the athlete came from," said one producer. It took athletes "out of their sports environment and personalize[d] them," showing viewers "the range and diversity of humanity that Olympic athletes represent."[29] It also filled time. In 1984 ABC showed thirty-one vignettes. It shot over sixty and spent at least $12,000 in travel and production costs on each.[30] The network recouped its money through commercials. In August 1983 the AP analyst Fred Rothenberg reported that ABC had presold $616 million in thirty-second commercial spots for the Winter Olympics in Sarajevo and the Summer Olympics in Los Angeles. Subtract from that $316.5 million in broadcast rights ($91.5 million for Sarajevo and $225 million for Los Angeles), $150 million in production costs, and $92 million in payments to ad agencies, and ABC stood to make $57.5 million.[31] This was big money, but the really big money was in the sweeps, the three month-long periods of February, May, and November in which the A. C. Nielsen Company measured ratings. Nielsen measured ratings in America's six biggest markets every day, but the sweeps involved local markets, even the small ones. Tabulated through TV-monitoring systems and diaries, the sweeps told networks exactly how much, in terms of advertising, they could charge.

"February," wrote one journalist, "like November or May, is one of those key ratings sweeps months when the networks set out in search of a bigger pot of gold at the end of the ad revenue rainbow."[32] The competition was fierce, but ABC promised advertisers a 32 percent share for its primetime Olympic broadcasts, which meant 32 percent of all American households with a television would be watching. The network charged accordingly: a thirty-second primetime spot cost between $200,000 and $225,000.[33] There was, however, a problem. Sarajevo was in the Central European Time Zone, six hours ahead of New York and nine hours ahead of Los Angeles. Therefore, ABC broadcast the games via delay, but that meant that by evening everyone knew the scores. A case in point: on Tuesday, 7 February, ABC ran an ad in the *New York Post* for that evening's USA–Canada hockey match, but the *Post* had already printed the result: Canada 4, USA 2.[34] The "uncertainty of sports is really the beauty of sports," wrote one columnist, which is why "American viewers [aren't] bothering to view . . . videotapes of what they already know are defeats. . . . That's human nature."[35] The USA–Canada hockey match, for example, had a truly pathetic eighteen share, down 43 percent from its opening-night thirty-one share in 1980. In fact, the USA–Canada hockey match was the fourth most-watched program that night.

"It's one of those things that happens," said Arledge. "Hockey has always been a question mark, and on a delay it has never done well. If the same situation had existed at Calgary," the site of the 1988 Winter Olympics, "the first two games . . . would have had huge live audiences. But we really didn't count on what happened . . . Obviously, you hope the United States doesn't bomb out [in hockey]."[36] Unfortunately, it did. Day two at Sarajevo was better. On Wednesday, 8 February, the games' opening ceremonies drew a twenty-nine share, below estimates but good enough for first place. But then disaster struck. On Thursday, 9 February, the American hockey team lost to Czechoslovakia and was eliminated, and blizzard-like conditions on Bjelašnica forced the postponement of the men's downhill. Rather than show the game in its entirety, ABC ran highlights. It then previewed the men's downhill for a second time, ran "Up Close and Personals" on the skiers Bill Johnson and Franz Klammer, and showed a total of three events: the women's 1,500-meter speed skating, the women's 10-kilometer cross-country race, and the first runs of the men's and women's luge competition.[37] Apart from John Denver, the network had nothing left to show, so at 10 p.m., two hours into primetime, ABC left Sarajevo and showed *20/20*, a prerecorded news program from New York.

"It was a . . . nightmare," said Arledge. "It was [like] having the first game of a World Series rained out and having to keep the audience interested for three hours. At least if you have a regular event you can postpone it or give people's money back. We could do neither."[38] According to Nielsen, Thursday's six-city ratings revealed, at best, a twenty-seven share, with three cities reporting a twenty. In fact, Thursday's show drew 16.7 million fewer viewers than the equivalent night in 1980 and was ranked fifty-fourth in viewership that week.[39] Luckily for Arledge, on Friday, 10 February, things improved. The Americans Peter and Kitty Carruthers skated in the short program in pairs figure skating, while in ice dancing the Americans Michael Seibert and Judy Blumberg competed in the compulsory dances with the British stars Jayne Torvill and Christopher Dean. On Sunday the Carruthers won the bronze, and on Monday, the Americans Debbie Armstrong and Christin Cooper finished 1–2 in the women's giant slalom. Ratings picked up. "There was concern and frustration over the early ratings," said the publicist Donn Bernstein. "The last few days, though, we've found a lot out there to build around. The hockey is done and forgotten, but in its place we have Scott Hamilton" and "the girls' showing in the giant slalom we didn't even expect."[40]

Still, ABC's week one Olympic ratings were abysmal. For the second week of February, ending on the twelfth, ABC's primetime lineup earned a twenty-six share, which put it in third place after NBC and CBS. The network had been in first. Its primetime share for the prior week had been thirty, which meant it had shown the Olympics—presumably the second-most popular sports event on American television after the Super Bowl—but had lost viewers. "At no point," said a rival NBC executive, "did we anticipate [that]."[41] Finally, on Tuesday, 14 February, Torvill and Dean skated to *Bolero,* the famous orchestral piece by the French composer Maurice Ravel, and ABC had its first big night: an average thirty-five and a half share in four of six cities and a forty in Philadelphia.[42] It won all six cities on Wednesday; then on Thursday, with Scott Hamilton skating and Bill Johnson skiing, it landed a thirty-eight. As one producer explained, "[These] are events people don't mind seeing, even [via delay]. They love the speed and danger of downhill, and the beauty of figure skating. And anything involving a growing drama, they really get caught up in that."[43] Ratings dipped on Friday—there were no American medals and CBS aired *Dallas,* television's number one show—but on Saturday, 18 February, women's figure skating earned a forty.[44] For the week, ABC averaged a fairly impressive thirty share and finished in first place.

Unfortunately, ABC's two-week performance in Sarajevo, a twenty-eight share, was considerably lower than its thirty-seven share in 1980 at Lake Placid and its thirty-four share in 1976 at Innsbruck. The numbers didn't lie. In 1980 the Olympics ranked first, ratings-wise, on nine of thirteen days. In

1984 it ranked first on only five. Overall, ABC's Olympic viewing audience had decreased by 29 percent.[45] "We're extremely disappointed," said a spokesman for Ross Roy, a leading ad agency, and "we definitely expect . . . make-goods if the circumstances call for it."[46] A "make-good" was a credit, in this case free commercial time which ABC gave advertisers as compensation for bad ratings. It didn't have to do it, but make-goods were a common industry practice and were part of the business. According to the *Wall Street Journal*, ABC owed an estimated $50 million in airtime, but, using a formula which counted projected viewers versus actual viewers, it offered advertisers a third of that amount. In March 1984 they accepted.[47] For ABC, in short, the 1984 Winter Olympics were a disaster. They'd paid perhaps $200 million in rights and production fees as well as make-good refunds but had lost the February sweeps. The worst thing? In January 1984, a month before Sarajevo, ABC had paid $309 million for the 1988 Calgary Olympics, the most any network had ever paid for a single event in the history of television. "It was unfortunate timing," said one ABC exec. "[We] were probably too optimistic."[48]

Now, for the politics. Believe it or not, the 1984 Winter Olympics were almost politics free. There were no boycotts, no fights between China and Taiwan, and no apartheid disputes. The only issue of substance, really, was the IOC's decision to deny press credentials to Radio Free Europe / Radio Liberty (RFE/RL), the U.S.-backed broadcasting service that beamed anti-communist news programs into Russia and Eastern Europe.[49] The SOOC had given credentials to eleven RFE/RL reporters, but in January 1984 Marat Gramov, the head of the Soviet Olympic Committee, complained. In a letter to Samaranch, Gramov wrote that RFE/RL was a regular source of "hostile propaganda" whose aims as a network had "nothing to do with the Olympic Movement."[50] He asked, therefore, that its credentials be revoked. Opposing Gramov was the RFE/RL president, James L. Buckley, a former Republican senator from New York and the brother of William F. Buckley Jr., the conservative author and television personality. Buckley was an anti-Soviet critic who claimed that "a reporter's passport [was] irrelevant to his right to cover news" and that the freedom of information and the right to broadcast information across borders were fundamental human rights.[51] He called on Senator Charles H. Percy, the chairman of the Senate Foreign Relations Committee, to intervene.

In early February, Percy sent a letter of inquiry to Samaranch, but Samaranch referred the matter to the IOC's nine-person Executive Board for a decision. The board included Julian Roosevelt, an American IOC member and former gold medalist in yachting who was a distant relative of President Theodore Roosevelt. In 1980 Roosevelt "resolutely opposed" the American boycott of Moscow on the grounds that Washington was using Olympic sport "as a political weapon."[52] He also favored the readmission of South Africa to the IOC—apartheid or no apartheid—and the right of Taiwanese athletes to call themselves the Republic of China. Sports "should not interfere in political situations," he said, "nor should politics interfere in sports."[53] That's why, on 8 February, Roosevelt voted, along with all eight other board members, to deny accreditation to RFE/RL. The reason, Roosevelt said, was that press credentials were given out on a per-country basis. But since RFE/RL was an American network broadcasting outside of America in languages other than English it had "no discernible benefit" for audiences in the United States.[54]

At a press conference in Washington, Buckley slammed the decision as a "collapse of political spine." He then criticized Roosevelt directly: "It is appalling, frankly, that any American would allow himself to act a patsy to such obvious Soviet objectives," he said. Roosevelt has "bought the line" that RFE/RL is a "spy organization."[55] In truth, RFE/RL wasn't a spy organization. It was a propaganda organization. But contrary to what Buckley claimed, RFE/RL wasn't free either. Until 1973 it had been funded by the CIA, then, starting in 1973, by an organization known as the Board for International Broadcasting, whose own board was appointed by the president and confirmed by the Senate. Established through an act of Congress, the Board for International Broadcasting declared that Radio Free Europe and Radio Liberty (they once were two networks) were "an independent broadcast media operating in a manner not inconsistent with the broad foreign policy objectives of the United States."[56] As a network, RFE/RL is "neither free nor . . . liberating," the *St. Louis Post-Dispatch* joked in 1972. It is "a Cold War relic."[57] Relic or not, the network was, from the IOC's perspective, unnecessary, for Sarajevo's Olympic organizers had given out press credentials to over 7,850 people. The countries of Eastern Europe, for example, where RFE/RL broadcast, sent 26 editors, 54 photographers, 177 radio and TV commentators, and 231 journalists.[58]

They were all in Sarajevo, on Thursday, 9 February, when the Soviet premier, Yuri Andropov, died. A former KGB chief and successor to Leonid Brezhnev, the sixty-nine-year-old Andropov had suffered from kidney failure for more than a year. "I just can't find the words because it's so sad," said the Soviet figure-skating coach Tamara Moskvina. "I'm very sad. The death of our president is a great sorrow for everyone."[59] The Soviet team heard the news on Friday, 10 February, and held an impromptu memorial service in a private room at Olympic Village A in Mojmilo. Standing in front of a framed portrait of Andropov draped in black, more than two hundred Soviet and East European athletes and coaches listened to eulogies by the goalie Vladislav Tretiak, the speed skater Natalia Petruseva, the luger Sergei Danilin, and Gramov. There was talk that IOC or perhaps SOOC officials would postpone the games—Yugoslav law called for a period of mourning when a world leader died—but neither party considered it. Instead, Olympic officials flew the Soviet and Yugoslav flags as well as those of eight other countries, most of them communist, at half-staff.[60] "We expected the worst," said Sabahudin Seleskovič, the SOOC official who managed the Olympic Villages. "We thought the Soviets would mourn for a day and refuse to participate, perhaps even drink. But they didn't. The truth was, Andropov or no Andropov, they'd come to Sarajevo to compete."[61]

II

Citius, Altius, Fortius

6

Do You Believe in Debacles?

FEBRUARY 1980. The seconds tick away at a USA–Soviet hockey match in Lake Placid, New York. The score is 4 to 3 in favor of the Americans. As the clock runs down to a minute, the USSR, the best hockey team in the world at any level, is losing. But they aren't just losing: they're losing to Americans, to a team they'd beaten 10–3 just a week earlier and whose average age was twenty-two. By contrast, the Soviets were so-called professional amateurs, men in their late twenties and early thirties whose only job was playing hockey.[1] Terrified of losing, they attacked. "Now Petrov controls," said ABC's play-by-play announcer, Al Michaels, "back to Karlamov. . . . Fifty-five seconds . . . Mikhailov has the puck. Sweeping in. . . . Out in front. The backhander goes wide." The intensity was palpable. There were eighty-five hundred fans crammed into Lake Placid's Olympic Center. Twenty-three million more, one out of every ten Americans, watched via delay on television. "Forty-three seconds remaining. . . . [The puck] comes back to center ice. Thirty-eight, thirty-seven. . . . The Americans on top four to three. A long shot . . . Craig able to . . . sweep it away. Twenty-eight seconds." The noise was deafening, Michaels a play-by-play machine. "Nineteen seconds. Now Johnson, over to Ramsey . . . McClanahan is there, the puck is still loose. . . . Eleven seconds. You've got ten seconds, the countdown going on right now! Morrow, up to Silk. . . . Five seconds left in the game. Do you believe in miracles?! YES!!"[2]

Ecstasy. Team USA pours onto the ice. Players weep and laugh, while Coach Herb Brooks, overcome by emotion, runs into the bathroom and cries.[3] It is the greatest upset in American sports history. The Soviet hockey team had won four Olympics in a row. They'd won fourteen of the last seventeen world championships, and in 1979 had beaten the NHL all-stars 6–0.[4] " 'When it was over,' said the team captain, Mike Eruzione, 'all I could think about was, "We beat the Russians! We beat the Russians!" It was unbelievable.' "[5] It *was* unbelievable. For millions of Americans the "Miracle on Ice" hockey game of 1980 became a where-were-you? moment, as in, Where were you when Kennedy was shot?[6] Vice President Walter Mondale, who watched the game in person, called it "one of the greatest moments [he'd] been through in [his] life."[7] The small-town sports reporter Frank Corkin described "a strange sense of elation . . . unlike anything [he could] remember in a half century of sports. It was almost like Christmas or the day World War II ended," he wrote. "People walked around grinning and there was talk of a miracle. The high price of gas was forgotten, and it seemed good to be alive. More important, it was great to be an American."[8]

In cities and towns throughout the United States strangers embraced. People at home cried. In Raleigh, North Carolina, fans at a college swim meet heard the news and began chanting in unison, "USA! USA!"[9] At a basketball game in Philadelphia, five thousand people "burst into song."[10] "It's a real great thing to see this outpouring of nationalism," said Brooks. "This team startled the athletic world. I don't mean the hockey world. I mean the sports world. As years go by, you'll remember these people."[11] Two days later the Americans beat Finland for the gold. The players visited the White House, but that was it—everyone went home. "The starkest realization that hits you," wrote one journalist, "is that this is no longer a hockey team. It's still—and probably will be for some time—a close group of friends, but it is no longer a team."[12] Indeed, America's Miracle on Ice hockey team never played together again. Most turned pro and joined teams in the National Hockey League (NHL) and some went to work or college, while Eruzione joined ABC as a commentator. Even Brooks turned pro. The surly coach spent a year with HC Davos in Switzerland and then became head coach of the New York Rangers.

In 1982 the Amateur Hockey Association (AHAUS) hired a new coach, Lou Vairo. He held tryouts and selected a new Olympic team for Sarajevo in July 1983. A thirty-seven-year-old former air-conditioning repairman from New York, Vairo was an unlikely choice. For one thing, he'd never played hockey. He'd played roller hockey and had learned to coach by volunteering in various youth leagues. Vairo was from Brooklyn, which was not what anyone would call a hockey hotspot. He was, however, enamored of the sport. He never missed a Rangers game and once paid his own way to a coaching clinic held by the Soviet coach Anatoly Tarasov in Moscow. "It was excellent," he said. "On-ice and off-ice lectures and demonstrations. Tactics. Conditioning. It reminded me of American football, the way they had specialists in different areas."[13] In 1973 Vairo took a paying job as coach of the club team at the City College of New York, then coached the Austin (Minnesota) Mavericks of the junior-level U.S. Hockey League (USHL). "I thought it was Austin, Texas," said Vairo in his thick Brooklyn accent. "I didn't even know where it was."[14] Yet in Austin, Vairo thrived. The Mavericks went from worst to first and won both the USHL championship and the national championship in 1976. From there, Vairo joined the Amateur Hockey Association in Colorado Springs, where he headed its coaching education program from 1978 until 1982. He also coached the U.S. Junior National Team and scouted for Brooks during the 1980 Olympics.[15]

Still, Vairo was an outsider. He'd never coached a professional team and, unlike Brooks or Brooks's predecessor, Bob Johnson, had never coached in college. Brooks had been head coach at the University of Minnesota, Johnson at the University of Wisconsin. Vairo was also ethnic; his language and mannerisms, his "Brooklyn-ness," seemed somehow foreign. "Born in East New York, raised in Carnarsie, moved to Bensonhurst," he liked to say. As one writer put it, Vairo was "an Italian Pete Rose."[16] Then, there was the hockey thing. He'd never played it. Detractors called him a book-taught coach, a wannabe, but Vairo defended himself vociferously. "I don't think a person should be penalized because he didn't grow up in an area that had the luxury of ice," he said. "Yeah, we played on roller skates. But it was the same game other people played. You give a pass, you receive a pass, you shoot, you check. In principle, it's the same."[17] Roller hockey was "like bandy," said Vairo, "a game Russians played on frozen soccer fields with a small orange ball."[18] And besides, he wasn't playing the game, he was teaching it, and the last he checked no one wanted the job. It had been offered to Johnson, but in May 1982 Johnson became head coach of the Calgary Flames. The AHAUS then offered the job to several other coaches, but each, in turn, said no. Finally, in June 1982, it hired Vairo.

"I was ready," he said. "Real men accept challenges. Real women accept challenges. I shouldn't say real men. I'm sorry. I don't mean that. Real people accept challenges."[19] What Vairo didn't say was that winning a gold medal, or rather a second gold medal, wasn't a challenge; it was an impossibility. One writer described it as "winning the lottery twice."[20] The Soviets were that good. Since losing at Lake Placid they'd won two world championships, two Izvestia Cups, two Rude Pravo Cups, a Sweden Cup, and a Canada Cup, in which they trounced pro teams from America not once but two times. They'd also beaten a Canadian squad featuring the NHL greats Guy Lafleur and Wayne Gretzky 8–1. From the game it lost in Lake Placid in February 1980 to the day Vairo was hired, the Soviet hockey team had a mind-boggling record of 56 wins, 3 losses, and 5 ties.[21] In December 1982 it beat the NHL's Quebec Nordiques 3–0 and the Montreal Canadiens 5–0, in Canada, *on consecutive days*. The NHL goaltender Pelle Lindbergh, who played for the Swedish national team, said, "We used to get beat real bad [by them], usually by more than five goals. In a tournament, we'd work on beating the Czech team or the Finnish team because the Russians were in a class by themselves."[22]

The question was, why? Why were the Soviets so good? One reason was that in Russia hockey was a national pastime. As the USSR's largest republic, Russia had 140 million people, more than Canada, Sweden, Finland, Czecho-slovakia, and the hockey-crazed states of Minnesota, Wisconsin, Michigan, New York, and Massachusetts combined. According to the USSR's official Olympic guide, 865,900 people played hockey on 27,000 clubs in Russia and in other Soviet republics. Each year, over 30,000 boys ages eight to eighteen trained in hockey at special sports schools, where they practiced "ninety minutes a day, six days a week, twelve months a year."[23] "We saw the hockey school in action," said Larry Clark, an official with the Ontario Hockey Association who visited Russia in 1982. "[It was] unbelievable. . . . Next to breathing, [hockey] seems to be the most important thing in their lives. You should have seen these youngsters skate."[24] In all, there were 157 junior-league teams. As players aged and showed promise, they were called up to one of 67 "top-class" teams in three leagues, the most famous of which was CSKA Moscow, the Central Sports Club of the Army. By law, males in the Soviet Union were required to spend two years in the military; therefore, CSKA simply con-scripted the players it wanted. Its coach, Viktor Tikhonov, who also coached the national team, was a colonel. Hockey was Tikhonov's religion, said one observer: "His attitude is that only fanatics can succeed on his team, and he demands perfection in everything, in tactics, in skills, in fitness, in men-tal preparation. He is a hockey genius, only a genius who achieves his goal through hard work."[25]

The Russian national team practiced and played games eleven months a year. The best club teams and hence the best players were in Moscow, which made it easier to keep the team together as a unit. By contrast, the American squad held tryouts in June and then practiced and played exhibition games from August to February. That was it. The team was temporary. However, the Soviets played on the same team with the same coach for years. By 1984, for example, the now-legendary goalie Vladislav Tretiak had played fourteen seasons with CSKA, capturing ten World Championships, nine European Championships, and two Olympic golds. The stars Viacheslav Fetisov had played seven years; Sergei Makarov, six; Nikolai Drozdetsky, three. "[They're] pros," one journalist noted. "Hockey is their year-round business. Seven of the players . . . [in] Lake Placid were on the Soviet team that flew the Atlantic in 1972 for a series with Team Canada. Some [were] in their thirties."[26] That was the truth. They were pros. Virtually every member of the Soviet national team had a military commission, but his job wasn't to serve. It was to play hockey. The handful of players who weren't in the army played for Moscow's Dynamo club, which was bankrolled by the Interior Ministry. Clearly, the state used the players for PR purposes. This was the Cold War. Victories in sport were "irrefutable proof," said the party, of the social, cultural, physical, and political superiority of Russia's socialist society.[27] That's why Tretiak received the Order of Lenin for his efforts, as did Fetisov and Tikhonov.

The players were a privileged class, receiving good pay by Soviet standards, apartments, cars, scarce consumer goods, and the chance to travel abroad. But as hockey players the Soviets were keenly aware of what NHL players made and what they would make if they defected—millions. In August 1980 the Slovak brothers Peter and Anton Stastny defected during the European club championships in Innsbruck, and each signed a $1.5-million contract with the Quebec Nordiques. "Do you want me and my brother to play for [you]?" Peter asked in a frantic call to Quebec. "We only come in pairs."[28] With defection a very real possibility for Soviet athletes, NHL teams drafted five Soviets in the amateur draft of 1983. The league hoped they would come legally, with Moscow's permission, but as one general manager put it, there was always the "possibility of an unconventional departure."[29] Yet more than money, what the players wanted was freedom, freedom not from communism per se but from Tikhonov. Tikhonov was "a strict disciplinarian," wrote the analyst Jeff Merron. He "drove his players hard year-round, and was considered by many . . . to be cruel, harsh, surly, and ruthless."[30]

Tikhonov billeted the team eleven months a year. But *billet* isn't the right word. A billet is temporary whereas Tikhonov's camps were permanent. Players lived in special team apartments and saw their wives and family members only one day a week. They ate and trained under the watchful eye of doctors and nutritionists; smoking was forbidden, drinking proscribed. To leave camp they needed Tikhonov's permission. He didn't give it. According to a Glasnost-era media report, Tikhonov actually prevented a player from visiting his wife and child in the hospital after a difficult birth. "You aren't a doctor," he said. "You cannot help."[31] At foreign venues Tikhonov kept the team as isolated as possible. At the 1988 Winter Olympics in Calgary he permitted the team one hour of sightseeing during a two-week stay.[32] The players were forbidden to speak English and answered questions only through team interpreters. No private contact with any reporter, for any reason, was allowed.[33] "They were paranoid," one journalist said. "They thought everyone was out to get them to defect."[34] Maybe so, but players were far more paranoid about Tikhonov. He berated them on and off the ice, called them names, and sometimes hit them. Once, when the forward Alexander Mogilny made a mistake during a game, Tikhonov pulled him off the ice and punched him.[35] Mogilny, one of the best players in the world, got fed up with Tikhonov and defected in 1989.

Vairo said he used to tell the Russians they were "fifty percent coaches. . . . [I'd say,] 'I'd like to see you treat an NHL player like [that]. . . . I'd like to see you coach if you had players who could tell you to screw off. . . . Then I'd call you a great coach.'"[36] But Tikhonov didn't coach in the NHL; he coached in Russia. The rules there were different. The expectations were different. "People just don't understand [that] he was driven by a crazy Soviet system," said Tikhonov's son Vasily. "The government thought only gold was good enough. . . . Silver medals were very bad. He had to win every time out. It was difficult but he did what he thought was necessary to be successful."[37] If, for example, a player didn't perform to Tikhonov's standards, he would suspend him, without pay, or confiscate his car. On several occasions he left players at home during international trips as punishment—"There is a problem with your passport," he'd say—or he'd banish unruly players, such as Helmuts Balderis, to the provinces. Balderis's crime was that in 1980 he had congratulated Brooks.[38] In 1983 Balderis was the leading scorer in the Soviet league but was not on the Olympic squad. Tikhonov "destroyed the careers of many, many players," said the Soviet great Yevgeny Mishakov, who described the coach as "a terrible man."[39] He was also petty. In 1992 the nineteen-year-old Nikolai Khabibulin was a backup goaltender on Tikhonov's Olympic team at

Albertville, France. The team won the gold but since medals weren't award-ed to coaches, Tikhonov took Khabibulin's medal for himself. "I didn't even touch it," said Khabibulin. "I didn't even have it in my hands."[40]

That was Tikhonov. The Soviet coach had a singular approach to winning. Yet even he had fears. He absolutely could not lose in the Olympics again. In fact, he was lucky to have a job after Lake Placid. In 1969 the Soviet hockey federation had suspended his predecessor, Anatoly Tarasov, for losing twice to Czechoslovakia in the same tournament. Although the Soviet team won the tournament, Tarasov, the "father of Soviet hockey," stepped down.[41] His successor, Boris Kulagin, won world championships in 1974 and 1975 and a gold medal in 1976, but he too was fired after a single bad season. His re-placement was Tikhonov. "Unlike coaches in other Soviet sports debacles," the correspondent John Burns wrote, Tikhonov and his assistant Vladimir Yurzinov "have kept their jobs." However, "no one here is betting they'll sur-vive another failure"[42]

In Tikhonov's view, the Soviet team hadn't taken the Americans seriously; they weren't fit physically and had what one coach called a "parasitic atti-tude."[43] They were also old. Of the six starters on Tikhonov's Lake Placid team, the average age was twenty-eight. The team's top three forwards were thirty-two, thirty-two, and thirty-five. To bring youth to the squad, Tikhonov added nine new players, including a twenty-three-year-old superstar named Igor Larianov. In addition, the Soviet hockey federation condensed its club schedule to give players an extra three months of conditioning, while so-called problem players like Vyacheslav Bykov were left off the squad.[44] "There were mistakes in preparations for the Lake Placid games," one official rea-soned, but "after a thorough analysis, we drew up a plan . . . and [that] plan [was] fulfilled."[45]

The American plan was simple: assemble a squad. In late June and ear-ly July 1983 Vairo held tryouts at the National Sports Festival in Colorado Springs. He selected the very best amateur players in America, but when practice opened in August several of them, including Brian Lawton, a high-schooler from Rhode Island and the first American ever picked first in the NHL draft, didn't show up. Stars like Lawton faced a choice: they could play for the Olympic team for seven months with no pay or go pro. The NHL's Minnesota North Stars had offered Lawton a four-year, $800,000 contract, nearly $2 million in today's terms, but Lawton was torn. "It was a great, great struggle," he said. "I [knew] a lot of guys on the team from the Sports Festival" and "gave it a lot of thought. . . . [This all] would have been easier if [it] hadn't been an Olympic year."[46]

Team USA's biggest loss, perhaps, was Tom Barrasso, a goalie from Massachusetts and the fifth player chosen in the NHL draft. Barrasso played with the team through August but left camp and signed with the Buffalo Sabres.[47] Viewed by many as a money-grubber and un-American, he was pilloried in the press. "It really didn't bother me," Barrasso insisted. "That's their opinion, they're entitled to that. But, for me, I can't say that the Olympic players are any more American than I am. They're playing for the Olympic team because that's what they chose to do. And I'm playing pro hockey because that's what I chose. Isn't that what living in the United States is all about, the right to choose?"[48] Barrasso was better than Lawton. But as Team USA entered its pre-Olympic schedule, both were playing in the pros. In fact, in his rookie year Barrasso won the NHL's Vezina Trophy as its top goaltender and was a first-team NHL all-star. Missing, too, were the NHL stars Bobby Carpenter and Phil Housley, players selected, respectively, in the 1981 and 1982 amateur drafts. "They should have been Olympians," said Vairo. "They should have been college kids and [thus] part of our team. But in 1979 the NHL changed its draft rules to let eighteen-year-olds in. The age used to be twenty. At first, it wasn't a big deal because the NHL folks rarely chose Americans. But after '80, after we beat the Soviets, they started to take more kids—including high school kids—in the draft."[49]

Fortunately for Vairo, the Detroit phenom Pat LaFontaine chose in August 1983 to play for the team. A center with the Verdun Juniors of the Quebec Major Junior Hockey League, LaFontaine was the third pick of the New York Islanders in the 1983 draft. In his only season with Verdun, LaFontaine had an eye-popping 224 points. He also had at least 1 point in forty-three straight games, breaking a record held by Lafleur.[50] Although just eighteen at the time, LaFontaine was the senior member of Team USA's "Diaper Line," a front three of LaFontaine at center and the seventeen-year-olds Ed Olczyk and David A. Jensen on the wings. Olczyk and Jensen were in high school, as was the sixteen-year-old defenseman Al Iafrate. There were two former Olympians on the squad, John Harrington and Phil Verchota, while the team's fifteen other members, including the goaltender Marc Behrend and the defenseman Chris Chelios, were either in college or had recently graduated. The team's average age of 20.7 made it the youngest one in U.S. Olympic history. However, experts claimed that talent-wise they were probably the best. Age isn't as "big a deal as everyone thinks," Vairo said. "You can have a twenty-six-year-old guy who can vote but can't play. Then you can have a seventeen-year-old guy who can play like hell but can't drink a beer. So what? When we go up against the Soviets . . . they won't be asking to see . . . [a] driver's license."[51]

His team intact, in August 1983 Vairo announced a grueling, six-month, sixty-five-game schedule with visits to forty-forty cities from Finland to Alaska. They'd play college teams, NHL teams, and minor league teams; they'd also play the Moscow Wings, a Soviet elite team funded by the air force, a Soviet B team called the Selects, and Canada's Olympic team. During one six-day stretch, they'd play five games and travel eight hundred miles by bus. Team USA had had a similar schedule in 1979. The difference, said the veteran Verchota, was that "four years ago . . . we'd go into a city, play, and leave. That was it. Now there's the media, there's the fans, [there's also] the expectations. Things are a lot different."[52] At the opener in Alaska, for example, the state's governor and two senators attended, and the arena was sold out. "USA! USA!" chanted the crowd. A band played the national anthem.

"Born on the Fourth of July, the 1984 U.S. Olympic Hockey team saunters into our expectations," wrote Jane Leavy, a reporter for the *Washington Post.* "Wherever they go, wherever they play . . . USA! USA!"[53] It didn't stop. The squad finished its series in Alaska 1–2–1, then played two games in Finland versus the Finish national team for a record of 0–1–1. It didn't matter. This was the U.S. hockey team, the Miracle on Ice team—even if it wasn't. "We're in demand," said one official, who noted that Team USA had a $1.4-million travel budget, nearly twice what it had in 1980.[54] There were banquets, luncheons, photo shoots, autograph sessions, press conferences, and commercials, even a visit to the White House. Then, there were interviews, hundreds and hundreds of interviews. "[They're] exhausting," said Vairo. "[We] could do interviews from six a.m. to midnight and still not please everyone. That's what's worrying us most. What to do about it."[55]

The atmosphere heated up in September 1983, when the Soviet military shot down Korean Air Lines Flight 007, a civilian airliner with 269 passengers, including 22 children and a sitting U.S. representative, on board. The plane had been flying from New York to Seoul via Anchorage and had accidentally flown into Soviet airspace. It had blinking lights and the silhouette of a Boeing 747, but the Soviet pilot, Gennadi Osipovich, on orders from an air defense base on Sakhalin Island, shot it down. "I was just next to [it],"

Osipovich said, maybe "two hundred meters away. I saw two rows of windows and knew [it] was a Boeing. I knew [it] was a civilian plane. But for me that meant nothing. It is easy to turn a civilian . . . plane into one for military use."[56] President Ronald Reagan condemned the attack as barbaric but refused to enact any but the smallest of sanctions. Among other things, Reagan had a $1.6-billion U.S.–Soviet grain deal to consider as well as a new round of impending missile defense talks in Geneva. The public saw it differently. According to *Newsweek*, 52 percent of Americans felt Reagan had been soft on the Soviets, while anger at the incident was, in a word, profound.[57]

Within a week, anti-Soviet protests had taken place nationwide. In New York, for example, more than two thousand protestors skirted police barricades and "ignored pleas" from Mayor Ed Koch not to picket the Soviet mission to the UN.[58] At Glen Cove, a beachfront community on Long Island, an angry mob of more than one thousand people carrying bats and banners that read "Kill the Soviets" stormed a Soviet retreat.[59] Residents of Los Angeles formed the International Stolichnaya Boycott Committee, which urged Americans not to buy Soviet vodka, while members of the Local 13 International Longshoremen's Union refused to unload Soviet ships.[60] "Nyet, nyet, Soviet!" chanted workers. "Nyet, nyet, Soviet!" Two weeks later, in late September 1983, the U.S. Amateur Basketball Association canceled a seven-game tour by the Soviets when all seven opponents, including the Universities of Kentucky and Kansas, refused to play.[61]

Protests engulfed the hockey world when the owners of two NHL teams, the Philadelphia Flyers and the Detroit Red Wings, announced that their home arenas would not be available for Team USA's pre-Olympic series in December versus the Selects. A "few days after" the Flight 007 incident, said the Red Wings' owner, Mark Ilitch, "I was sitting on a 747, the same kind of plane that was shot down, flying home with my family over the Atlantic. I couldn't help but think about all those people who were just blown out of the sky. It started eating at me and it kept eating at me after I got back to my home in Detroit. Finally, in good conscience, I just couldn't do it."[62] Shortly thereafter, a third game in Los Angeles was canceled when American Isuzu, a car manufacturer based in Whittier, California, who had promised to sponsor the game, backed out. U.S. hockey officials were livid. "I think it's kind of stupid," said Larry Johnson, general manager of the U.S. team. "They're not punishing the Russians [by canceling the games], they're punishing us. . . . We're trying to get our team ready to play in the Olympics, and to do that we have to play the best. The Russians happen to be the best. By cancelling the games, they're punishing us."[63]

Indeed, Team USA's schedule featured games with six NHL teams and the Canadian national team, but the Selects, said Vairo, were "probably the number two team in the world."[64] Therefore, in October 1983 the AHAUS announced that, protest or no protest, it would replace each and every city that had pulled out. The six-game series scheduled for December 1983 was on.[65] "I don't think the political ramifications are that great," said the defenseman Mark Fusco. "I think it's unfortunate that hockey players have been thrown into the breach. I'm twenty-two years old. I don't make our foreign policy, and the [Soviet] players don't make theirs. . . . [We're] thankful . . . [they'd even] play us."[66] However, some Americans, including the Jewish Community Relations Council (JCRC) of Cincinnati, the radio host Bob Trumpy of WLW Cincinnati, and the well-known journalist Mark Purdy of the *Enquirer* disagreed. The JCRC picketed a game on 15 December at Riverfront Coliseum in Cincinnati, while Trumpy and Purdy urged residents not to attend. "My problem," wrote Purdy," "[is that] whenever I think of the Soviet Union, I think of dead children lying at the bottom of the Pacific Ocean. If I can express my revulsion by not buying a ticket to a hockey game, I will."[67]

Although Team USA entered the series 26–12–7, it'd gone 3–4–3 against Team Canada and 1–2–1 against the Moscow Wings. Slumping badly, it had also lost four of its last five and been thumped by Colorado, a so-so member of the Central Hockey League. Vairo said the team was "80 percent" there, but "the most important thing on our schedule" wasn't the Soviets. It was Christmas.[68] The team needed a break, yet, girded by huge crowds, including sixteen thousand in Cleveland and eighteen thousand in St. Louis—the most spectators to ever watch a U.S. Olympic hockey team—the upstart Americans won the series against the Selects 3–2–1. "USA! USA!," chanted fans, who waved flags and sang songs and who, wrote one journalist, were "intent on turning the games into a political statement."[69] Case in point: in St. Louis, officials paused the game momentarily after one demonstrative fan threw a missile made of cardboard on the ice. Far from being chastised, the Soviets were confused. "We are sportsmen," said the Selects coach Anatoli Bogdanov. "We came here to strengthen our ties with American sportsmen. The political problems, let them be decided by diplomats."[70]

Nevertheless, in beating the Selects in Cleveland in game three of the series, the young American squad played its best hockey of the year. Led by

LaFontaine and Scott Bjugstad, Team USA scored three first-period goals to defeat the Soviets 4–2. "If we could bottle that first period and take it to the Olympics," said an enthused Vairo, "I could sit on the bench, open up the bottle and watch."[71] The team played its first game at the Olympics on 7 February 1984, the evening before the opening ceremonies. (With twelve teams in two brackets, the Olympic hockey tournament was thirteen days long, while the games themselves were twelve.) Team USA was in the Blue Division, which included the hockey powers Canada and Czechoslovakia and the lower-tiered teams from Norway, Austria, and Finland. The Red Division was composed of Sweden, the USSR, West Germany, Poland, Italy, and Yugoslavia.

Interestingly, Team USA was the seventh seed, the result of a poor showing at the 1982 World Championships. In hockey, seeds are determined through pre-Olympic qualifiers, in this case the World Championships, but in 1982 a ragtag American squad of pros, college kids, and minor leaguers went 0–6–1 to finish in last place. (According to International Ice Hockey Federation [IIHF] rules, professionals could play in World Championship games but not in the Olympics.) That meant that in 1983 Team USA was relegated to Group B, in which it was forced to play second-tiered teams at the Group B World Championships in Tokyo. It won the championship, but as a Group B qualifier it received a seventh seed for the Olympics.

"We would have liked to have started with Norway or Austria," said Vairo, referring to two lower-tiered teams. "But what can you do? You've got to play who they tell you to play."[72] In its first two games Team USA faced the number two and number three teams from the 1983 World Championships, Canada and Czechoslovakia. Because only two teams from each group made it into the medal round, it was possible that Team USA could lose twice and be finished at the Olympics in three days. "Hey, I believe in miracles," said ABC's Eruzione, but "the opening ceremonies [haven't even been] held yet and already the U.S. is in a must game. They have to beat Canada . . . [or] they may never even see the Russians."[73]

Complicating matters was a bitter dispute between the AHAUS and Hockey Canada over the amateur status of four Canadian players. In 1983 Hockey Canada rewrote its eligibility rules to include players who had signed NHL contracts but who had played fewer than ten professional games. The IIHF agreed to the plan, but the AHAUS claimed that the use of anyone who had signed a pro contract violated the Olympic Charter. "Our interpretation is that if you signed a pro contract you are a pro," said one official. "It's that simple."[74] But who, exactly, was a pro? An NHL player? A player in the minor leagues who earned a salary? A teenager with a housing stipend in the junior league? They'd all signed contracts.

For some reason, the IIHF felt that only NHL players were pros, not anyone below that level, such as LaFontaine or even players who played professionally in Europe. Since the NHL was the world's preeminent league, the IIHF considered all other leagues to be minor, in other words, not professional. That meant Tretiak was an amateur, as was Erich Kühnhackl, a center with Germany's EV Landshut who made $200,000 a year. "Kühnhackl makes two hundred grand and [our guy] fifteen thousand," a Canadian official said, and "[our guy] is a professional. That doesn't make sense."[75] Therefore, Hockey Canada's IIHF-approved rule change allowed four Canadian NHL players to play in the Olympics in 1984. "It is safe to assume that [these four players] are little more than a test case for the Canadians," wrote the reporter Hal Bock. "If these four are approved . . . what's to prevent the people who make the rules from extending [a player's amateur status] to ten months—or even ten seasons—in the NHL?"[76] Nothing really, except IOC traditionalists who defended amateur sports and . . . the Americans. In November 1983 the AHAUS announced that it would formally oppose "anyone using pro players . . . in the Olympic Games."[77]

The Canadians called the Americans' stance foolish and claimed the real reason the AHAUS was protesting the plan was that Team USA faced a difficult game versus Canada. "We know what you [Americans] want," Bud Estey, chairman of Hockey Canada, said derisively. "You want us to bring girls, maybe fourteen girls and have two of them in nets. You want to play girls."[78] That's when the Hockey Canada negotiator, Alan Eagleson, went for the jugular: the American stars Eruzione and Ken Morrow, he claimed, had both signed pro contracts before the 1980 Olympics. "More bits and pieces are coming out," Eagleson alleged, but the "last thing we want to do is have players give back medals."[79] The implication was that if the AHAUS didn't agree to the plan, then Hockey Canada would ask the IIHF to investigate two key players on the greatest team in U.S. Olympic history.

The issue came to a head in January 1984 when the Finnish Olympic Committee filed a complaint. The Finns had a player, Hannu Kamppuri, who'd played one game in the defunct World Hockey Association (WHA) but whom the IIHF declared ineligible. The reason, it seems, was that Kamppuri had the misfortune of playing for the Edmonton Oilers, a WHA team that merged, eventually, with the NHL. Because the Oilers were now an NHL team, Kamppuri was ruled to be a pro. The Finns maintained that the ruling was unfair. They submitted the names of eleven players from four countries who they contended were ineligible too. On 6 February, one day before the U.S.–Canada matchup, the IIHF reviewed the complaint and ruled that five of the players, including two Canadians, were pros.

The Canadians were incensed. Although Finland had filed the protest, Canada's Olympic team blamed the Americans. "After all the stuff we had been through," said the goaltender Mario Gosselin, "we decided to set things right again on the ice."[80] Interestingly enough, the Canadians had been flat. In January they'd lost three straight to West Germany, a Group B squad, and 8–2 to the Americans. But grudges are grudges, and nothing inspires a team like anger over a slight. By game time the Canadians were fired up. The two teams met on Tuesday, 7 February, in Zetra Hall. "I'm not making excuses," Vairo said, "but everything that could go wrong went wrong. Pat LaFontaine was sick. He had a virus. Mark Fusco was sick. He had a virus. David A. Jensen was hurt. He played against Canada, but his knee was hurt. And then the weirdest thing happened. We were going to the arena, and the bus took a wrong turn. The games hadn't started yet, remember, and we got stuck in traffic behind the torch. They're running the torch relay, and everyone's clapping and we're trying to make it to the game. We got there but had like twenty minutes to warm up."[81]

Reporters would note afterward that Team USA was tight. That was understandable. But rather than pushing the Canadians offensively, the Americans surrendered a goal twenty-seven seconds into the game. "[Our] emotions [just] flattened," said David A. Jensen. "And from then on," the Canadians were "more intense."[82] The center Dave Tippett hounded LaFontaine relentlessly. Gosselin blocked thirty-seven shots, while Carey Wilson, a Dartmouth star from Winnipeg, had three goals and an assist. Although Team USA nearly tied the game late in the third period—a shot by Tom Hirsch hit the crossbar—the final score was 4–2. "There is no hiding the fact that we were outworked and outplayed," said Vairo. "[But] we still have a chance. If we beat the Czechs, it changes the tournament."[83]

The only problem was that Czechoslovakia was the second-best team in the world. Since February 1980 the Czechs had tied the Soviets six times, no small feat given that the Soviet record between the two Olympics was 96–3–9. "I look at the Czechs," said the Boston Bruins' general manager Harry Sinden, "and I'd like to see thirteen or fourteen of them on my team. You know, I don't think there's a single [Czech] player . . . who couldn't play in the NHL."[84] Known as exceptionally good skaters, the Czechoslovaks played an up-tempo brand of hockey in which they constantly attacked. In game one versus Norway, for example, a 10–4 blowout by the Czechs, they had sixty-six shots on goal. By contrast, the average NHL team took thirty to thirty-two. "[You] can't get off the lead against them," said the Canadian coach, Dave King. "When they get in front they just take off. . . . [They] go whoosh."[85] Thus if Team USA had even the slightest chance of beating Czechoslovakia, it had to "knock them off the puck," in other words, be physical. At least that was the plan. Yet game two, played on Thursday, 9 February, at Zetra Hall, quickly devolved into a fight. "We thought it would be to our advantage to intimidate them," said the goalie Marc Behrend, "unfortunately . . . [we drew] penalties."[86]

Penalties? The Americans had ten penalties. As the journalist Bob Verdi quipped, they "sounded like an excerpt from a police blotter: cross-checking, interference, hooking, cross-checking, elbowing, hooking, slashing, roughing, holding, tripping."[87] Chelios had three penalties in one period. But instead of riling the Czechs, America's rough play meant that players sat in the penalty box while their opponents scored and scored and scored. The final was 4–1. "U-S-A, gute-bye," chanted the fans from Czechoslovakia. "U-S-A, gute-bye."[88] The players were stunned. Six months and two lightning-fast losses later, it was over. "We blinked, and [it] ended," said Olczyk. "You can't beat a world-class team by spending the night in the box."[89]

The criticism was unbelievably harsh. "Do you believe in debacles?," the *San Diego Union* mocked, riffing scornfully on Michaels's ecstatic victory call in 1980, "Do you believe in miracles?" One paper called Vairo a "Lou-ser."[90] Vairo tried to explain: "I told [the team] that masses of people and some of the media were going to make distinct comparisons between this and 1980. . . . I told them to be big boys about it. . . . [The] world's going to get on their case. . . . [That's] all right. . . . [The] world's going to get on my case, too."[91] The hardest thing, perhaps, was that Team USA still had games to play. Over the next week it faced the Blue Division squads Norway, Austria, and Finland, and then, if it qualified, a playoff game for either fifth or seventh place. With an 0–2 record and no points, it had a minuscule chance of making the medal round. That chance ended when Canada and Czechoslovakia won their games and America tied Norway.

If the first two losses were bad—and they were bad—Norway was a disaster. The Norwegians were the worst team in the division. They'd never beaten the Americans, and their best Olympic finish was eighth. "We went against the Czechs in the second game with our backs against the wall," said U.S. assistant coach Dave Peterson. "When we didn't win there it was basically over. The first day compounded the second day which compounded our tie with Norway, which finally ended our hopes."[92] By this point, Team USA was defeated. It went 1–0–1 in its remaining games to finish its Blue Division schedule in fourth place. It then beat Poland, the Red Division fourth-place finisher, in a meaningless game for seventh. It was the worst finish by a hockey team in U.S. Olympic history.

"I can sit here and make all kinds of excuses," said Vairo, "but we just haven't played up to our capabilities. It's unfortunate, a disappointment to all of us, but that's life."[93] Looking back, Vairo has no regrets. "I don't care what people say about me," he says. "Really, I don't. But that was a great team, just a young team. LaFontaine, Chelios, Olczyk . . . those guys are hall-of-famers. That says it right there. Jensen woulda been but got hurt. What else can I tell ya? They had a bad week. Things didn't go right. But those were great kids who gave everything they had. People should've embraced 'em. Instead, they treated [them like] Vietnam vets. It wasn't fair."[94]

Now, for the Soviets. The Soviets did what everyone knew the Soviets would do: they annihilated their opponents. In round one they were a perfect 5–0 and outscored the Red Division teams 42 to 5. Their most impressive win was a 10–1 blowout of Sweden, a top-four team internationally that later won the bronze. "I've seen all their games so far," said King, "and they've yet to play more than ten minutes of hockey. The game was over in the first ten minutes every time."[95] In the Soviet game versus Yugoslavia, the crowd gave the Yugoslav goalie, Cveto Pretnar, a standing ovation when he "held" the Soviets to nine goals. In the semifinals, the Soviets defeated Canada 4–0. Then, in a close game that wasn't really close, they shut out Czechoslovakia 2–0 for the gold. Although Drozdetsky led the Soviets with ten Olympic goals, the real star was Tretiak. The thirty-two-year-old goaltender, playing in his last Olympics, held his opponents scoreless for two hours and ten minutes straight, including the final two games of the medal round. It was a masterful effort. "I would say he played like Tretiak," said Tikhonov, "not worse than that."[96] By then, the Americans had gone home. In fact, they arrived in Minneapolis the same day the Soviets won the gold. As one reporter noted, there were no flags or banners, no one was singing, and fewer than fifty people were there to greet them.[97]

7

Nine Times First Place

SHIRLEY MCBURNEY was a seventy-year-old retiree from East Liverpool, Ohio, who had just watched the 1984 Olympic figure-skating competitions on television. She'd watched as the British skaters Jayne Torvill and Christopher Dean wowed judges in the ice-dancing competition and as the singles favorite, the American Scott Hamilton, squeaked his way to the gold. Like millions of Americans, she loved the artistry; she loved the glamour and the costumes. But what she hated were the judges—in particular, the Soviet judges. She hated them so much that she composed a letter to Juan Antonio Samaranch, the president of the IOC. "Dear Mr. Samaranch," she wrote,

> This letter is in reference to the Winter Olympics. I hope that when the Summer Olympics take place, you [will] have selected better qualified judges than the ones you had for the Winter Olympics and that they . . . leave politics out of it. After all, the performers do their very best, and then to be knocked down by one or two votes, out of winning a medal, [is unfair]. For example, Tiffany Chin should [have won] a bronze medal, instead of the tall, awkward, gawky girl from Russia. To loads of people she was not in the same class as the Chin girl. Chin outskated her and she was given a fourth. . . . There were some other fourths . . . [given to] the United States . . . [and it was] evident to the whole world what the judges were doing. . . . I hope it is on their conscience, and [that] they certainly will not be judges for the next Winter Olympics, because . . . they stink.[1]

Ahhh . . . figure skating: the subjectively judged, demandingly athletic, curiously artistic, and always controversial semisport. In 1984 the *New York Times* columnist Dave Anderson insisted that figure skating wasn't a sport. It was "a show," he wrote, "not a competition," and if ballet wasn't in the Olympics, then figure skating shouldn't be either. "It's beautiful," claimed Anderson.

"It's appealing. Its practitioners should be applauded and cherished for their skill, but it is not an Olympic sport."[2] The reason was the judging. It was subjective. Unlike other sports, in which there were goals to score or times to beat, in figure skating the winner was determined by a judge, or rather nine judges appointed by the International Skating Union (ISU). At the time, four other Olympic sports had judges—two summer sports, gymnastics and diving, and the winter sports of ski jumping and Nordic combined—but here, wrote Anderson, "the highest and lowest scores . . . [were] discarded for balance."[3] Not so in skating, where all nine scores were counted. That meant that biased scores were counted with the rest. In a study published in the journal *Perspectives on Politics* in March 2007, the political scientists Brian R. Sala, John T. Scott, and James F. Spriggs III scrutinized the rankings of 407 judges from 29 countries between 1948 and 2002.[4] They found that judges awarded higher scores to skaters from their own countries and lower scores to those they viewed as enemies.

During the Cold War, for example, Soviet judges awarded medal contenders from NATO countries scores that were nearly two places lower than those other judges gave. But "NATO [judges] returned the favor," they wrote, "punishing USSR and Warsaw Pact skaters by 0.6 ordinal places."[5] Overall, during the Cold War judges gave contenders from their own countries a 2.5 place advantage: the Americans 1.5, the Soviets 3.8. In 1977 the Soviets were so biased that the ISU banned Soviet judges from European and world competitions for a year for what it called "repeated national partiality."[6] As one westerner put it, that's "the way the Communist bloc operated, I would have had to levitate and fly over the ice to win."[7] Yet Americans were biased, too. So were the Canadians. One of the most infamous judges in history, in fact, was a Canadian named Suzanne Morrow Francis, who was suspended not once but twice by the ISU for "nationalistic bias." In 1964 irate West German fans gave Francis the nickname "Red Devil" when she placed a Canadian pair ahead of the German favorites, Marika Kilius and Hans-Jürgen Bäumler. Although the Canadians were third overall, Francis's vote allowed a Soviet couple to win while dropping Kilius and Bäumler to second. Francis gave overly high marks to Canadian skaters at the World Championships in 1966 and again at the Winter Olympics in 1976 and was suspended both times.[8]

The ISU chose judges by country according to a country's order of finish at the previous year's World Championships. If skaters from Western countries placed higher in, say, 1983, there would be more Western judges chosen by the ISU for 1984. "What it means," explained a Canadian skater, "[is that when we win, we'll have] more rug traders at the market than they do."[9] In addition, the ISU appointed different judges for each skating event, for the men's and women's singles, for the pair's competition, and for ice dancing. They judged by means of a complicated system in which winners were determined by the highest ranking that a majority of judges gave them. Judges scored skaters on a zero to six scale, zero being the worst and six the best. This gave them the ranking. The ranking was known as an ordinal, and on panels with nine judges, five made up a majority. So, if Skater A received five first-place ordinals and four second-place ordinals, that meant a majority of judges, five, had given her first place. Her "total ordinals of majority" score was five—five times one, or five times first place. Skater B, however, received four firsts and five seconds, which meant a majority of judges had given her *at least* second place. Therefore, her total ordinals of majority score was ten—five times second place. Since Skater A had five points and Skater B had ten points, Skater A was the winner. Confusing, right? It gets worse.[10]

In 1984 the men's and women's singles competitions had three component parts: the compulsory figures, the short program, and the long program, or free skate. The compulsory figures were worth 30 percent, the short program 20 percent, the free skate 50. However, instead of multiplying the compulsory, short program, and free-skate standings by .3, .2, and .5, respectively, the ISU used "placement factors" of .6, .4, and 1. They were mathematically the same, but it meant that Katarina Witt, the East German women's champion, had the bizarre score of 3.2. She was third in the compulsories (3 times .6), first in the short program (1 times .4), and first in the free skate (1 times 1), for a total score of 3.2. Her rival Rosalynn Sumners, the silver medalist, was first, fifth, and second, for a score of 4.6. "Figure skating," one writer observed, has "style and grace. But nothing is simple about the sport's scoring system, which . . . [is like] filling out an income tax form with an abacus."[11]

The first event in the men's and women's singles competitions was the compulsory figures. A throwback to an earlier age in which skaters etched figures on a clean patch of ice, the compulsory, or school, figures were a bore. In empty arenas with no television cameras and in front of nine judges standing on the ice, skaters traced three different figures chosen randomly by draw. In Sarajevo the figures were the inside rocker, the forward paragraph double three, and the backward change loop.[12] Each was a variation of the Figure 8, and skaters were evaluated by the shape and symmetry of circles and the cleanness of turns. "Basically," wrote one author, "skaters perform Figure 8's on the ice and then stand by nervously as the judges scrutinize the circles. [They then] . . . do it again, twice more."[13]

In the fifties and sixties the Olympic figures competition was worth 60 percent of the total score. There were just two events: the figures and the free skate. Trouble came at the 1972 Winter Olympics in Sapporo, Japan, when the Austrian skater Beatrix "Trixie" Schuba was seventh in the free skate but still managed to win. Schuba was tall at 5 feet, 9 inches and downright corpulent by skating standards at 145 pounds.[14] She "has the build of a lumberjack and the free-skating grace of a camel," wrote one reporter, rudely, but she is "a champion in the compulsories." In "the eye-appealing free-skating competition," however, the "ballet on ice, she creates consternation among [spectators] because she is so outclassed."[15] In 1971, in Lyon, France, Schuba won the World Championships but was booed by the crowd. "What can I do [about it]?" she cried. "I'm better in figures than in free skating, but that doesn't make me any less [of] a champion. Skiers, too, can win by being proficient in only one event."[16]

Tell that to the spectators. They didn't get it. Viewers at home didn't either. The free skate was the most popular part of any broadcast. In fact, it was the only part because compulsory figures were not shown on television. "There's a reason . . . [it's] compulsory," one journalist joked. That's because "no one in their right mind would do it. . . . More interesting than this is cattle judging at the Iowa State Fair."[17] Because viewers didn't see the compulsories, the scoring made no sense, such as when the American Janet Lynn took six firsts in Sapporo but finished with a bronze. "Janet was the best free skater in the world," wrote the skater Dorothy Hamill, "and Trixie had the best figures in the world, but the audience did not realize that figures [had] set the placements before Janet had [taken] . . . the ice."[18] The solution, adopted in 1973, was the introduction of the short program, a two-and-a-half-minute free-skating session with required elements worth 20 percent. The formula now was 40 percent for the figures, 20 percent for the short program, and 40 percent for the four-minute long program (the men's long was four and a half minutes). However, in 1976 the ISU reduced figures even further, to 30 percent. The 30–20–50 formula was in place in 1984.

That year the favorite in the men's competition was Hamilton, who'd won three World Championships and four U.S. Championships in a row. At 5 feet, 3 inches and 115 pounds, the twenty-six-year-old Hamilton was slight yet sinewy, his small size the result of a childhood eating disorder that had stunted his growth. "I'm this size because of my childhood," he explained in an interview in 1984. "I lost a lot of the years until I was nine. The only good thing to come out of it is that I've never developed any excess poundage, like some other athletes. It ain't much, but everything I've got here is a skating muscle."[19] Hamilton went to dozens of doctors. In his memoir of 2008, Hamilton wrote that at the age of nine he hadn't grown in four and a half years. His belly was distended, and every day he ate through a feeding tube that went up his nose and into his stomach. It "was not pleasant," he said. Even worse, doctors had misdiagnosed a food allergy, which meant that for years he "had no wheat, no flour, no sugar, [and] no dairy." Hamilton nearly died. When that happened a doctor at the Children's Hospital in Boston tried a new technique: Hamilton should go home and do nothing. He should eat what he wanted to eat and "see what happens."[20] Soon, Hamilton was healthy again and growing. He became a normal kid and in 1967 joined a skating class at the new rink at Bowling Green State University, where his father taught biology.

"The other kids, of course, said, 'Eww!'" he wrote, "[because] I showed up ... [with a] tube dangling out of my nose." However, he "soon discovered that skating was something [he] could do as well as the other kids," so he stuck with it.[21] By the age of eleven Hamilton was regularly competing in regional championships and in 1973 moved to Rockton, Illinois, to train with the former French gold medalist Pierre Brunet. In 1976 Hamilton won the U.S. national junior title but was "flat broke."[22] "My folks had spent all the money they could possibly afford to keep me going," said Hamilton, who estimated his training fees at $12,000 a year. "Dad had remortgaged the big house; Mom had been teaching. So I decided to quit skating and start college at Bowling Green."[23] In 1977 Hamilton earned a sponsorship from the Chicago-area philanthropists Frank and Helen McLoraine. The McLoraines were wealthy skate fans who sponsored dozens of skaters, including Tonya Harding and Johnny Weir. Over the next several years the McLoraines gave Hamilton tens of thousands of dollars, which he used for living expenses and for coaching fees, which were $45 an hour.

Hamilton practiced Monday through Friday from 8:45 a.m. until 2 p.m. and again from 5:30 p.m. until 8 p.m. Saturday was a half day, and Sunday he had off. "You can't miss a practice," he said. "You don't want to. You want everyone to think you're a machine."[24] To his opponents, Hamilton was a machine. He won his first U.S. Figure Skating Championship in 1981 and coming into Sarajevo had won sixteen competitions in a row. At his last Olympic tune-up, the U.S. Championships in Salt Lake City in January 1984, Hamilton received first-place votes from every judge in every vote in every event— forty-five judges in all. In the long program, four of the nine judges gave him a perfect 6.0.[25] For a small man in a sport many saw as effeminate, Hamilton looked athletic. He "was built for what he was doing," said Hamilton's longtime coach Don Laws. "He was compact and muscularly balanced, with great strength in his upper body and arms."[26] On the ice, Hamilton strived for what he called the "ballistic effect," a joining of speed and flow with the explosiveness of a gymnast. He was a showman, too, but what stood out was his physicality; he was somehow solid. "Athletics in men's figure skating has been neglected," he told *Time* magazine. "Sure, there's some dance in it, but we [are] athletes first. They call it an Olympic sport, not an Olympic art, don't they?"[27] To emphasize his point, Hamilton wore a specially designed uniform that looked like a speed skater's. It did not have sequins.

Although the long skate, lasting four and a half minutes, was his best event by far, Hamilton took his compulsory figures seriously. He spent four hours a day practicing Figure 8's.[28] He had to. As of 1984 Hamilton had never won the compulsory figures competition at the World Championships. Finishing fourth at the 1981 Worlds and runner-up in both 1982 and 1983, he had used his short and long programs to win. Not so in Sarajevo, where Hamilton placed first in all three figures. His total ordinals of majority score was nine, as in *nine times first place.* "Yahoo!" he exclaimed. "I've been second all the time. Always second, second, second. I guess this sets me up pretty good [for the short program]."[29] Just two and a half minutes in length, the short program had seven required elements, and the judges scored skaters in two categories, technical merit and artistic impression. Here, Hamilton played it safe, as his closest competitor in the short and long programs was Brian Orser, a rising star from Canada who'd finished the compulsories in seventh place. Orser outskated Hamilton in technical merit, receiving eight 5.9's and a 5.8 to Hamilton's one 5.9, three 5.8's, and five 5.7's. In artistic impression, Hamilton won, but when the two scores were added together Orser was the winner.[30]

It didn't matter. For Orser to beat Hamilton overall, he needed to win the long program and Hamilton had to finish fifth. They skated on Thursday, 16 February, in Zetra Hall, which was packed, mostly with Americans. Dressed in a blue and red skin suit reminiscent of the body-hugging uniforms speed skaters wore and skating to *Swan Lake,* Hamilton began his program with a difficult triple lutz. It was flawless, but his next move, a triple flip, wasn't. Instead of spinning three times in the air, he spun once, tentatively, and his leg opened, resulting in a minor score deduction.[31] It wasn't a bad mistake, but for the next four minutes he seemed nervous, even wooden. Toward the end of the program, he missed a second jump and finished in second place. His scores were so-so: for technical merit, one 5.9, three 5.8's, two 5.7's, and three 5.6's; and for artistic impression, five 5.9's and four 5.8's. "It might not have been pretty," wrote Hamilton, "but I survived."[32]

For his part, Orser was spectacular. He defeated Hamilton with eight 5.9's in technical merit and was second in artistic impression. Overall, his total ordinals of majority score for the long program was eight, while Hamilton's was eleven. But when all three finishes for the compulsory figures, the short program, and the long program were multiplied by factored placements and added together, Hamilton was the winner. He'd been second in two of the three events but had a gold medal score of 3.4. Orser was second at 5.6, while Jozef Sabovčík of Czechoslovakia was third at 7.4. Hamilton "backed into it," one journalist wrote, and when he "accepted his medal on the victory stand, he shed no tears of joy." Instead, "he took the deepest of breaths, filling his cheeks like a chipmunk. Then he exhaled with gale force, his face gone from swollen to slack in an instant."[33] Orser was overjoyed. It was his best performance ever, and the system, he said, was fair. "To win you have to be consistent in all [three] disciplines," he said, and "Scott is . . . consistent at everything."[34] It was a good thing he was, too. In 1990 the ISU did away with compulsory figures and instituted a one-third/two-thirds split for the short and long programs. Had the two men competed at the 1992 Olympics in Albertville, Orser would have won.

Hamilton had been the odds-on favorite. His chances had been better even than those of the Soviet hockey team. He was that good. However, the women's competition was a four-way contest between Rosalynn Sumners, Elaine Zayak, and Tiffany Chin of the United States and Katarina Witt. Their resumes were amazing: Sumners and Zayak had both won World Championships—Zayak in 1982 and Sumners in 1983—while Chin had finished second to Sumners at the U.S. Championships in January 1984. Not to be outdone, Witt had been second at the 1982 Worlds and had won two European championships in a row. "In forty years of figure skating, I've never seen anything as hard to call," said the commentator and two-time Olympic champion Dick

Button. "I just don't know what's going to happen . . . Anyone could blow up at any time."[35] The favorite, perhaps, was Sumners, an elegant skater known less for her athleticism than for her smooth, artistic style. Yet Sumners, a nineteen-year-old from Edmonds, Washington, was notoriously nervous. She's "a head skater," said Button. "She can psych herself into or out of a good performance. . . . Sumners moves beautifully. She's Grace Kelly on ice, but she admits she feels pressure."[36]

Sumners's chief rival was Zayak, a plainspoken eighteen-year-old from Paramus, New Jersey. The daughter of a barkeep, Zayak had lost part of her foot in a lawn-mower accident when she was two and began skating as a form of physical therapy. In spite of her injury she was exceptionally athletic. In 1981, as a sophomore in high school, Zayak landed seven triple jumps in one program at the World Championships. But because triple jumps earned higher scores in technical merit, the more artistic skaters complained. "People have said what I do isn't figure skating," said Zayak, "but they're into ballet. I think the sport is changing, becoming more athletic. I think people like my way better. I think they fall asleep with slow skating."[37] In 1982 Zayak upped the ante by landing four triple toe loops and two triple salchows in the long program at the World Championships. By doing so, she jumped seven places in one day, winning the title on factored placements by just .4. It was unheard of. Many skaters were indignant. "They weren't looking like ladies," said Rosalynn Sumners. "They were looking like [skaters in] the men's program. It was a jumping contest."[38] Zayak's improbable win forced the ISU to implement what's now known as the Zayak rule, which prohibited skaters from performing the same triple jump more than once per program. The Zayak rule essentially forced Zayak to change her program. She never recovered. In 1983 she suffered an ankle injury and was sidelined for four months. When she returned she was twenty pounds heavier—a no-no in the svelte world of figure skating—and finished third at the U.S. Championships in January 1984.[39]

Tiffany Chin, a sixteen-year-old Chinese American from Toluca Lake, California, finished second. Measuring 5 feet, 1 inch tall and weighing just 90 pounds, Chin was the future of women's skating. In 1980, at the age of thirteen, she had won the World Junior Championships by inserting an unchoreographed triple salchow into her routine.[40] She was graceful and athletic, but experts predicted her Olympic gold would come in 1988, in Calgary, not in 1984. "There's no question that once she gets stronger she'll be able to jump higher and become even faster," said her coach, John Nicks. "And if she can get mentally strong, she'll get more consistent. . . . I don't think she's reached her full potential."[41]

The final contender at Sarajevo was Witt, an eighteen-year-old star from Karl-Marx-Stadt, a grim, industrial city three hours south of Berlin. A product of the East German sports system, Witt joined a skating club at five and, showing promise, had been funneled through a sports school and into the arms of Jutta Müller, the GDR's most demanding coach. "Any other skater would have been totally thrilled," wrote Witt, "but I burst into tears, because I knew, even [then] . . . the fun times were over."[42] Described by writers as "Jutta the Hutt," Müller had coached her own daughter, Gabriele Seyfert, to World Championships in 1969 and 1970 and Anett Pötzsch to an Olympic gold medal in 1980. She was the best in the business, but she was also, as Witt put it, "severe."[43] Witt trained with Müller six days a week for six and sometimes seven hours a day, eleven months a year. In fact, as a teenager she saw Müller more than she did her parents. Although just 5 feet, 5 inches and 114 pounds, Witt was big, said Müller. She forced the girl to lose weight. "If Katarina has put on a little extra," she said, "I see it immediately. It's not that she can't jump anymore. It's just that I want that ideal look. I want the skater's figure to have absolutely no fault. For esthetic reasons, it must be absolutely perfect. And that takes discipline."[44]

If Müller was invasive, the Stasi, the Ministry for State Security, was worse. In 1992 Witt discovered that her Stasi file was three thousand pages long. One of the first entries was, "She's eight years old and . . . has lots of talent." The Stasi spied on Witt through paid informants, including, most notably, her fellow Olympic medalist Ingo Steuer, and put listening devices in the music consoles on the sides of the ice rink. A stickler for details, the Stasi also documented Witt's sex life and saw to it that when her boyfriend served in the army, he did so as far away from Karl-Marx-Stadt as possible.[45] Renowned for her beauty, Witt as a teenager bore a striking resemblance to the American model and *Blue Lagoon* star Brooke Shields. Knowing she'd make millions in America as a professional, the Stasi made sure through inducements and restrictions that Witt didn't defect. It gave her a car, for example, a blue Russian Lada from the Stasi motor pool, but kept her under twenty-four-hour surveillance.[46] She could travel to international skating events with Frau Müller, but her parents could not. In fact, the first time they saw her outside of East Germany was at the 1988 World Championships in Budapest,

Hungary. They did not come to Sarajevo. "We live[d] in the GDR," Witt once said, "and my parents . . . witnessed the major part of my . . . career from their living room."[47] In 1984 they watched from Karl-Marx-Stadt as Witt competed in the figures.

Held at Skenderija II, the women's figures were the same as the men's. They were the inside rocker, the forward paragraph double three, and the backward change loop. The winner was Sumners. Yelena Vodorezova of the USSR was second, while Witt was third. "I felt great," said Sumners. "It was the most relaxed and confident I've ever felt with compulsory figures. I had a good pep talk with my mom last night" and was "oblivious to the judges."[48] Sumners's two American competitors, Chin and Zayak, finished twelfth and thirteenth. Standing on the ice, Zayak broke down and cried. With a factored placement score of 7.8 for the compulsories (13 times .6), she had twice what the winner would have for all three events. Her Olympics were over.[49] Next up was the short program, which, as everyone knew, was a two-woman race between Sumners and Witt. Witt skated flawlessly, but Sumners made a clear mistake on a required element known as a double axel. On technical merit, Witt had five 5.8's and finished first on eight ballots to Sumners's majority 5.3. Where Witt stood out, though, was in presentation. Dressed in a folk costume from old Germany, she skated to a vibrant gypsy tune as the audience clapped along. "I thought the costume on its own was gaudy," said Carol Heiss Jenkins, the gold medalist from 1960. "But when it started, it was the whole package. It all fit in. Everyone does the same doubles, the same triples. [So] anything you can do to capture the judge's eye, which is usually what captures anyone's [eye], is good. To me, she was the whole picture. The ice princess."[50] Witt's scores were indicative: four 5.9's, four 5.8's, and a 5.7 for artistic impression. First in technical merit and first in presentation, Witt was the winner. In second was Chin, with Kira Ivanova, a Soviet skater, in third. Sumners finished fifth.

That left the free skate. Going into the event, Witt and Sumners had factored placement scores of 2.2 and 2.6, respectively. Whichever skater won the event won the gold. "This is where I want to be," said Sumners. "The long program is my strong point."[51] Skating before a capacity crowd at Zetra Hall, Witt and Sumners were the last two skaters to take the ice. Witt went first. She had seven 5.8's, a 5.7, and a 5.9 for artistic impression, and four 5.8s, four 5.9s, and a 5.7 for technical merit. These "were very good but not utterly great marks," one observer explained. "With a great performance, Sumners

... could [win]."[52] Indeed, for four minutes of a four-minute, eleven-second program Sumners did win. But as she came to the finish, she opened up on a double axel and completed the jump as a single. Technically, it wasn't a mistake—there were no required jumps in the long program—but the judges voted her down. Her scores for technical merit included four 5.8's, two 5.6's, a 5.7, and a 5.9. Although Sumners had outscored Witt in artistic impression, it wasn't enough. When the scores for the long program were added together, Witt was first on five ballots for a total ordinals of majority score of five. "It may haunt me tonight," said Sumners, "but I can't let it haunt me the rest of my life. . . . If I'd landed that end triple, I think I could have won."[53] In the final standings for the women's singles, Witt won the gold. Sumners was the silver medalist, while Ivanova was third.

In the pairs competition the winners were Elena Valova and Oleg Vasiliev of the Soviet Union, who scored what was perhaps a mild upset over Barbara Underhill and Paul Martini of Canada. As the USOC puts it, "Pair skating is free skating with a partner."[54] It sounds simple enough, but skating with a partner is incredibly difficult and involves technical elements that singles skating does not, such as press lifts, twist lifts, and throw jumps. The goal is to skate in unison. The male partner lifts and throws the female partner; therefore, he's strong, physically, and a foot taller, on average, than she is. There are no compulsories and just two judged events. In 1984 these included a two-minute, fifteen-second short program with seven required elements and a four-and-half-minute free skate. The short program had a placement factor of .4 for 28.57 percent of the total, while the free skate had a placement factor of 1.0 for 71.43 percent. (Again, the scoring system for figure skating was bizarre. Why the ISU didn't use placement factors of .6 and 1.4 for a clean 30/70 percent split is unknown.)

In any case, going into the short program the five-time Canadian champions Underhill and Martini were favored for the gold. After falling during a simple sit-spin maneuver, however, the couple finished the program in sixth. "I'm really not sure what happened," said a dazed Underhill. "It all happened so quickly. . . . [It's just] one of those things I guess."[55] A second pair who struggled was Sabine Baess and Tassilo Thierbach of East Germany, who in 1983 were the number two pairs skaters in the world. In the short program Thierbach missed a double loop jump, a required element, which landed the Germans in fourth. The winners were Valova and Vasiliev, the latest in a long series of Soviet figure skaters who dominated in pairs. Beginning with

Ludmila Belousova and Oleg Protopopov at Innsbruck in 1964, Soviet pairs skaters had won five gold medals in a row. They also won fourteen World Championships in a row, and seventeen out of nineteen between 1965 and 1983.

The surprising second-place finishers were the Americans Kitty and Peter Carruthers, adopted siblings from Burlington, Massachusetts. Crowd favorites, the two Carruthers skated a mediocre yet clean routine in the short program and were thrilled at the result. In fact, they'd never once been second following the short program at a major international meet. Their plan for the long program was to skate conservatively. Barring a mishap, Valova and Vasiliev were unbeatable, but if the Carruthers pair skated a mistake-free long program, they'd probably win a bronze, maybe even a silver. In all, there were fifteen pairs in the free skate. Valova and Vasiliev captured nine firsts. Kitty and Peter Carruthers were second, and the Soviets Larisa Selezneva and Oleg Makarov were third.

Both the second- and third-place pairs had a total ordinals of majority score of fifteen, that is, five times third place. The Carruthers siblings had four seconds and three thirds, Selezneva and Makarov two seconds and five thirds. Thus, as a tiebreaker, the ISU added together the ordinal placements of all judges who voted with the majority, that is, all places third or higher. With four seconds and three thirds, the Carruthers pair had seventeen points (4 x 2 + 3 x 3), while Selezneva and Makarov, who had two seconds and five thirds (2 x 2 + 5 x 3), had nineteen points. Since seventeen was lower than nineteen, Kitty and Peter Carruthers finished in second. "They skated very sure of themselves, very sure of what they were doing," said Tamara Moskvina, who was Valova's and Vasiliev's coach. "But their contents were less difficult."[56]

The final event was ice dancing, a form of figure skating in which mixed pairs literally danced on the ice. Originating in Austria and France at the end of the nineteenth century, ice dancing held its first World Championship in 1952. It appeared as an exhibition event at the 1968 Grenoble Olympics and became a medal sport in 1976. Although confused, at times, with pair skating, ice dancing focuses on dance. As one expert put it, "Ice dancing programs involve continuity, transitions, and overall structure rather than the exclamation point abruptness of sudden big moves. . . . Judges take [into] account skating technique . . . while also considering more dancerly concerns, such as creativity, originality, and musicality."[57] It was, as everyone said, "ballroom dancing on ice." To guarantee that ice dancers were indeed dancing, the ISU specifically told skaters what they could and couldn't do. There were, for example, no jumps. The male partner was forbidden to lift the female partner over his head, and spins were performed as a team. There were also no throws, and the competitors were required to have at least one skate on the ice at all times.

"Ice dancing is ruled by a technical committee of the ISU," said Button, "and they have it in their minds that ice dancing should be ballroom dancing on ice, and that's what it's going to be. There are more rules regarding this event than all the rest of skating put together."[58]

In 1984 there were three ice-dancing events: the compulsory dance, factored by .6 and worth 30 percent; the original set pattern dance, factored by .4 and worth 20 percent; and a free dance, factored by 1.0 and worth 50 percent. The compulsory dance was first. Each season the ISU designated six dances that could be used in the compulsories. Then, at ISU events, such as the World Championships, it chose three of these dances from a hat. In Sarajevo they were the Westminster waltz, the *paso doble,* and the rhumba. Described as mind-numbing, migraine-inducing, tedious, and bizarre, the compulsory dance required every pair of skaters to perform the same sequences of steps to the same music. That meant nineteen waltzes in row— *one,* two, three, *one,* two, three, *one,* two, three; then nineteen double-steps in a row—*one,* two, *one,* two, *one,* two; and finally, nineteen rhumbas in a row—*one,* two, three, four, *one,* two, three, four. "I can understand they can be a little boring to watch if you're not into them," said one skater. But the compulsory dance "teaches us how to skate. The exact technique, the perfect technique, or at least that's what you hope."[59]

In the original set pattern dance, skaters performed a two-minute rendition of a dance chosen, a year or so earlier, by the ISU. In 1984 that dance was the *paso doble,* which skaters choreographed and chose music for on their own. The *paso doble* is a "duple meter" Spanish march. There are many versions, the most famous of which is *España Cañí,* or "Gypsy Spain." Another is *Bamboleo* by the Gypsy Kings. The ISU described the dance as original because the skaters themselves designed it. But it was a set pattern dance because they completed each series of steps three times. Although less restrictive than the compulsory dance, the original set pattern dance was still a prescribed dance that limited what skaters could do. The skaters' favorite, therefore, was the free dance, in which skaters chose the music, the tempo, and the dance, while focusing on interpretation. "The important thing is to bring something new," said the French skater Paul Duchesnay, whose free dance at the 1990 World Championships was, in the words of his partner, Isabelle Duchesnay, "a portrait of the life of the people in South America, some under the pressure of dictatorship."[60] The Duchesnays wore tattered, sequinless clothes and skated to music from the anti-Pinochet film *Missing* (1982). Others have interpreted *Riverdance, Phantom of the Opera,* and *Romeo and Juliet* plus countless classical numbers, rock and roll and blues medleys, and even disco.

The most famous free dance ever was *Bolero* by Torvill and Dean. In 1984 the British couple, partners since 1975, was the best ice-dancing duo in the world. Torvill was a twenty-six-year-old insurance clerk, and Dean a twenty-five-year-old constable. They'd been skating since they were kids. Both had won junior titles—Torvill in pairs, Dean in ice dancing—by the age of fourteen. They were brought together at their hometown ice rink in Nottingham, England, by a former British ice-dancing champion and coach named Janet Sawbridge, who trained the two skaters and led them to several regional titles and their first international championship in 1976. By 1979 they had a new coach, Betty Callaway, and were the best ice dancers in Britain. Unfortunately, they were broke. Torvill and Dean trained for two hours in the morning, worked their day jobs, then were back at the rink from 10:30 p.m. until 2 a.m. "It was getting to the stage [where] I feared having to take somebody into custody at, say, 9 o'clock on the 2 to 10 p.m. shift," wrote Constable Dean. "In one week alone I had to make three arrests which caused [me to cancel our] training."[61] In 1980 the couple placed fifth at the Winter Olympics in Lake Placid, using vacation time to be there. "We must have been the only skaters at that level still to hold full-time jobs," they wrote. "We had no sponsors, so it was the only way we could afford to skate."[62]

In the fall of 1980, after a fourth-place finish at the World Championships, their schedule came to a head. It was a "turning point," they wrote, when "every competition meant borrowing time against holidays, which had to be paid back with overtime, or being given time, or taking unpaid leave."[63] They couldn't do it anymore. Therefore, Torvill and Dean quit their jobs and began searching for a sponsor. That's when Jayne's mother had an idea. They would ask the Nottingham City Council for a three-year, £42,000 stipend to train for the Olympics.[64] It had never been done before. But in late 1980 the stipend was approved, and the pair went to Oberstdorf, West Germany, to train. In

February 1981 they won the European Championships at Innsbruck, then in March, the World Championships in Hartford, Connecticut. They would not lose, as amateurs, again. Torvill and Dean were outstanding technical dancers, but what set them apart were the soulful and innovative free dance programs choreographed by Dean. "All sports lay down . . . rules," he said, "and we have a lot of them in ours. In the free program—which counts for fifty percent of the score—we've got to wrap it all up in four minutes. Not much time. So there's only one thing to do: we turn on the music and try to lead the audience into fantasy."[65]

At the 1982 World Championships, for example, Dean broke with convention by using four straight minutes of music from a Broadway show entitled *Mack and Mabel*. Instead of three songs and three changes of rhythm, a scheme which everyone used and the ISU allowed, in Dean's program there were no breaks whatsoever. "The piece flowed and any changes of tempo were introduced by the music itself," the couple's biographer, John Hennessey, wrote. "It was revolutionary, and, as it turned out, revelational."[66] Their scores were seven 5.9's for technical merit, but five 6.0's for artistic impression. The next year Torvill and Dean worked closely with the famed stage actor Michael Crawford to bring *Barnum*, the Broadway musical about the life of the circus owner P. T. Barnum, to the ice. It was a huge success. At the World Championships in Helsinki, they scored nine 5.9's for technical merit, and nine 6.0's for artistic impression. A perfect 6.0 sweep had never been accomplished before, not in ice dancing, not in any skating event. They also won all three dances in the compulsories and the original set program. They were, without question, the greatest ice dancers in the world. "They're the best," said the coach and former ice-dance champion Bernard Ford. "I feel sorry for ice dancers [today]. . . . There's no way they can live up to what [Torvill and Dean] are doing. They are changing the directions of ice dancing in so many ways. With their choreography and what they're trying to do . . . it makes [coaches like me] re-evaluate what [we're] doing [too]."[67]

In Britain their fans called them Their Greatnesses. In 1981 they became Members of the British Empire, an award bestowed by the queen, and in 1983 they were the proud recipients of the Freedom of Nottingham award.[68] Given to persons "of distinction" who had "rendered eminent service" to the city, the award allowed the somewhat confused and cowless Torvill and Dean to graze cattle on city lands. To many Brits, they were as popular as Charles and Di. They were hounded for autographs and chased by paparazzi, and everyone wondered if they were a couple. "Their relationship is the subject of more guesses in England than the winning lottery number," wrote one reporter. "Will they or won't they? Were they or weren't they? On ice, he twirls her like a swizzle stick. Off the ice? Well, the tabloids can only speculate—and the public laps it up."[69] Adding fuel to the fire was Dean's newest free dance, a sultry interpretation of *Bolero.* Composed in the 1920s, *Bolero* was mildly popular among music fans until it appeared in the film *10* (1979), directed by Blake Edwards and starring the model and actress Bo Derek and the comedian Dudley Moore. After that it became a cliché. In the film's memorable sex scene, Derek and Moore cavort uncomfortably with *Bolero* playing in the background. "It's sex music from the sexiest movie of the past few years," said a music editor at *Billboard* magazine. "People are really buying it."[70] According to one writer, *Bolero* was "a sex aid," a "plain-brown-wrapper item."[71]

For Torvill and Dean, what the song was was brilliant. With help from an Oxford-trained musician named Bob Stewart, the ice dancers condensed the seventeen-and-a-half minute piece to four minutes and twenty-eight seconds. It was still eighteen seconds too long. As per ISU rules, the free dance could last a maximum of four minutes and ten seconds, but the skaters discovered that the clock started only when they began to skate. Therefore, they started the performance on their knees. Swaying back and forth eighteen seconds into *Bolero,* Dean lifted Torvill slowly, then brought her over his shoulder and down to the ice. When Torvill stood up, the free dance began. *Bolero* was unlike any music anyone had skated to before. It had no breaks and no changes of pace; it was one long melody leading to a crescendo. "From that . . . we evolved a romantic scenario," they wrote. "A man and a woman are in love . . . [but] they realize their love is doomed, that the only way they will be together is to be united in death, a dramatic, fiery end in the crater of a volcano." It was "over the top," admittedly, but "the narrative," they explained, "gave [them] a sense of purpose."[72] In Sarajevo they practiced the routine at six a.m. the day of the finals. It was Valentine's Day, 1984. Only Callaway, a sound engineer, and twenty or so people on the cleaning staff were there to see them. Zetra was empty.

"We ran through *Bolero* as if it were real," they wrote, "putting as much into it as we could—the expressions, the soulful, passionate looks—and as the music ended, we were astonished to hear applause. All the cleaners had put down their brushes and dusters, and had sat down to watch. They didn't have to do that, probably weren't allowed to, officially, so it was quite a tribute. We bowed, and took their applause as a good omen."[73] That night Torvill and Dean had the highest-scoring performance in ice dancing in Olympic history—six 5.9's and three 6.0's for technical merit, and nine 6.0's for artistic impression. Together with the compulsory dance and the original set pattern dance, judges had given the skaters twenty 6.0's. No other pair had received even one. In second place were Natalia Bestemianova and Andrei Bukin of the Soviet Union, while Marina Klimova and Sergei Ponomarenko, also of the Soviet Union, were third. Torvill and Dean went pro at the conclusion of the 1984 season. Although they skated together, created and choreographed shows together, and returned to the Olympics in 1994, where they won a bronze, they were never—at least publicly—a couple. "It's very hard for other people to understand what we [had]," said Dean in an interview in 2006. It was "a unique partnership. [We were] almost a brand name."[74]

8

The *Nasenbohrer*

Bᴵᴸᴸ. Wild Bill. Bad Billy. The judge had seen it before: a local kid too smart for his own good, divorced parents, alone, and bored. He smoked pot. He stole things. He ran with the wrong crowd. In 1977 Bill Johnson was a seventeen-year-old punk, in court in Clackamas County, Oregon, for stealing a car. "It looked like it had a nice engine," said Johnson, who'd stolen the car by tying a rope to its chassis and then simply towing it away. The judge gave him a choice: go to a juvenile detention center or ski. That's right. Go to a juvenile detention center or ski. "They wanted to take me to adult court," Johnson remembered. "I was seventeen, but real close to eighteen. That really threw a scare into me."[1] But Johnson had never been scared . . . or so it seemed. As a kid at Mount Hood Meadows ski resort, he flew down the slopes like a missile. He was a tiny, tucked-in prodigy, a speed demon who, as he put it, "never . . . learn[ed] how to turn."[2] Now he'd taken a wrong turn. His father, Wally, spoke to the judge. What Bill needed was structure, he said. There was a ski school near Wenatchee, Washington, where students worked, attended community college, and skied. It was highly regimented, and Wally knew the coach. Bill had planned to go there before his . . . uh, well, indiscretion. It's just what he needs. The school was the Mission Ridge Ski Academy; the coach, Dick Knowles. "Bill knew when he was there he was there to keep himself out of jail," Knowles said. "I had a reputation of being a very tough coach. We'd square off, I'd lay down the rules, and he'd follow them."[3]

Yet Bill was antisocial, a loner. He skied how he wanted to ski and was, as one teacher put it, "very individualistic." Coaches found him difficult to deal with. Teammates hated him. He was brash, arrogant, and vain. He was also insubordinate. "I can go straight faster than anybody," he once said. "It takes a lot of guts to go out there and throw yourself down the mountain."[4] At 5 feet, 9 inches and 170 pounds, Johnson had what experts called an aerodynamic profile, an excellent aerodynamic profile.[5] Knees bent, arms tucked tightly, he handled straightaways as well as anyone in the world. He was a glider—a gifted, gifted glider. But while downhill skiing is technically a speed event, there are turns, and Johnson couldn't turn. "He is essentially a soft-snow skier," wrote one journalist, "a glider who lets his skis run like the wind on the flat sections of any course. . . . However, most World Cup courses are . . . full of tight, technical turns that are not [his] forte."[6] Johnson could learn how to turn, but only if he listened to a coach.

He was "fairly receptive," said Knowles, but in 1979 Johnson accepted a scholarship from the Whiteface Alpine Training Center in Lake Placid, New York, where he met coaches from the U.S. Alpine Ski Team.[7] "They told me what to do and where to go," sneered Johnson. "[They] thought I was arrogant because I didn't want to watch myself [on video] while they pointed out what I was doing wrong. But . . . why should I watch myself doing things wrong when I could watch [other skiers] doing things right?"[8]

In coach-speak, Johnson was uncoachable but too talented not to be a member of the national team. He was given a spot in 1980. In 1981, however, he was cut by the director of the U.S. Alpine Ski Team, Bill Marolt, for being out of shape. "I think Bill needed to know that we were serious about developing a good program, and the discipline it took to do it," said Marolt.[9] Unsponsored and unaffiliated, through the winter of 1981 Johnson paid his own way to ski events and in 1982 finished fifth at the U.S. Nationals. That put him back on the team. In 1982–83 he won three of four downhills on the Europa Cup circuit, a kind of junior league, but finished his senior events as the sixty-fifth-place skier in the world. Then, in 1983–84 he finished a mediocre forty-first, twenty-sixth, twentieth, forty-fifth, and twenty-third before shocking the field in January 1984 with a first-place finish at the legendary Lauberhorn course near Wengen, Switzerland. It was the first-ever victory by an American male in a downhill World Cup.

Critics said Johnson's victory was a fluke. For one thing, the weather was so bad that the twisting Lauberhorn course had been shortened by eight hundred meters. Then, as the top-seeded competitors went first, they encountered foggy conditions and snow. "The conditions were just terrible," complained one skier. "We couldn't see anything when we started; there was new snow all over the place. . . . [The] race shouldn't have been run."[10]

Urs Raber, the Swiss star who had won at Laax the previous week, fell to fifteenth, while the Austrian great Franz Klammer, who placed second at Laax, was thirteenth. Steve Podborski, a star skier from Canada, was twentieth. "Right at the start," said Podborski, "I turned to my serviceman . . . and said 'unbelievable' to him in German. He agreed. That's what it was like. If I had [started] number twenty or twenty-five, I think I could have won."[11] That wasn't a boast. Skiers who had low seeds had an advantage on bad weather days because the top seeds, skiing first, essentially plowed the snow. Twenty-one people skied before Johnson, but only two of the first fifteen skiers finished in the top ten. "I won't say he is a bad skier," said Podborski. "I won't even say I'm a good one. But just look at the standings. . . . [The] starters were at a disadvantage."[12] Johnson finished in 2:10.89, even after losing nearly a second on a difficult turn near the finish. That meant he was flying. In downhill skiing, winners are determined by hundredths of a second. To lose a second and still win is virtually unheard of. Tucked low and seemingly in control, Johnson, at the 1:50 mark, landed a small jump but splayed awkwardly. He righted himself on one leg, exited the course briefly, then returned to it as if nothing had happened. He did this in .8 seconds at sixty miles per hour.

Still, competitors like Klammer were unimpressed, even bitter. "When the course is hard and icy," said Klammer, "Johnson is nowhere. He can't make the turns."[13] Although nearing the end of his career at age thirty, Klammer was the greatest downhill skier in the world. Known simply as the Kaiser, Klammer had won the World Cup downhill title five times. He'd won twenty-five races in all, including, at one point, ten in a row. "Oh yeah?" said Johnson. "That's too bad. . . . Wait'll they see me [next week] at Kitzbühel."[14] Klammer could only laugh. High in the Austrian Alps, Kitzbühel was home to the Hahnenkamm race course, perhaps the most difficult course in all of downhill skiing. Johnson would never win. "[He's] a nose picker," said Klammer, a *nasenbohrer*. In German, *nasenbohrer* is an idiomatic word meaning beginner, someone who's wet behind the ears. But Johnson saw it as an insult. He lashed out at Klammer, a hero of his he now had "little respect for." He said if he was a nose picker he'd be "the fastest nose picker" Klammer had ever seen.[15] Soon the Klammer–Johnson dispute was big news. "I enjoy sticking it to the Austrians," said Johnson. "Those Austrians are spoiled brats. They think they should win every time. They have trouble accepting that someone from another country can win too."[16]

Johnson had won one race but chose to insult the Austrians in Austria, where skiing was a national sport. Things got nasty. When Johnson returned to Kitzbühel in 1985, people pounded on the windshield of his car and beat at the windows with their fists.[17] "Billy had . . . [a] big mouth," the twin ski racers Phil and Steve Mahre wrote. "[Talk like that] upsets a lot of people."[18] It was risky, too, for if Johnson lost the next race or even had his usual result of, say, thirtieth place, he would be a laughingstock in his sport or, in Klammer's words, a *nasenbohrer*. With all of Austria watching, Johnson came in forty-fifth. Klammer was first, Erwin Resch was second, and Anton Steiner was third—a clean sweep for the Austrians. The next week at Garmisch-Partenkirchen in Germany, Johnson was thirty-second. This time Podborski was first, Resch was second, and Klammer was third. "Bill has a lot to learn on hard-turning, icy courses," said the coach Theo Nadig. "But he is a fast learner."[19] It's a good thing he was, too, because in less than a week he'd be on the slopes at Cortina d'Ampezzo, Italy, and after that at Mount Bjelašnica in Sarajevo. By this point, the media and members of the ski world had largely forgotten Johnson, but at Cortina he was fourth.

This time it wasn't a fluke. It was the course, said critics. It wasn't technical enough. Cortina starts with "extremely steep slopes and a series of well-iced turns," Matthew Fisher wrote in the *Toronto Globe and Mail*. "Unfortunately, these are followed by a two-hundred-meter stretch that is as level and as interesting as a banquet table. The final fifty seconds are straight and smooth. A racer must stay in a gentle, aerodynamically sound tuck all the way to the finish"—in other words, ski like Johnson.[20] Then it dawned on everyone: if Johnson finished fourth at Cortina, what would he do at Bjelašnica, a course *Ski* magazine called "a glider's dream"?[21] Bjelašnica had been dangerous, but the organizers "corrected" the course by improving the straightaways and smoothing out several large bumps. Now it had "a twisty technical section" at the top, two turns in the middle, then a straight, straight run to the bottom.[22] Bjelašnica "is my kind of course," said Johnson. "I think most everybody knows it."[23] If they didn't know it, he told them. "I'm going to win the gold medal," he boasted. "They might as well give it to me now."[24] No one had ever seen such bravado. This was skiing, not boxing, and no American male had ever won the Olympic downhill. But Johnson was sure of it. All he needed was snow—new snow—which would make gliding a breeze. "On new snow . . . you have to glide a lot," said Peter Mueller, a Swiss skier who, like Johnson, was a glider. "Standing too hard on [your] skis only makes you lose time."[25]

If it snowed, Johnson and Mueller were the favorites; if it stayed dry, specifically, cold and dry, Klammer. In the end, it snowed. It snowed and snowed and snowed, nearly sixty straight hours of snow over three days. According to the Yugoslav press agency Tanjug, snowdrifts in parts of Yugoslavia were seventeen feet high. The country's main highway was closed, and in Vojvodina some fifteen hundred people were trapped in their cars for three days on a six-mile stretch of road.[26] This was a major European storm: in Switzerland there were thirty avalanches, a ship sank in the English Channel, and wind and snow closed airports from Glasgow to Dubrovnik. "The Europeans were freaking out," said the American coach Erik Steinberg, but "[Bill] was cooling his heels in the Olympic Village, chewing Copenhagen and playing pinball." Whenever Johnson saw the Austrians, he'd say, "Hi guys! It's still snowing up there."[27] It was an annoying taunt. "I don't know an athlete in [the] village who actually like[d] the guy," said Phil Mahre. The Austrians despised Johnson. They "were out for blood."[28] When an Austrian TV crew asked him if he'd seen the film *Downhill Racer,* Johnson replied, "I've seen it many times, and that's exactly the way it'll happen now. You can [write] your story."[29] Released in 1969, *Downhill Racer* starred Robert Redford, whose character, Dave Chappellet, was a devil-may-care speed freak who won the Olympics.

The Austrians "think I'm crazy to talk like this," explained Johnson. "But they've seen I can ski. . . . I have them worried."[30] The Austrians were worried, for instead of racing their race all they could think of was Johnson. For example, when Johnson said Bjelašnica was "[his] kind of course," Klammer replied that yes it was, "a course for eight-year-olds." The Austrian great then went out, in his third training run, and fell. "[Bill did it] by design," said his teammate Blake Lewis. His incessant talking "was a way to tick people off, to make them think harder about it."[31] To ABC, Johnson was a godsend. After two straight losses in hockey and a week of weather delays, the network was in third place. On Thursday, 9 February, for example, ABC opened its broadcast with the USA–Czechoslovakia hockey match, but with no other competition to air, it stuck viewers with a series of unpopular Bosnian travelogues and "Up Close and Personal" vignettes. Klammer had one, Podborski had one, but Johnson's was filmed before his victory at Lauberhorn, when the upstart skier seemed to have little hope. Now, as ABC claimed, Johnson was America's hope. He raced, finally, on Thursday, 16 February 1984.

"I was nervous twenty minutes before the race," said Johnson, "but I started to cool down. In the starting gate I just said, 'Relax. Relax. You've got it.' "[32] Johnson started sixth but had only the fourth-fastest time through the second interval, two-thirds of the way down the course. He was .44 of a second slower than Steiner but blazed through the final third to finish first. His time was 1:45.59. Mueller was second at 1:45.86, while Steiner, at 1:45.95, was third. Klammer finished tenth. "You've got to give [Johnson] credit," said the Canadian Todd Brooker, who finished ninth. "It's one thing to be so goddamn sure of yourself and another to be absolutely right."[33] Still, Brooker couldn't resist: "It's just too bad the . . . downhill [was] held on [such] an easy course." "Easy?" replied Johnson. "If it's so easy why didn't [he] win it?"[34] Klammer was gracious. "It was a very good time," he said. "I was a little surprised. But he was the best in the training runs. . . . He skied extremely well."[35] Johnson had skied well. He'd skied so well that when reporters asked what the medal meant to him, he quipped, "Millions. We're talking about millions."[36] Observers weren't so sure. Johnson was too brash, too headstrong to be a spokesperson for commercial products. In the year or so following his victory, he was also a jerk—to his fans, teammates, coaches, sponsors, and, particularly, the officials of the U.S. Ski Team.

Not wishing to share his earnings, as he was obligated to do, Johnson threatened at one point to ski for Botswana. "I told [the U.S. Ski Team] to take a hike," he said in 1985. "They only sell the team, not the individual. They ruin racers by taking their money. The latest is they're trying to get a piece of . . . my movie."[37] The movie was a made-for-television stinker entitled *Going for Gold: The Bill Johnson Story*, starring Anthony Edwards as Bill Johnson and Sarah Jessica Parker as Maggie, Bill's fictional girlfriend. Johnson received $200,000 for the film plus maybe a million in sponsorships, but he blew through the money and was out of skiing by 1989. In the weeks after Sarajevo he won three more races, once at the U.S. Nationals and twice at the World Cup. Johnson's two World Cup victories were in Aspen, Colorado, and Whistler, British Columbia, on curvy, technical courses for which he had been ill-equipped. Yet somehow, wrote Johnson's biographer Jennifer Woodlief, "Bill had learned [how] to turn."[38] It was an amazing run: three World Cup victories (including Lauberhorn in January), a U.S. National Championship, and a gold medal in three months. Johnson had come from nowhere to finish third in the World Cup downhill standings and says he would have won the title had he had one more chance. However, Johnson spent the summer of 1984 on what he called "the champagne circuit." There were parades, banquets, luncheons, and parties—lots of parties. He returned in the fall amidst rumors of a drug problem and a gambling problem and was ten pounds overweight.

Johnson never skied well again. He had five top-ten finishes in six tumultuous years and failed to make the 1988 Olympic team. In his private life Johnson experienced one tragedy after another: in 1991 his infant son Ryan drowned tragically in a hot tub accident, in 1995 he lost his job as a "ski ambassador" at the Crested Butte Resort in Colorado, and in 2000 his wife, Gina, filed for divorce. By that point Johnson was a carpenter. He drove from job to job and lived alone in a Winnebago. In 2000, drunk at a party in San Diego, the thirty-nine-year-old Johnson got a tattoo. Etched on his right bicep, the tattoo featured a crudely drawn skull with flames coming out of it that read, "Ski to Die." "Johnson's crash-and-burn style," wrote one journalist, "was better suited to the slopes than to daily life. . . . In the end, the fire that propelled him, that youthful fearlessness, would devolve into a sort of desperation—nihilism, even. He would become the stereotypical ex-jock who destroys himself trying to act young, and his life would serve as proof that you cannot burn on forever."[39] Yet Johnson tried. In 2000, unemployed and with no permanent address, he announced a comeback. By competing at various FIS events in America and Canada, he'd return to the World Cup and win a spot, he said, at the 2002 Olympics.

To raise money Johnson asked for donations through his website, www .billjohnson1984gold.com, and sold the skis he'd worn in Sarajevo to his mother. (He had tried eBay, but his mother talked him out of that and instead bought the skis herself for four thousand dollars.) His goal, he said, was to be back on the U.S. Ski Team by the end of the 2000–01 season and to finish ranked in the top 100 in the world.[40] "When I heard he wanted to make a comeback," said one of his former coaches, "my reaction was he's got the talent. But . . . there's a reason people don't come back to downhill racing at forty. [The swimmer] Mark Spitz tries a comeback, and what's the worst that can happen to him? In our sport people can kill themselves."[41] Johnson appeared in over a dozen races, finishing in the thirties and forties, typically; his best result, in a downhill in January 2001, was fourteenth place. He wasn't bad, but he was racing mainly with teenagers on a midlevel circuit known as the Nor-Am Cup, a circuit two levels below the World Cup. "It's a long road back," Johnson admitted. "I'm doing okay. [In North America] I'm in the top whatever. Top fifty I think. Two weeks ago I started 115th. Now, what [am] I? Thirty-second. That's better, isn't it?"[42] It was better, but in March 2001, on a training run in Big Mountain, Montana, Johnson lost control on a section of course known as the Corkscrew. Going fifty miles an hour, he slammed face-first into the ice and careened through two layers of safety netting before landing in a third. "Help me," he groaned before passing out.[43]

Johnson was flown via helicopter to the hospital. "I knew he was a ski racer," said the emergency room doctor, Keith Lara. "He had the suit, a helmet, and the number thirty-four bib. I looked at his tongue and knew I had not seen a worse airway injury in [my entire career]."[44] Johnson had bitten through his tongue. Blood poured into his lungs, and he began to suffocate. Paramedics at the scene had used a tracheal tube to get him breathing again, but Johnson had suffered three separate brain injuries, including one, called shearing, in which his brain had rotated inside his head and slammed into his skull.[45] (Known as diffuse axonal injury, shearing happens frequently in car wrecks.) Johnson spent three weeks and his forty-first birthday in a coma. He awoke with severe memory loss—he had no idea where or when he'd crashed or why at his age he'd even come back. "I don't remember a lot of things," he said. "I don't remember 1990 . . . [or] 1991. I don't remember 2000 . . . [But] I do know I won an Olympic medal. . . . What's that area I skied in? It starts with a Y."[46] Although forced to relearn simple tasks such as eating and brushing his teeth, Johnson had good muscle memory and by 2002 could even ski again. Yet work was out of the question. His mother became his guardian, and Johnson survived for a time on disability checks and donations, including one in 2004 from the Franz Klammer Foundation of Austria. By 2008, however, his injuries had caught up with him. That year he suffered the first of several strokes and lost the use of his right arm and right leg. Today he lives in a nursing home in Gresham, Oregon.[47]

To his critics, Bill Johnson was a flash in the pan. According to the alpine ski database ski-db.com, as of 2014 Johnson's three career victories in the downhill put him in thirty-fourth place.[48] Even then, he's tied with seventeen others and has since been eclipsed by the Americans Daron Rahlves, who has nine downhill victories, and Bode Miller, who has eight. But Johnson did what no American had ever done before: he'd not only won a World Cup downhill, itself an accomplishment, he'd won the Olympics. "What [Bill] did that day was amazing," said Marolt. "In retrospect, it's still amazing."[49]

To many Americans, Bill Johnson was *the* story of the Sarajevo games, but his medal was America's third alpine medal in three days. On Monday, 13 February, Debbie Armstrong and Christin Cooper finished one–two in the women's giant slalom, while Tamara McKinney, the presumed favorite, was fourth. Just twenty at the time, the peppy Armstrong was an even bigger long shot than Johnson. Whereas Johnson had won in January 1984 at Lauberhorn, Armstrong had yet to win even a single World Cup event. She'd placed in the top ten five times, but, as one analyst put it, she was in Sarajevo "for the experience."[50] After all, her teammates were three of the best skiers, male or female, in U.S. history. In 1983, for example, McKinney became the first American woman to win the overall World Cup title, with season finishes of second in the slalom and first in the giant slalom. In 1982 Cooper finished third overall, while her teammate Cindy Nelson was fifth. At the age of twenty-eight, Nelson was the "grande dame" of American skiing.[51] Since 1974 she had had eight top-ten finishes in the overall World Cup standings and was the last American woman to have won an alpine medal—a bronze in the downhill at Innsbruck—in the Olympics. Experts predicted a one–two finish for McKinney and Nelson in the giant slalom and a first-place finish for Cooper in the slalom. Armstrong wasn't even mentioned.[52]

Yet Armstrong was peaking at the right time. In January 1984 she finished third in the Super G (super giant slalom) at Puy St. Vincent, France, which was a speed event similar to the downhill. She also finished fifth in the giant slalom and sixth in the combined downhill and slalom at St. Gervais, France. "Debbie is no fluke," Nelson said. "She's going to be around for a lot of years. She reminds me of myself. . . . She's got a healthy head."[53] A native of Seattle, Armstrong was a natural athlete who excelled in soccer and basketball at Garfield High School—the same school Jimi Hendrix, Quincy Jones, and Bruce Lee attended—but whose real gift was skiing. "The sport chose her," said her father, Hugh, a professor of psychology at the University of Washington. Hugh was an avid skier; he and his wife, Dollie, actually taught skiing on weekends in the Alpental Valley east of Seattle, which is where Armstrong learned to ski. "We started racing Mighty Mites when I was ten," she said, "but I was never one of the hot kids. The best I'd do was usually third because Kelly Davis, who was supposed to be third, fell down."[54] When Armstrong was twelve, her father took the family to Malaysia for two years—he was teaching on an exchange program—and Armstrong forgot how to ski. "I couldn't stop crying," she said. "My first time back on skis . . . I couldn't do it anymore. . . . I thought I'd never be able to do it again."[55]

Nevertheless, by the spring of 1981, at the age of seventeen, Armstrong was the U.S. Junior Olympic champion in the giant slalom and was promoted to the national team for the 1981–82 season. Armstrong's World Cup debut, in the downhill, came in Saalbach, Austria, where she stunned the other competitors by finishing first in her first training run, an amazing 2.4 seconds ahead of the second-place finisher, Doris De Agostini of Switzerland.[56] A few weeks later, during a training run at the World Championships in Schladming, Austria, Armstrong broke her leg. "I think it was a plus," she said. "It was my first year on the World Cup [circuit] and so much was going on. My head was spinning. . . . Before I broke my leg, I didn't know if skiing was my favorite sport. . . . [But once] I was [away from skiing], I realized how much I loved it."[57] Armstrong returned to the slopes in late 1982. Her best finish was fifth, in the downhill, and she finished the 1982–83 season ranked nineteenth in the world. She was also twenty-sixth in the giant slalom, and thirty-third overall. Although Armstrong started the 1983–84 season with three top-ten finishes and six in the top fifteen, to coaches she was a project, an "up-and-comer." Her bio in the 1984 U.S. Olympic media guide listed her as belonging to the B team. "Her coaches [said] she [had] a lot of potential," a family member said. "[But] she wasn't sure she'd even be on the team as late as Christmas."[58]

IOC rules stated that the combined U.S. Alpine Ski Team, male and female, could have at most fourteen competitors and no more than eight of either sex. Thus, it was possible, though not probable, that Armstrong would be left out. She wasn't. In fact, she was picked to compete in two events: the downhill and the giant slalom. (In contrast to the one-run speed event of the downhill, the slalom and giant slalom are technical events in which skiers maneuver through gates and make short, quick turns. For each slalom event, skiers make one run on two consecutive days, and the fastest aggregate time wins.) The downhill at Mount Jahorina was originally scheduled for Saturday, 11 February, and the giant slalom for Monday and Tuesday, 13 and 14 February. But the same storm that hit Bjelašnica hit Jahorina. By the end of week one of the games, Jahorina had had two avalanches.[59] Winds of one hundred miles per hour whipped through the course, and both the downhill and slalom events were postponed. By late Monday the weather had cleared, and the organizers decided to hold the two giant slalom runs on one day, Tuesday, and to move the downhill to Wednesday. "I couldn't wait to get on my skis," said Armstrong, who spent Monday night shooting hoops at the gym in the Olympic village.[60] As more than one person noted, every shot she took went in.

The Olympics are "a once in a lifetime opportunity," she said, "and I didn't want to get to the finish line wishing I had a chance to do it again. So . . . I just let loose [mentally] and everything clicked. . . . I was in tune with myself more than I've ever been in my life."[61] Using mental techniques taught to her by her father, Armstrong was oddly ebullient but also calm at the starting gate. "I was behind her," Cooper said, "and I heard her say 'Okay, Deb. Have a good time. Have a good time. Have the race of your life.' Then she turned to me and said, 'Have the run of your life, Coop. Have a good time.' She was so hyped up it was funny."[62] Her "hyperpsych boiling merrily inside," as one author put it, Armstrong blew through the course in 1:08.97. At the end of the first run she was in second place, one-tenth of a second behind Cooper. McKinney was eighth at 1:10.11. In run two Armstrong was fourth at 1:12.01, but Cooper slipped at gate five and finished a half second behind her. McKinney bounced back and won the second run, but with an aggregate time of 2:20.98 Armstrong was the winner. Cooper was second at 2:21.38, Perrine Pelen of France was third at 2:21.40, and McKinney was fourth at 2:21.83.

At the finish line, after the last skier had come down and the final results were known, Armstrong was mobbed by the press. "Yaaaaaaaaaaaaaweeeeeeee!," she yelled, as her friends and teammates lifted her in the air. "I can't believe it! I can't believe it! I wish I could always be this happy. I feel so good for everyone who had anything to do with it and who is happy for me right now!"[63] The 1–2–4 finish was the best alpine finish in U.S. Olympic history. Armstrong's gold medal was also the thousandth Olympic gold medal won by an American (in both the Winter and Summer Games) and the first of the Sarajevo Olympics. "You could hear Americans howling in the streets downtown when they announced it," said Pat Ahern, a member of the U.S. Nordic team.[64] Almost unbelievably, the United States had gone five full days and sixteen events without a gold. In fact, America's only medal was a silver in pairs figure skating won by Peter and Kitty Carruthers. Team USA was disappointed, but the press was apoplectic. By this point, the hated Soviets had won thirteen medals, including three golds. The East Germans had won fourteen medals, including six golds. "What happened to the U.S. team's burning desire?" read one headline, as if world-class athletes training year-round lacked motivation.[65] The columnist Bob Sudyk was especially glib. Writing for the *Hartford Courant,* the patriotic Sudyk issued a dimwitted attack on the skier Phil Mahre. Mahre was the best skier on the U.S. Alpine Ski Team, and in 1983 was the overall World Cup leader and the number one skier in the world. In fact, Mahre had been the world's number one skier three years in a row and was undeniably the greatest skier America had ever produced. Yet Mahre was at the end of his career. At twenty-six, he and his brother Steve had been skiing the World Cup circuit since 1976. The Mahres wanted to win, but the 1983–84 season, prior to Sarajevo, had been the worst of their careers. In January, for example, Steve had two "did not finish" results because of falls or disqualifications and one nineteenth place. Phil was better, with two top-ten finishes, but he also had a "did not finish" as well as a fourteenth and a twenty-sixth place. "We knew exactly what we were capable of doing," the brothers wrote in their coautobiography of 1985, "but we also acknowledged the challenge, considering" that just prior to the Olympics "[we'd] placed in the top ten only twice. So we told the truth—we said that we weren't necessarily expecting to win a gold medal. But the press heard us say that we weren't trying to win a gold medal."[66] What made Sudyk mad, in particular, was Phil's assertion that there was "too much emphasis on gold" and that his focus wasn't "to peak for the Olympics" but to win the World Cup. "It only matters in the public's eye whether you win gold medals," Phil said. "It's unfortunate . . . [but] that's the way it is. . . . I've never thought a medal was that important and I can't understand why people think [they are]. You lose, so what? Life goes on."[67]

Not good enough, cried Sudyk. "If the nation had the same will to win that the Mahre twins are currently expressing, Adolf Hitler . . . [would] be playing the fluegelhorn in the White House today."[68] It was a stupid comparison, but Bob Lochner of the *Los Angeles Times* agreed. So did Bob Verdi of the *Chicago Tribune* and Dan Barreiro of the *Dallas Morning News*. The jingoistic low point, perhaps, occurred when Phil finished eighth in Sarajevo in the giant slalom. "That's the good news," wrote Barreiro. "The bad news is that Mahre gets another chance Sunday in the slalom. I hope he chokes again."[69] To be fair, the Mahres were free spirits who had a love–hate relationship with coaches, Olympic and World Cup officials, and the press.

Born in Yakima, Washington, Phil and Steve Mahre were numbers four and five in a family of nine children. Their father, Dave, was the resident manager of the White Pass Ski Area, and the Mahres grew up in the manager's house at the bottom of a ski slope. "Each morning a bus would drive to the Pass to pick up a half dozen or so of the Mahre kids and transport us to school," they wrote. "We got home about five. Mom would have dinner ready and afterward we would go upstairs to put our ski gear on. Night after night, we skied on an illuminated ramp beside the house, climbing [up] . . . and skiing down."[70]

By 1974 the two sixteen-year-old Mahre brothers had made the U.S. Ski Team, and in 1975 Phil won the giant slalom and Steve the slalom at the U.S. Nationals in Washington. By 1976 they were World Cup regulars—Phil was fourteenth overall in the standings, while Steve was twenty-seventh—and both competed in the Innsbruck Olympics. Phil's breakthrough year came in 1978, when he finished second overall in the World Cup standings and emerged as a serious rival to Sweden's Ingemar Stenmark, who at the time was the greatest slalom skier in the world. Just a year older than the Mahres, Stenmark would win every World Cup slalom and giant slalom title between 1975 and 1981 as well as a gold medal in both events in the 1980 Olympics. In 1981, however, Phil narrowly beat Stenmark for the overall World Cup title; Phil won again in 1982 and 1983, with Stenmark finishing second each time. Yet critics contended that while Phil Mahre was good, even great, Stenmark was better. Since 1978–79 the FIS had included combined points for downhill and slalom events in its overall World Cup standings. Since Stenmark didn't ski downhill and Mahre did, however, Mahre edged him on points. In 1981, for example, Stenmark was first in the slalom and first in the giant slalom and had more tour wins, ten, than anyone else that season but finished second overall.[71] "It was as if baseball had shut the doors to the hall of fame to Joe DiMaggio," wrote one author, "because [DiMaggio] refused to bunt."[72]

In 1982, though, Phil Mahre finished ahead of Stenmark in both the slalom and giant slalom and was the number one skier in the world. There was no doubt about it. Mahre had finished ahead of Stenmark in eleven of sixteen races and had won five. He was first in the slalom standings, first in the giant slalom standings, and first in the combined standings for a number one finish overall. Stenmark was second, while Steve, in his best year on the World Cup circuit, was third. "I'd like to win the World Cup myself," Steve said in an interview in 1982, "but right now Phil is the best."[73] Notoriously independent, the Mahres utterly refused to either ski or train formally during the summer. Instead, they water-skied. They jogged and played basketball and competed in their second-favorite sport, motocross. "Our lives are ours to lead," said one brother. "We both love ski racing, but we've got to do it our way. We have to get away from skiing for a while each year."[74] In the summer of 1981, for example, the Mahres eschewed training altogether to build Phil and his soon-to-be-wife, Holly, a house. "We liked working on it so much," said Phil, "that it was almost hard to get skiing again. I [couldn't] wait to get back at it."[75]

Although terse and introverted—one writer judged them to be laconic—the Mahres aired their grievances in the press. There was a frankness to them. They said what they meant, and meant what they said. "Fame and glory aren't something we really like much," said Steve. "We haven't sought a lot of money. We'll take an endorsement here and there, but we won't go for a million dollars or anything like that."[76] They described Bill Johnson as arrogant, said Marolt was a dictator, and nearly quit the team in 1982 over a clothing dispute. Apparently, Phil gave an interview while not wearing team-approved attire. When officials told him to change into something with a sponsor's logo on it, he threatened to quit. "I was ready to hang it up," said Phil. "I mean, I'd dressed myself for twenty years or more and didn't need to be told how to do it."[77] Phil was "as principled as Gandhi and as defiant as Cool Hand Luke," one author avowed.[78] Steve was quieter, but his opinions, at least his ski-related opinions, were the same. "It's sometimes like he's an extension of myself," said Phil. "When Steve wins, it's almost like a victory for me. It just doesn't feel as if I've been beaten when he wins. So if I can't win, I want him to win."[79] A common Mahre tactic was for one brother to radio the other brother after he'd skied the course. Phil, for example, would tell Steve where the trouble spots were, when and where to turn, and what lines to run. "It's not fair," said Stenmark, on more than one occasion. "You are two to one against me!"[80]

Yet both Mahres wanted to win. In March 1981 in Borovets, Bulgaria, Steve shocked competitors by beating Phil in the slalom—Steve was second while Phil was third—when a second-place finish would have given Phil the overall World Cup title, America's first. But because he'd lost to Steve, Phil was required to finish in the top three, while skiing against Stenmark, in the very last race of the season. Luckily, he did. "Steve was out there skiing for himself," said Phil. "He wasn't skiing for me. If he didn't try to do the best he could, no matter what the situation was, he wouldn't be much of a skier."[81] Although technically amateurs, the Mahres made six-figure salaries through sponsorships and "broken time" payments provided by the U.S. Alpine Ski Team. Rule 26 of the Olympic Charter stated that athletes could accept "compensation authorized by his or her National Olympic Committee or National Foundation"—in this case the U.S. Ski Association, which oversaw the U.S. Ski Team—"to cover financial loss resulting from his or her absence from work or basic occupation on account of preparation for, or participation in, the Olympic Games." The one condition was that all monies paid to the Mahres flow through the U.S. Ski Team, which took a cut.[82]

"It's laundering money, basically," said one company rep. "We do it. Every federation worldwide does it. But it's allowable under the rules."[83] The trouble came when elite skiers like Stenmark and Johnson grew unhappy with the rules. In May 1984 Johnson asserted publicly that the U.S. Ski Team had kept 85 percent of the Mahres' endorsement money. He would hold out, he said, to negotiate a better cut.[84] Stenmark faced two blows: first, he had to share his income with the Swedish Ski Association, and, second, he faced higher-than-average taxes from the Swedish government. According to one report, Stenmark's tax rate was 90 percent.[85] In 1980, therefore, he petitioned the FIS for a B-license, a permit which allowed him to negotiate his own contracts while skiing on the World Cup circuit for Sweden. He also moved to and established residency in Monaco, the well-known tax haven where his fellow Swede the tennis player Bjorn Borg lived. In return, Stenmark promised the Swedish Ski Association a percentage of his earnings and gave up his eligibility for the Olympics. He was now, in the bizarre world of presumably amateur skiing, a professional. "I knew I had only two or three years of good skiing left," Stenmark said. "I decided it was time to capitalize on [it]."[86] Who could begrudge him? By pulling a B-license and moving to Monaco, Stenmark made at least a million dollars a year. But as Sarajevo approached, he was ineligible for the Olympics—bad for Stenmark, good for the Mahres.

A second Mahre rival missing from Sarajevo was Marc Girardelli, an Austrian-born skier who lived in Luxembourg. Although just twenty, Girardelli was a star. In 1983 he'd finished fourth in the overall World Cup standings, and in January 1984 was the number-one ranked slalom skier in the world. That month he had two firsts and a second. In February he was also first in the slalom and second in the giant slalom at Borovets. But Girardelli was ineligible because when he was twelve, his father, Helmut, had fought with the Austrian Ski Federation and had moved the boy to Luxembourg.[87] As Marc got older, he skied for Luxembourg on the World Cup circuit but was not, at the time, a citizen. "It's unfortunate that Ingemar and Marc aren't here," said Phil Mahre. "They're skiing flawlessly right now. But that's something we can't do anything about. That was their decision."[88]

It was both Phil and Steve Mahre's decision to retire after the games. The brothers had been skiing on the World Cup circuit since 1976. Each had a wife and daughter, and Phil's wife was expecting her second child a week after the games. "Skiing doesn't hold the mystique for me it once did," Phil said. "My family is going to swell to four people in about two weeks, and my family is more important than skiing right now. . . . That's causing me some problems; that, and a lack of concentration, mainly."[89]

On Tuesday, 14 February 1984, Phil finished eighth and Steve seventeenth in the giant slalom. The winner was Max Julen of Switzerland, a giant slalom specialist and perennial top-ten finisher. Julen had edged out Jure Franko, a twenty-one-year-old Slovene skier from Nova Gorica, who was fourth following round one. Andreas Wenzel of Liechtenstein was third. "YU-go-SLAV-ia! YU-go-SLAV-ia!" chanted the crowd. "Yoo-Ray! Yoo-Ray!" There were at least seven thousand people, almost all locals, ringing the slopes. In the crowd was a four-piece band in folk costume, and everywhere there were flags. "Hop! Hop! Hop!" they yelled, which meant "Go! Go! Go!"[90] So Franko went. In run two he skied faster than anyone in either run but lost to Julen in the combined times by .23 of a second. It didn't matter. Sarajevo went nuts. "Lake Placid was nothing until the Americans beat the Soviets," said Pavle Lukač, the SOOC's press director, "and then it became a real Olympics. No one likes to provide the stage for someone else's Games. Now these are our Games."[91] Franko was a good skier. He'd finished twelfth in the giant slalom at Lake Placid and during the 1983–84 season had had seven top-ten finishes prior to the Olympics. But this—this was an upset. Franko's medal was Yugoslavia's first-ever medal in the Winter Games. "It was a great show," he said. "I had two very good runs, but I really didn't believe I would win the silver. What a joy."[92]

In the women's downhill the big story was Michela Figini, a seventeen-year-old Swiss star who narrowly defeated her teammate Maria Walliser. Olga Charvatova, Czechoslovakia's first women's alpine medalist, was third. Figini, like Johnson, was a glider who had won her first World Cup downhill just weeks prior to the games and in training runs was skiing better than anyone. When the downhill opened on Wednesday, 15 February, she out-skied the first ten competitors and led the second-place finisher, Holly Flanders, an American, by an astonishing 1.52 seconds. That's when fog and heavy snow forced the organizers to postpone the race until Thursday. Figini was unperturbed. In the second race she was slower but still managed to win by .05 of a second. In the women's slalom, held on Friday the seventeenth, the U.S. team was unexpectedly shut out. In a race in which twenty-four of the forty-five competitors either did not finish or were disqualified, Tamara McKinney and Christin Cooper both missed gates. "In slalom, you have to take as many chances as possible," said McKinney, "as many chances as you can get away with. I just took one too many."[93] The winner, in an upset, was Paoletta Magoni of Italy, an unheralded racer whose best World Cup finish had been a sixth. The runner-up was Perrine Pelen of France, who won her second Sarajevo medal, while Ursula Konzett of Liechtenstein finished third.

That left the Mahres. The American twins had one event left, the slalom on 19 February, the last event of the Sarajevo Olympics. "We wanted to win as much as anyone," they wrote, "but millions of Americans watching television at home had already pegged us as losers. Billy Johnson looked like a winner, and so did the girls' team. . . . [But we did not]."[94] For days, the press had ravaged the Mahres for their "bad attitude," while in story after story the loutish Johnson was a hero. It didn't matter. The Mahres attacked the fifty-eight-gate course and finished the first run with Steve in first, at 50.85 seconds, and Phil in third, at 51.55 seconds. In the second run Phil skied a scorching fast 47.86 seconds to move into first place. His combined time was 1:39.41. "I mean there Phil was, with the gold medal almost in his hands," said Steve, "[but still he radioed up to me] telling me what I had to do to beat him."[95] Unfortunately, Steve made three small mistakes at the bottom of the course to finish .21 of a second behind Phil and in second place. Didier Bouvet of France was third at 1:40.20. It was a fascinating finish. The Mahres were the first brothers in history to finish one-two in a single Olympic event. After the race, as Phil was leaving the Olympic Village for the medal ceremony, he heard the news: his wife had given birth to a boy. He thanked the person who told him, "took a few steps," and started to cry.[96]

Sarajevo mayor Anto Sučić (seated, center) signs a formal agreement in May 1978 to host the 1984 Winter Olympics. IOC president Lord Killanin (seated, left) and IOC executive director Monique Berlioux (seated, right) look on. *All photos used with permission from the IOC and the Olympic Committee of Bosnia and Herzegovina unless otherwise credited.*

IOC president Juan Antonio Samaranch (center) inspects Olympic sites during a visit to Sarajevo in 1982.

Ahmed Karabegović, the secretary general of the Sarajevo Olympic Organizing Committee, socializes with Roone Arledge, the president of ABC Sports, at a 1981 reception in New York. ABC paid a then-record $91.5 million for the broadcast rights to the Sarajevo games.

A view of the yet-to-be-finished speed-skating oval at the Zetra Sports Complex, circa 1982. Zetra Hall, the site of figure skating and hockey competitions and the closing ceremonies, and Koševo Stadium, the site of the opening ceremonies, are in the background.

In addition to hundreds of construction firms, both foreign and domestic, the Sarajevo Olympic Organizing Committee used over 3,000 volunteer workers from communist youth brigades to construct its facilities.

The mascot and emblem of the 1984 Winter Olympic Games. The mascot was known as Vučko (Wolfie), and the emblem was a stylized snowflake.

A scene from the torch run in February 1984. Starting in Dubrovnik, runners followed an eastern route and a western route and visited each of Yugoslavia's six republics before meeting in Sarajevo.

A view of the opening ceremonies at Koševo Stadium. A then-record 1,272 athletes from 49 countries took part.

Avenging its upset loss to an American team in 1980, the Soviet Union dominated the ice hockey competition. Led by star goalie Vladislav Tretiak, the Soviets won all seven of their matches and outscored their opponents 48 to 5.

An impressively athletic skater, American Scott Hamilton competes in the long program at Zetra Hall. Hamilton defeated the Canadian Brian Orser and the Czechoslovakian skater Jozef Sabovčík for the gold.

East German sensation Katarina Witt hugs coach Jutta Müller following a gold medal performance at Zetra Hall. Witt narrowly beat the talented American skater and silver medalist Rosalynn Sumners.

Perhaps the most beloved medalists in Winter Olympic history, British ice dancers Jayne Torvill and Christopher Dean, wowed judges with a flawless performance in the free dance portion of the competition.

Ranked 65th in the world during the 1982–83 World Cup season, the brash American skier Bill Johnson promised to win, and then won, the men's Alpine downhill. For many Americans, Johnson was *the* story of the Sarajevo games.

An instant hero, the Slovene Jure Franko celebrates after winning Yugoslavia's first-ever Winter Olympic medal, a silver in the men's giant slalom.

The twin American Mahre brothers, Phil and Steve, finished 1 and 2 in the men's slalom. Tired after years on the World Cup circuit and ready to retire, they were criticized as lackadaisical by the American press.

West German biathlete Peter Angerer competes in the 20km individual competition in Sarajevo. Angerer won a gold in the 20km individual, a silver in the sprint competition, and a bronze in the 4 x 7.5 km relay.

Underfunded and completely outmanned, the US bobsled team purchased a technologically superior Swiss sled for $10,000 from a disgruntled Swiss alternate just days before the competition commenced. The sled, painted blue in a Sarajevo Volkswagen shop, finished fifth.

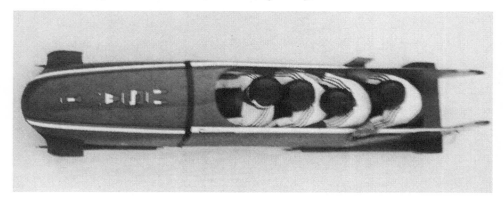

Canadian speed skater Gaetan Boucher won two golds, one in the 1,000-meter competition, the other in 1,500-meter competition, and was third in the 500 meter.

At the Games' closing ceremony, IOC president Juan Antonio Samaranch presents Bosnian president Branko Mikulić with the golden Olympic Order, the organization's highest award.

The bobsled and luge run on Mount Trebević housed Serbian sniper and mortar positions during the Siege of Sarajevo from 1992 to 1996. As of 2015, the track is still ruined and surrounded in parts by land mines. (*Photo courtesy of author*)

Destroyed during the Bosnian War but rebuilt by the IOC and various donor organizations in 1999, Zetra Hall remains one of the best indoor sports facilities in the Balkans. Note the cemetery in the foreground. (*Photo courtesy of author*)

9

The "Minor Sports"

Minsk, Belarus. February 1982. Seventy competitors from twenty countries are here to compete in the World Biathlon Championships. It's bitterly cold, but two hundred thousand people are in attendance.[1] That was the equivalent of four Yankees–Dodgers World Series games at Yankee Stadium in 1981 or three times the attendance of the 1982 Super Bowl. But these fans weren't here to see Reggie Jackson. They had never heard of Joe Montana. Instead, they had come to Minsk, a city behind the Iron Curtain deep in the USSR, to watch biathletes, men who skied long distances while stopping periodically to shoot at targets. The word *biathlon* is Greek for "two tests," skiing and shooting, and no one was better in 1981 at skiing and shooting than Frank Ullrich, an East German. Ullrich's event was the 10km sprint, which he'd won here three years in a row. He'd also won a gold medal in the sprint in 1980 and led World Championship relay teams in 1978, 1979, and 1981. Ullrich was the best biathlete in the world and to East Germans a sports god, a national hero.

For that he was a paid accordingly: he had a good job, better living conditions than most people in the GDR, the freedom to train year-round as well as travel, and lodging expenses for competitions and training sessions throughout Europe. Ullrich's support staff included trainers, coaches, nutritionists, pharmacists, and doctors. He even had a "waxing scientist" to ready his skis. Now, contrast all that to the Americans. In 1982 the U.S. Biathlon Association had a total budget of $62,000.[2] In addition to administrative costs, the money covered two coaches' salaries, a single training session in West Yellowstone, Montana, and a trip to Europe. For all other expenses, including their rifles, America's biathletes were on their own. They were "self-supervised and self-financed," wrote *Sport* magazine. They were "adept scramblers."[3] The team's best biathlete mortgaged his family farm just to train for the Olympics and financed a five-week session in Europe by selling a "car, a dump truck, four chain saws, and a bicycle."[4] All for forty-fourth place. His teammates finished forty-fifth, fifty-second, and fifty-fifth. "We [were] international laughingstocks," one biathlete recalled. The "spectators [in Minsk] yelled, 'U-S-Ah! Ha-Ha-Ha!'" and whistled whenever Americans missed a shot.[5]

Welcome to what one journalist called the "minor sports ghetto," the 1980s home of biathlon, bobsled, cross-country skiing, ski jumping, and luge.[6] "Far from the flash and golden glamour [of America's] alpine skiers, figure skaters and hockey players," wrote *Time* magazine, "another breed of home-grown Olympians will drive themselves beyond reason . . . without so much as a pat on the back, or, for most, even a faint hope" of medaling.[7] These five Olympic teams had won just two medals in twenty-eight years. Two of the teams, biathlon and luge, had never medaled, while America's only ski-jumping medal came in 1924. (Even then, the IOC awarded the medal some fifty years later after a Norwegian ski fan found a mistake.) There was one bobsled run in the United States, one luge run in the United States, and not a single member of the USA Luge team in 1983 had trained on a genuine luge run before 1979.[8] According to one analyst, they'd all ended up in the Olympics by "winning contests and accepting dares."[9]

America's best minor sports were cross-country skiing and ski jumping. In 1976 the cross-country skier Bill Koch surprised the Olympic world by winning a silver at Innsbruck. When he crossed the finish line, not a single American reporter was there to greet him.[10] In the Nordic combined, a mixture of ski jumping and cross-country skiing, the American Kerry Lynch was perhaps the best performer in the world in 1983, while that same year Jeff Hastings and Mike Holland placed third and fourth at the World Ski Jumping Championships.[11] These guys were good, really good, but no one knew who they were. In 1984 the minor-sports athlete most widely and regularly seen by Americans wasn't even an American: he was a Yugoslav named Vinko Bogataj. Since 1971 ABC's *Wide World of Sports* had beamed Bogataj twice a week into American living rooms. "Spanning the globe to bring you the constant variety of sports," the show began, "the thrill of victory and the agony of defeat." The "thrill" scene showed four or five Little Leaguers celebrating a championship: nice but prosaic. The "agony" scene was *awesome*—Bogataj flying down a ski jump at what seemed like Mach 2, losing his balance just before the jump, and careening into the crowd.

Miraculously, he survived. The ABC producer Doug Wilson witnessed the crash in Oberstdorf, West Germany, in March 1971. "My first thought was— oh, my God—is he seriously hurt, is he mortally hurt? I knew right away that this was going to be something extraordinary on the air."[12] Indeed it was. In late 1971 *Wide World of Sports* began broadcasting Bogataj's accident in its opening montage. Twice a week he crashed, brutally, a ski-jumping Sisyphus pushing a stone. The image stuck. The show ran for decades, and Bogataj became a star. "He is undoubtedly the most recognized skier in America," a reporter for the *Boston Globe* wrote. "He has never won a downhill. Never skied through a set of slalom gates. Never huffed or puffed his way over a 50k cross-country course. . . . Yet perhaps three or four of every five Americans [can] identify Vinko Bogataj."[13] Well, sort of. He was more like that dude from *Wide World of Sports* who wiped out on the ski jump, a kind of minor-sports meme. "I get calls at least every other day asking, 'Who is that man?'" recalled a publicist at ABC. "I surmise it's probably a trivia game or someone has a bet."[14]

The real Vinko Bogataj was an average Joe who worked as a forklift driver in Lesce, Slovenia. He retired from ski jumping in 1975 and was shocked when ABC invited him to New York in 1980 to attend a *Wide World of Sports* anniversary dinner at the luxurious Waldorf-Astoria Hotel. There he met the host of the show, Jim McKay, the car racer Jackie Stewart, the golfer Arnold Palmer, the track great Wilma Rudolph, and the boxing legend Muhammad Ali. In fact, Ali asked for his autograph. That night there were two standing ovations: one for the 1980 "Miracle on Ice" hockey team, the other for Vinko Bogataj. "I couldn't believe it," he said. "Ali was there. Jackie Stewart was there. But they applaud[ed] me."[15] Applauded, yes. Took up ski jumping? No. "It's not like you and I are going to get together and say, 'Hey, let's go ski jumping!'" said Greg Windsperger, coach of the 1984 team. "Ski jumping wasn't a recreational sport—it's never been. It's a competitive sport. So you and I would go alpine skiing at a resort, but we wouldn't do a 70m together."[16]

We wouldn't ski fifty kilometers either or blast down an icy track in a six-hundred-pound bobsled at eighty-five miles per hour. Who would? "People [thought I was] either a hotdog or a whacko," said Jeff Hastings, a ski jumper. "But [that was] okay. I [wasn't] doing this to be famous. I [didn't] expect to have streets named after me. . . . I loved being an amateur."[17] The manager of

USA Luge called them "the last real amateurs," men and women who scraped by on minuscule budgets competing in odd and obscure sports that Americans didn't do.[18]

"Let's face it," said one biathlon official. "[It's] never been the most natural thing in the world for an American to ski and shoot at the same time. You don't see much of that on your average ski slope."[19] In 1984 there were two hundred biathletes total in America. The sport's lack of popularity and obscurity stemmed from the fact that biathlon was a military endeavor, originating in eighteenth-century Scandinavia as a competition sport between ski troops stationed on the Swedish–Norwegian border. Biathlon was known, alternatively, as the "military patrol ski competition" and first appeared in the Olympics as a demonstration sport in 1924. It became a formal Olympic sport in 1960.[20]

America's first biathlon team was founded in 1956 and housed at the U.S. Army's Biathlon Training Center in Fort Richardson, Alaska. In theory, the Olympic biathlon team was open to civilians, but owing to the remoteness of "Fort Rich" and the uniqueness of the sport America's first biathletes were almost always soldiers. John Morton, a veteran of two Olympics and the coach of the Dartmouth ski team, was stationed at Fort Richardson in the 1960s. "The Vietnam War was on," said Morton, "so the ironic part was that virtually all of our commanders and colleagues . . . thought we were flunkies who were trying to wiggle our way out of Vietnam. We weren't."[21] Lt. Col. Bill Spencer competed in the 1964 and 1968 Olympics, spent four years at Fort Richardson, and did two tours of duty in Vietnam.[22] Morton himself did a tour in 1970–71 and made the Olympic biathlon team in 1976. In all, approximately 120 soldiers filtered through the biathlon center before the army withdrew funding and transferred the program to Vermont in 1973. There, it "foundered for several years" in a National Guard armory, with no money, no connection to the military, and a ragtag mixture of "civilians who could ski and shoot."[23]

The team's best Olympic finish came in 1972, when it placed sixth in the 4 x 7.5 km relay. In 1976, though, it placed eleventh out of fifteen teams, then, in 1980, eighth out of fourteen teams. Its best individual finish ever was fourteenth place. Marie Alkire, the shooting coach of the 1984 team, said, "I know there was a question after one of the Olympics in which the media people asked: 'You know we have skiers, and we have shooters. . . . So why don't we do better in this sport?' And I thought, 'I could make you a list, guy!'"

In Alkire's estimation, funding was the key issue: there simply wasn't any. Founded in 1980, the U.S. Biathlon Association (USBA) subsisted on small fundraisers and a paltry contribution from the USOC. It had so little money that Alkire saw her biathletes only twice a year—once in training and once at the World Championships or the Olympics. "That was frustrating," she says. "We'd finish up somewhere in Europe, usually by March, and then the kids would go back to wherever they lived. They'd try to train, but we never had a spring camp to get them ready for the next year. . . . Plus, they had to get jobs to make it through the winter."[24]

Josh Thompson dug fence-post holes and pounded nails. Don Nielsen "taught skiing and high school English from Boulder, [Colorado,] to the Canadian Yukon," while Lyle Nelson worked at logging camps, gave motivational speeches, and joined the National Guard.[25] "You'll notice that not one of us on the biathlon team has written an autobiography," Thompson joked. "But that's just the way it was. The USBA had the best intentions. They wanted to help us, but what can you do with a dollar?" Actually, a lot. In 1987 Thompson shocked the biathlon world by placing second at the World Championships, currently still the highest finish ever by an American.[26] After the race Thompson had dinner with the West German biathlete Peter Angerer, who asked him, "How much will you get for your medal?" To which Thompson replied, " 'Dude, I'm not going to sell it!' Angerer looked at me like I was the biggest ding-dong in the world. 'Of course you're not going to sell it!' he said. 'No! How much is your federation giving you for second place? How much money?' I just looked at him and said, 'Nothing. Zero. I won't get anything.' Angerer was shocked. He said, 'Why then do you even do this sport?' He thought I was from another planet."[27]

In 1984 Thompson's World Championship medal was three years in the future. Like the rest of his teammates, he had no hope in Sarajevo and finished a disappointing fortieth in the 10km. Willie Carow was the best American finisher at twentieth, while the team placed eleventh in the 4 x 7.5 km relay. "I was in over my head," Thompson said. "I really stunk it up. But people said, hey, you made it to the Olympic Games! You finished . . . you weren't last! Get ready for the next one. And I always told myself that the British team had it worse. Those guys, no matter how much we bitched about funding. . . . They had a legitimate gripe. They didn't even have snow in their country."[28] However, the Brits did have Princess Anne, the president of the British Olympic Association, who came to the biathlon events and cheered from the coach's box. She sat with King Carl XVI of Sweden and King Olav V of Norway. "No one came for us," said Alkire. "The USOC didn't even meet us at the airport, and the guy they sent to take pictures of us forgot to put film in his camera. What else can I say? The biathlon team was always at the back of the bus."[29]

So was luge. As late as 1975 the coach of the American luge team earned three dollars a day. He was an immigrant Pole named Piotr Rogowski, who once said, "This is Olympic team? I am surprise."[30] The headlines didn't lie: "Lugers, More Often Than Not, Are Losers," read one. "U.S. Finds Tough Sledding in Olympic Luge," said another. Even Johnson, the Olympic expert at *Sports Illustrated* who liked winter sports, wrote, "Some Win, and Some Luge."[31] If biathlon was obscure, luge was a sport that Americans had never heard of—literally. In May 1984 the winning word in the Scripps Howard National Spelling Bee, believe it or not, was "luge . . . L-U-G-E . . . luge."[32] The sport was so foreign that journalists often instructed readers in how to pronounce it. There was "loozh," "looj," "lewj," "Scrooge," "huge," "booze," "bruise," "rouge," even "Baton Rouge." One journalist wrote, lugers "rhymes with Hoosiers."[33] According to Maura Jo Haponski, a member of the luge team in 1976, there were American athletes competing in other winter sports who had no idea what luge was. "'What do you do?' they'd ask her. "I say 'luge' and . . . they give [me] that 'oh yeah' look. On the other hand, if they [knew] anything about it, [they'd probably] think [I] was crazy."[34]

Crazy enough to slide feet-first down a 1,000m track on a fifty-pound sled with no brakes and a strap for a steering wheel? Yeah . . . that was crazy. Since 1964, the year luge entered the Olympics, it had been widely known as the most dangerous Olympic sport. In fact, the first death of an athlete at the Winter Olympics occurred in 1964, when a Polish-born slider from Britain named Kazimierz Kay-Skrzypecki lost control of his luge, slid up and over a curve, and flew from the track. He "ruptured his aorta, fractured his skull . . . and died of a heart attack twenty-seven hours later."[35] That same year America's two-man luge team crashed as well. No one was killed, but the luger Jim Higgins was knocked unconscious. (Another luger died in a non-Olympic event in 1975.) "Of all the ways to get down a mountain," wrote one journalist, luge "is the looniest. . . . [It's] the bungee jump[ing] of sports."[36] In a way, luge was an extreme sport, some would argue the first extreme sport to be included in the Olympics. "The luge run gives me such an adrenaline rush that my eyes are flicking like a tape recorder on fast-forward," said John

Fee, a member of the 1980 team and president of the U.S. Luge Association. "It's often terrorizing, [but it's] always exhilarating."[37]

Luge was so exhilarating that several Olympic sliders first fell in love with the sport after watching it on television. In 1976, Frank Masley, a fourteen-year-old high school freshman from Newark, Delaware, watched the Innsbruck Olympics, then used money from his paper route to attend a three-day beginners' workshop in Lake Placid. "They started us on short runs, about three hundred yards," Masley remembers. "I was surprised I did so well."[38] Masley returned to Lake Placid in 1977 for a two-week training program. He was one of two eighteen-and-under junior sliders to receive three weeks of additional training in Germany and Austria. By 1983 he was tenth in the world. Masley's teammate Ron Rossi watched luge on television during the 1968 games. "I would have been eleven then," he says. "My dad woke me up at five o'clock in the morning—there was no tape delay in those days—and said, 'You gotta see this.'"[39] Bonny Warner, America's best female slider and a field hockey player from California, first learned of the sport while serving as a volunteer torch bearer at the 1980 Winter Olympics. "Like millions of other Americans, [I'd] never heard of [luge]," she said, "[but] one ride and I was hooked."[40]

The U.S. Luge Association prayed that other Warners were out there. "There may be only two hundred people in the country who have ever been on a [luge] sled," said one official. "[So] tell kids if they want to make the Olympics, try luge."[41] The *New York Times* reported that in 1983, at the luge national championships in Mount Van Hoevenberg, New York, the announcer said, "Remember, ladies and gentlemen, you are watching the sport of luge, the fastest, most exhilarating event on the planet. [And] by the way, if any of you are interested in trying out for the U.S. luge team, here's a number to call."[42] Like biathlon, luge was an exotic sport practiced in complete anonymity by a core of devotees. The team's budget for 1983 was $150,000. It had one van, its coach was a twenty-four-year-old undergraduate, and its manager, "Bullet" Bob Hughes, worked in the parts department of a Cadillac dealership.[43] "Luge is never going to be baseball," said Hughes. But "we need another $150,000 to $200,000 [a year just] to run a top-drawer [program]. We're doing well without it, but the athletes bear . . . the burden."[44]

As it stood, the 1984 team was respectable—not good, but respectable. At one World Cup event in 1983, for example, Masley placed seventh in the men's singles, Warner placed eighth in the women's, and three other Americans placed in the top fifteen. Gone were the days when European sliders insulted each other by saying, "You drive like an American." Gone, too, was free European advice.[45] Still, the best the Americans could hope for in Sarajevo was a top-ten finish in the men's and women's singles and a top-five finish in men's doubles. It wasn't to be. Masley finished fourteenth out of thirty, Warner fifteenth out of twenty-four, while Rossi and Doug Bateman were ninth out of fifteen. One very bright spot for luge was the unexpected announcement that Masley would be carrying the American flag at the games' opening ceremonies. He'd been chosen by a meeting of team captains, who had decided that luge was "an up-and-coming sport" that needed publicity. "This is the greatest honor I've ever had," said Masley. "[This is] the proudest I've ever been. . . . When we got back, and told the rest of the guys about it, the seventh-floor lugers went wild. . . . Luge has never carried the flag before. . . . [But this is for] biathlon and the Nordic people, [too. . . . This is for] the unknowns."[46]

Ironically, the one luger who was known in Sarajevo was George Tucker, a paunchy, thirty-six-year-old doctoral student from Connecticut who competed for Puerto Rico. Tucker was 100 percent American; he'd been born in San Juan to American parents, spoke no Spanish, and had lived in the United States since he was five. He was a terrible luger, the result, perhaps, of a truly Olympian regimen of donuts and no exercise as well as the fact that he'd been luging for less than year. Tucker began practicing the sport in February 1983 and realized somehow that as a Puerto Rican "native" he was eligible for the Olympics. He wrote a letter to the island's Olympic committee and soon found himself the first Puerto Rican participant ever in the Winter Olympics. "I got the name of the president of the Puerto Rican Olympic Committee out of the *New York Times*," said Tucker. "[He] sent me a beret."[47] To the press, Tucker was "flabby," the "blunt bullet of Olympic luge" who finished an astonishingly bad thirty out of thirty in men's singles, twenty-nine seconds behind the winner.[48] "I was coming down during practice the other day," Tucker recalled, "and the guy announced me as 'George Turkey.' I think he [knew] a little more English than he [let on]."[49]

If Tucker was bad, the eighteen-year-old Jamil Omar Hatem Abdullaleem Jamiul Abdulmalik Omar Mohammed el Reedy was even worse. A resident of Plattsburgh, New York, el Reedy was the heart and soul, really the only soul, of the Egyptian ski team. Like Tucker, el Reedy had been born abroad and brought to the United States as a child. El Reedy was a novice skier, a beginner, who prepared for the Olympics by spending forty days and forty nights in a cave in the Sahara Desert, "the Trial of Fears," he called it, an ancient practice meant to "purge the mind and soul."[50] What el Reedy really needed was physical training, and lots of it. He finished last in two practice runs in Sarajevo, then roared through the gates in the men's downhill in sixtieth place. His time: 3:13.83, a full 1:10 behind the fifty-ninth place finisher and almost 1:30 behind the winner. El Reedy even lost to the Senegalese demon skier Lamine Gueye, the first black Winter Olympian ever from Africa, who had trained for Sarajevo by skiing just fifteen days that year.[51] Also present were Erroll Fraser, a speed skater and fashion designer from the British Virgin Islands; Prince Hubertus von Hohenlohe, an Austrian blue blood skiing for Mexico; and Lina Aristodimou, a two-time last-place slalom skier from Cyprus.

Critics called them exotics, men and women from "exotic countries" who had come to the Olympics "despite their homelands' lack of snow and their own lack of talent."[52] In a way, these exotic Sarajevo Olympians were just the tip of a bad athlete iceberg. In 1988, at Calgary, Tucker, Gueye, and von Hohenlohe were joined by a long list of odd, even eccentric, characters. Who could forget Rusiate Rogoyawa of Fiji, who rocketed through the men's 15km cross-country course in 1 hour, 1 minute, 26.3 seconds to capture eighty-third place? Rogoyawa finished just two places behind the legendary Burgos brothers of Guatemala. Said one Burgos, "This is the first time Guatemala has been in the Winter Olympics. I am happy for my country and happy with myself. I did well. I passed a Mexican."[53] And who could forget Eddie "the Eagle" Edwards, the loony, thickly bespectacled ski jumper from England who once, while training, slept in a mental hospital because his NOC refused to fund him?[54] Perhaps the goofiest athletes at Calgary were the beachcombing bobsledders, men from such "winter sports meccas" as Australia, New Zealand, Mexico, Monaco, Portugal, the Netherlands Antilles, the U.S. Virgin Islands, and Jamaica. "Me first thought?" said one Jamaican bobsledder. "It was 'Oh, mon. What's this, mon?'"[55]

Although no exotic bobsledders took part in the Sarajevo games, it seemed that America's bobsled team was exotic enough. Its best pusher, for example, was Joe Briski, a twenty-eight-year-old San Diego State grad and hammer thrower who'd only been practicing the sport for less than a year. He's "put in so much effort for so many years into the hammer throw," one track coach said, "and then in a span of about six months [he's] become an

Olympian in an entirely different sport. I'm not sure what that says about our bobsled program, but I think it says something."[56] What it said, for the most part, was that Briski was a pusher—a very good pusher. At the U.S. Bobsledding Trials in January 1984 his four-man bobsled team set an American push record of 4.87 seconds for the first fifty meters. But Briski's sudden rise in the sport also said that USA bobsled was a joke. America hadn't medaled in the sport since 1956; it possessed a single bobsled run, near Lake Placid, which meant, traditionally, the American bobsled team was *from* Lake Placid. In 1980 seven of its nine members hailed from upstate New York.[57] "It's been tough for Americans to get into bobsledding if they're from outside the area," said one Olympian. "There has been talk of building new runs [elsewhere], but right now, this is it."[58]

USA bobsled was so insular that two or three generations of athletes tended to congregate in just one bar, the Dew Drop Inn in Saranac Lake, New York, which was owned by Forrest "Dew Drop" Morgan, the manager of the 1976 team and the father of the Olympic bobsledder Jim Morgan. Forrest's other son, John, was a bobsled commentator for *Wide World of Sports*. In February 1981 John was in Cortina d'Ampezzo, Italy, to cover the World Bobsled Championships. It was his first assignment, and he watched from the booth as a four-man sled driven by his brother Jim flipped on its side and slid 150 feet. The other sledders were unhurt, but Jim Morgan suffered a broken neck and his throat was severed. He died at the scene. "I reached over to check Jimmy's pulse," John remembered, "[but] there was none. There's a picture of me leaning over and holding his wrist."[59] A death like Morgan's, though tragic, was not unknown in bobsled. By 1981 no fewer than five athletes had been killed competing in the sport; three at the old Mount Van Hoevenberg run near Lake Placid and two in Cortina. Morgan was the sixth, but less than two weeks after his death an Italian stuntman shooting a bobsled scene for the James Bond film *For Your Eyes Only* was killed on the same track.[60]

"I think when you're in a sport like this, you realize the dangers but you don't really pay any attention to them," the bobsledder Jeff Jost reasoned. Jost rode with Morgan that day. "You just have to wash them out of your mind."[61] Jost was a New York state trooper; he knew danger, but bobsled was a different animal altogether. In its first month of operation, for example, the new Olympic bobsled run on Mount Van Hoevenberg witnessed thirty-seven wrecks. There were six in one day, including a sled full of tourists, who had paid five dollars apiece for the privilege, and a sled manned by four Morgan brothers, including Jim and John, who all went to the hospital. "It's nobody's fault," said Jim Morgan. "The track is just so fast. I'm as experienced a driver as anyone on this hill, and I have my hands full. . . . But that's the name of the game: Go fast."[62] In 1980, taking advantage of its new track and several competent drivers, the American bobsled team went fast. It placed fifth and sixth in the two-man division, the best finishes by American bobsled teams, two- or four-man, since 1968. However, America's two four-man teams were terrible, finishing twelfth and thirteenth (out of fifteen), behind Great Britain.

"With the exception of the two two-man bobsled teams," wrote the *Boston Globe*, "the bobbers . . . did no better than they ever do."[63] Well, maybe a bit better. They'd finished fourteenth and nineteenth in 1976, with only one sled finishing, in fourteenth place, in 1972. (The other was disqualified.) Critics claimed that USA bobsled was too parochial; that, in effect, it was a men's club in the Adirondacks that kept athletes out and locals in. The *Washington Post* columnist Michael Wilbon called bobsledders quasi-athletes who felt it was their "birthright to qualify for the Olympics because they live[d] ten minutes from Lake Placid."[64] However, in its defense, the bobsled team did try on several occasions to incorporate outside talent. There was the hurdler Willie Davenport in 1980, Joe Briski in 1984, the wide receiver Willie Gault in 1988, and the running back Herschel Walker in 1992. Good athletes were always a necessity, but what USA bobsled really needed was technology, not manpower. In 1984 a new bobsled cost between fifteen and twenty thousand dollars. A high-tech Soviet sled unveiled in 1983 reportedly cost one hundred thousand dollars. It had been designed in a Soviet space center and was too advanced, said one official, for the Soviets "had taken an exciting sport and turned it into an icy gray science."[65]

The world's leading bobsled teams raced to catch up. East Germany modified its sled by adding independent front suspension, while the Swiss copied the Soviet sled with help from the missile manufacturer Oerlikon-Buehrle. "This just can't go on," Jost complained. "[It'll] cost a fortune to keep up" or "drive a lot of bobsledders out of business."[66] The American team had Budweiser as a sponsor, but even then, said the bobsledder Fred Fritsch, "we're running stock Italian sleds [and] they're running race cars."[67] One East German observer said jokingly, "You Americans can send a man to the moon . . . [but] you still drive down the mountain on this?"[68] Wisely, the American four-man team led by Jost leveled the playing field somewhat by buying a used sled from the Swiss bobsledder Hans Hiltebrand. Hiltebrand had come to Sarajevo as a reserve driver but posted the fastest training times on Mount Trebević in his own personal sled. When, in spite of this, the Swiss coach Werner Camichel refused to name Hiltebrand to the team, Hiltebrand got mad and sold his sled to the Americans for ten thousand dollars.[69] It was the sled, painted blue in a nearby Volkswagen shop, that Jost, Briski, Tom Barnes, and Hal Hoye rode to a respectable fifth place. America's other four-man sled finished sixteenth, while its two two-man sleds were fifteenth and seventeenth.

In the Nordic events Team USA earned its best results in ski jumping, the visually stunning sport in which athletes glide down a 70m or 90m ski jump and launch themselves into the air. The jumps on Mount Igman were towering, but, unbeknownst to television viewers, the ski jumpers rarely flew more than ten or fifteen feet off the ground. They landed, or attempted to land, at the very bottom of the hill's downward slope, for if they "out-jumped the hill" and flew past the slope, they'd crash onto level ground. This rarely happened; architects designed ski jumps so the slope of the hill followed the jumper's trajectory, and judges had the right to lower the starting gate if jumpers, in windy conditions, jumped too far. "There's a point on every hill where the hill begins to level out," one ski jumper explained, "so you can imagine that when you take off from a point one hundred vertical meters above the point where you're landing, you want to avoid flattish ground. If you don't, it's dangerous. That's one reason the judges are there, to keep an eye on things. They watch practices all week to make sure that the best jumper lands right at the bottom of the hill and everyone else lands above him."[70]

On rare occasions judges halted ski-jumping events in midcompetition, as they did during the Nordic combined events on Mount Igman. In 1984 Nordic combined involved three 70m ski jumps and a 15km cross-country race. The jumps came first. Judges awarded points for distance and style—two points per meter and style points of between three and thirty per jump. They discounted the shortest of the three jumps. In the cross-country race, the jumper with the most points started first, and for every fifteen points he led he was given a one-minute head start. The problem was that every once in a while a middle-of-the-pack skier uncorked a truly massive jump. In 1984, in jump one of the competition, the American skier Pat Ahern sailed 89 meters (292 feet), good enough for first place. However, the judges feared that since Ahern had gone that far, other, higher-ranked skiers would go even further, perhaps to the base of the hill, where they would slam into flat ground and get hurt. Therefore, they stopped the competition, moved the starting gate down, and rejumped. This time the jump stood: Ahern went 83.5 meters (273 feet), which put him in third place.

Then, in what officially was jump two, Ahern flew 86 meters (282 feet) to retake the lead. But shortly after Ahern's jump, a so-so West German skier flew an astounding 92 meters (301 feet). The judges, again citing safety, moved the starting gate down and rejumped. This time Ahern flew a mediocre 78.5 meters (257 feet) and followed that with a third jump of 81 meters (265 feet). As a result, he dropped in the standings from first to sixteenth place. "When I got that first one taken away," he said, "I thought, 'Well, that's part of the game. I can still do [this].' When they took the second jump away, "[I thought] there's some politics going on [here]. . . . This [is] bogus. . . . Somebody's pulling strings."[71] By "somebody," Ahern meant the judges from East Germany and Norway, whose athletes hadn't jumped very well and who would benefit from a second or even a third rejump. "They were embarrassed," said Kerry Lynch, a teammate of Ahern. "Having the Americans come in and do something like that in Nordic combined skiing [was] like having the South Pole win the Super Bowl."[72]

Lynch may have been right. The chief beneficiary of both restarts was Norway's Tom Sandberg, the number-one Nordic combined skier in the world, who improved, interestingly enough, from twentieth to first place. With 214.7 points in the jump competition, Sandberg started 2 minutes, 10 seconds ahead of Ahern, and 3 minutes, 39 seconds ahead of Lynch. They've got "no shot," said Jim Page, the head of America's Nordic programs, but we "can't do anything about it. . . . It's kind of a helpless feeling. [There's] a bunch of turkeys running the tournament" who "saw an opportunity . . . and took advantage of it. . . . That kind of stuff has no place in sports. . . . It just kills [the] spirit."[73] Ahern likened it "to being kicked in the crotch," but he and Lynch had no choice but to finish the competition. "It's really hard to run your guts out when you've had something like that taken away," he said. "[I wasn't] given a fair shake."[74] In the end, Lynch and Ahern finished thirteenth and seventeenth, respectively, though Lynch ran an impressive third in the cross-country race and nearly overtook Sandberg, the gold medalist.

As in Nordic combined, in the ski-jumping competition the American team experienced another near miss when Jeff Hastings placed fourth in the 90m competition with a grand total of 201.2 points. Hastings was the best ski jumper in America; he'd won the National Championships three years running and in 1984 was the number six ski jumper in the world. Hastings learned to jump as a youngster in Vermont, on a hill, he says, that "wasn't even a mogul."[75] By the age of twenty-one he was jumping for the varsity team at Williams College in Williamstown, Massachusetts, which disbanded its program in 1980 when the NCAA decided to drop ski jumping as an intercollegiate sport. Luckily, Hastings "broke out a bit" that year and was added to the national team following the Winter Olympics in Lake Placid. "Ski jumping, like biathlon for Josh Thompson, was truly an amateur sport," Hastings observed. "You could make a little money if you were the top guy . . . maybe a few thousand, [but] nowhere near enough to live on. So you had to work." Hastings worked as a management trainee at the Denver Sheraton Airport Hotel, which gave him flexible hours and the freedom to train on the 90m jump in nearby Steamboat Springs, Colorado.

Although money was tight, Hastings has no complaints. "We had enough money to field a full team with a great training program," he said. "We had a great coach, too. We definitely cut corners" and were "less professional in some ways than the Austrians and Finns were. But what we didn't have we took as a challenge."[76] Hastings practiced his takeoffs, for example, by attaching an eight-foot-long bungee cord to the top of a basketball hoop, wrapping the cord around his waist and shoulders, and using it to launch himself into the air. His teammate Jon Denney jerry-rigged a wind tunnel by cutting off the front end of a rear-engine school bus. As *Sport* magazine explained, Denney practiced "in-flight maneuvers" up and down the highway while his brother drove.[77] Greg Windsperger, the coach of the 1984 team, said, "As far as true amateurs go, you're looking at them. They're [right] here. You compare what ski jumpers from other countries get in the way of [compensation] and then compare that to ours. I think Norway is on the low end, and they each get twenty-five dollars a day for every day they're away from home for a meet or training. It's called broken time. You ask our guys what they get . . . [and they'll say, 'zero']."[78]

In retrospect, however, Windsperger thought this was fair. "If someone donated a dollar to the U.S. Ski Team," he insists, "the Alpine Team got maybe ninety-five cents, and we got a nickel. But they were drawing results. They were medaling. We weren't winning any medals. So I told my guys, 'Don't complain. We got a nickel! Just go with it and see what we can do. If we medal, maybe they'll give us a dime next year, or maybe someday a quarter.'"[79] It was good advice, and it helped, too, that Hastings was the best jumper the team had seen in a long, long while. As Hastings improved, the team's funding doubled from $90,000 in 1980 to $180,000 in 1984. Over that same period the team rose from twelfth to six in the world. "We are getting tougher, deeper," said Hastings. "But we [still] don't have a broad base. It's not a national pastime."[80] Not like in Finland, where the phlegmatic, at times ill-tempered Matti Nykaenen (pronounced "Nuke-an-en") was a star. Just twenty-one years old in 1984, Nykaenen won the 90m Junior World Championship in 1981, the World Championship in 1982, and both the Sarajevo pre-Olympics and the World Cup Championship in 1983. "When he's on, he's on," said Hastings. "Nobody can touch him."[81]

Nobody, that is, but Jens Weissflog, a nineteen-year-old East German prodigy who came to Sarajevo expecting to challenge Nykaenen for the gold. In the first competition, the 70m, Weissflog scored a mild upset when he out-jumped Nykaenen on jump two to outscore the "Flying Finn" by a mere 1.2 points (215.2 to 214.0). In the same event, Hastings was ninth, with three other Americans finishing back in the pack at twenty-eighth, thirty-third, and forty-first. To the press, the biggest news wasn't that Nykaenen had lost; it was that Bogataj had made an unannounced, seemingly random appearance as a volunteer starter at the 70m gate. As jumpers warmed up and skied past him, he told reporters, "I remember it well. I was doing fine previous to that jump, then . . . psshtt, I fell."[82] In the 90m jump, Nykaenen and Weissflog switched positions, Nykaenen taking the gold and Weissflog the silver. The two jumpers had out-jumped Hastings by a wide margin, but Hastings was still third in the standings with just one jumper to go—Pavel Ploc of Czechoslovakia, who had a good chance of beating him. "I watched him all the way," said Hastings. "Ploc hit a beauty, and when I saw him land I just said to myself, 'Well, there it goes. There goes the Olympics.'"[83] Nevertheless, Hastings's fourth-place finish in the 90m event was America's best Olympic finish in any ski-jumping event since 1924 and its second-best finish in history.

As for the men's and women's cross-country events, the best America could do was a seventeenth-place finish by Bill Koch in the men's 50km and an eighteenth-place finish by Dan Simoneau in the 15km. The women finished in the twenties and thirties in three different events and weren't close to medaling. Koch and Simoneau were two of the finest cross-country skiers America had ever produced, especially Koch, who not only won a silver at Innsbruck but also captured America's first and only World Cup Championship in 1982. Fiercely private, Koch had a love/hate relationship with the U.S.

Nordic team and was particularly cautious with the press. In 1980 at Lake Placid a horde of frothing journalists more or less demanded that Koch win a medal. When he didn't, and when he dropped out midway through his first race, they called him a quitter, a poor example, and a disgrace. Never mind that Koch had three more races to run, including a 50km, and that skiers quit races all the time. It was a tactic for saving energy. But Koch was skewered in the press. "That was a purely strategic decision on my part and one that I feel very good about," said Koch. "If it was the only race in the Olympics, I would have finished it if it had killed me. [But] I had three more races, for heaven's sakes. . . . I wanted to do well in the Olympics as a whole, not just one race."[84]

But Koch believed too that winning wasn't important—effort was. In a rare interview in 1984 with *Sports Illustrated,* Koch said, "It all boils down to this. The more I win, the more I believe that what's important isn't the winning itself but trying to do your best—to simply strive for your own excellence. Our society, in so much of its behavior and values, doesn't agree with that. It says something like 'It's gold or failure.'"[85] Gold or failure. That was the Olympics in a nutshell, a grim yet visible reality that explained, in part, why the U.S. hockey team had a $1.5-million budget, while biathletes, lugers, bobsledders, ski jumpers, and cross-country skiers worked odd jobs to eat. For America's "minor sports" athletes, none of it mattered. Win or lose, but mostly lose, they strived for personal bests. "It's what builds a person's character," said Koch. "No matter whether you come in last, [or] whether you quit the race, as long as you've put it on the line, that's all [you] can do."[86] Koch was serious. He told a journalist in Sarajevo that "I don't go by places. I go by feel." And though he finished a disappointing twenty-first in the men's 30km cross-country race, he felt "very good . . . like a winner."[87]

The odd sport out was speed skating. Speed skating was a minor sport—to an extent. Like biathlon, bobsled, cross-country skiing, ski jumping, and luge, it had no money and no participants, but it was miraculously successful. Between 1968 and 1980 the U.S. Speed Skating Team won 23 medals, more than all the other American teams in all other winter sports combined. From its first appearance at the 1924 Chamonix Olympics up to the 1984 Winter Olympics in Sarajevo, the U.S. Speed Skating Team had won 38 of America's 106 total winter medals, or 35.8 percent. At the 1968 Olympics in Grenoble, American speed skaters won 5 of America's total of 7 medals. In 1976 they won 6 of 10, and in 1980, 8 out of 12. "If it weren't for [America's] speed-skating team," wrote one journalist in 1980, "the faces of [our] athletes . . .

would be as red as the stripes of the nation's flag."[88] The headlines said it all: "Speed Skaters Save U.S. from Embarrassment," read one. "Skaters Soothe Smarting U.S. Pride."[89] You could argue that speed skaters won more medals because speed skating had more events. It did. It had nine. There was the 500m, the 1,000m, the 1,500m, the 5,000m, and the 10,000m race for men, and the 500m, the 1,000m, the 1,500m, and the 3,000m race for women—27 medals in all.

The International Skating Union, which governed speed skating, allowed each country to have three competitors in each event. Therefore, countries could sweep an event and win all 3 medals. In 1964, for example, the Soviet women swept the 500m race and finished one-two, one-two, and one-three in three other events. In 1968, also in the 500m race, three American women— Jenny Fish, Dianne Holum, and Mary Meyers—turned in identical times and tied for second place. As a result, the officials awarded 4 medals—1 gold and 3 silvers—for one race. Speed skating's 27 medals constituted roughly one-fourth of all medals awarded at the 1984 Winter Olympics. The next closest sport, cross-country skiing, had 24 potential medals, while alpine skiing had 18. Figure skating followed with 12; biathlon, 9; luge, 9; bobsled, 6; ski jumping, 6; Nordic combined, 3; and hockey, 3. In all, 117 medals were awarded. But because only one team per country could enter the hockey competition and because bobsled and luge allowed only two entries in certain events, the most medals any country could win was 112.

East Germany did the math. It realized that by focusing its attention on speed skating and its nine multimedal events, it could win more medals than anyone else. "We are not in a financial position to develop all sports to the Olympic level," said Karl-Heinz Bauersfeld, a leading sports official in Leipzig. "We concentrate on the sports which are traditionally strong in the GDR and which also have some prospect of success."[90] There were no alpine skiers from East Germany in Sarajevo. There wasn't an East German hockey team there either. But the GDR had three competitors in each speed-skating event. Culled at a young age and subjected to rigorous (not to say, abusive) training regimens at state-sponsored sports institutions, East Germany's speed skaters were the best in the world, particularly the women. As of 1984 its star skater was Karin Enke, the world-record holder in the 500m and the reigning All-Round World and Olympic champion. Her teammate Andrea Schoene had upset Enke in three of four events at the 1983 World Championships and was the world-record holder in the 5,000m. Behind Enke and

Schoene were emerging stars like Christa Rothenburger, who won a bronze medal at the 1983 World Sprint Championships, and Gabie Schoenbrunn, the world-record holder in the 3,000m.

The German women were so good that in January 1984, at the World All-Round Championships in Holland, they were first in all four events. In addition, they were second in three events and took eight of the championship's twelve total places. "It is definitely a very good group of girls," said the coach, Rainer Mund. "I would claim as a coach that you can hope to find this only once in [a] lifetime."[91] There were rumors that Enke and company were cheating. As Steven Ungerleider detailed in his book *Faust's Gold: Inside the East German Doping Machine* (2001), East Germany's "corrupt sports organization" gave thousands of athletes performance-enhancing steroids.[92] The most famous recipients were swimmers, who, like speed skaters, competed in multimedal events. At the 1980 Summer Olympics in Moscow, East Germany's women swimmers won twenty-seven medals, including eleven of thirteen golds. By contrast, Canada had sent over nine hundred athletes to the previous five Summer Olympics, where they had won just twenty-six medals and two golds. The reason was steroids. East German swimmers had "juiced-up," as noted in chapter 1, on Oral-Turinabol, an anabolic steroid created by an East German pharmaceutical company and given to them as "vitamin supplements" by trainers. The same drug was given to rowers, track and field athletes, cyclists, canoers, weight lifters, gymnasts, and, it is alleged, speed skaters.

In 2010 the Dutch television show *Andere Tijden Sport* (Different Times) aired a documentary in which it claimed that Enke had been doping. It interviewed Giselher Spitzer, a physician, German sport historian, and expert on doping in the GDR, and showed portions of a Stasi record to prove it.[93] Yet Enke had been tested dozens of times, and neither she nor her teammates had ever turned up positive—at least not outside of the GDR. As Ungerleider explains, East German officials maintained a "doping control research team" which tested urine specimens "from all areas of sport and from all areas [of the country]. . . . If a negative result was not returned before [an athlete's] departure, then that athlete was denied travel permission, effectively removing him or her from that competition."[94]

Although East Germany was an extreme case—it was, after all, the only country in the world where the systematic doping of athletes was state policy—the Americans were doping, too. Not all athletes, but enough that in

1984 the USOC began administering a pre-Olympics drug test of its own. Every athlete in every sport would be tested. Some sports, such as track and field, actually had a *pre*-pretest, that is, an informal, nonpunitive test to "let them know what was coming," said one official, "[and] what to expect."[95] The U.S. Speed Skating Team, twelve men and eight women, took its test in January 1984. "I'm really glad they're doing this," said Mary Docter, a three-race skater from Madison, Wisconsin. "I hope other countries are doing it too."[96]

Docter had been the only American to place at the January All-Round Championships and was arguably the U.S. team's lone hope for a medal. The team had talent. Three of its younger members, Bonnie Blair, Dan Jansen, and Nick Thometz, would all set records one day, Blair in particular. Between 1988 and 1994 Blair, a native of Champaign, Illinois, won five gold medals and a bronze, the most by an American female in Winter Olympic history.[97] "It would be stupid for us to believe that we would not win any medals [in Sarajevo]," said the team coach, Dianne Holum, optimistically. "If you understand skating, you should never say that because anything could happen."[98]

Indeed, anything could happen, but in 1984 America's speed skaters were either too young or too old, and they all missed Eric Heiden. In 1980 Heiden, a skater from Madison, Wisconsin, swept all five events in the men's competition, setting four Olympic records and a world record in the process. He also won eight World Championships and set fifteen world records. Heiden was and still is the greatest speed skater of all time, in any country, but in 1984 he was a premed student at Stanford and an analyst for ABC. He was retired from skating. "I got so I would start a race hurt," he said, "[from] inner pain, [from the] pressure I put on myself. . . . Near the end of my last race at Lake Placid, the 10,000, I started out thinking 'I've done well so far.' Then, I began saying to myself, 'How can I get out of it and save face?' That's when I knew it was time to quit."[99]

Although busy living his life and sick of speed skating, Heiden raised money for the team by persuading Atari, the video game manufacturer, to contribute $60,000. He also raised money to help bail out a 400m speed-skating oval in West Allis, Wisconsin, that the state was threatening to close. The only other 400m rink in America was in Lake Placid. "If the [West Allis] rink were closed," said one official in May 1982, "it would totally devastate speed skating as we have come to know it. We could probably field some kind of team in 1984 . . . [but] after that, the quality would drop to zero."[100] There were perhaps three hundred speed skaters in America, whose parent organization, the United States International Speedskating Association (USISA), had an annual budget of $110,000. The president of the USISA received $34,000 in salary, while the team's coach made $16,000. There was "never enough money," said one former official. Because speed skating "is not a national sport . . . [y]ou [couldn't] go out and say, 'Hey, skaters, drink Coca-Cola and . . . [have Coke] sell ten million more bottles [of the stuff].' "[101] It just didn't happen. There were sponsors—Kellogg's put Docter and Thometz on a cereal box, for example, and Rexnor, the industrial equipment company, cofunded the World Sprint Championships in Wisconsin—but the team was broke. "[In 1980] America took a lot of pride in speed skating," said the skater Mike Woods, but "it [sure] didn't pay . . . for it."[102]

The disgruntled coach, Bob Corby, blamed the USISA—it could have been better at fund-raising, he said—but Erik Henriksen, an alternate in 1980 and a starter on the 1984 team, blamed Heiden. "He disappeared from our sport for four years," said Henriksen, whose own sponsor was REO Speedwagon, the rock-and-roll band. "We could have used a personality, an Arnold Palmer-type personality. Someone who could court public exposure. . . . [But Eric] hurt the sport because of what he didn't do."[103] The charge was unfair. Heiden had raised money, he said, "but a whirlwind tour, promoting? [He'd] have a hard time doing that."[104] Still young and fit at twenty-five, Heiden could have contributed by skating. He belonged, for example, to the 7-Eleven pro-am cycling team and in 1981 won his first pro event. In 1985 he competed in the famed Giro d'Italia road race and in 1986 in the Tour de France. "[It's] kind of hard to compare," said Dianne Holum, but "if he was still skating and as strong as he was then, he'd do just as well now."[105]

Second to Heiden in the 1,000m race at Lake Placid was Gaetan Boucher of Canada, a twenty-five-year-old marketing student from Sainte-Foy, Quebec. Short, yet powerfully built and incredibly fast, Boucher set two world records at an international meet in Switzerland in 1981: one for the fastest time in the 1,000m, the other for the best combined time in the samalog sprint, a competition in which 500m and 1,000m times are added together.[106] "In 1980, [no one] was expecting to win because . . . [of] how good [Heiden] was," said Boucher in an interview in 1984. "[We] . . . were all shooting for silver."[107] Now, with Heiden gone, Boucher expected to win the 1,000m and to place in the 1,500m. He had a good shot at medaling in the 500m as well.

Although Boucher was a favorite in the short-track events, that is, those events that were 1,500 meters or shorter, in the men's field all five events were open. That was in contrast to the women's events, where Enke, Schoene, and Rothenburger were a lock. The races played out as expected. Rothenburger was first and Enke was second in the 500m, while Enke and Schoene were first and second in the 1,000m and the 1,500m events. In the 3,000m, Schoene, Enke, and Schoenbrunn finished one-two-three. It was a jaw-dropping performance. The GDR had won nine medals in four events. Enke herself had won two golds and two silvers. She also set two Olympic records and a world record in the 1,500m. "She's the women's Eric Heiden," said Docter, who led all American women with a finish of sixth. "I'm not saying she can't be beat. But there's nobody here today who'll do it."[108]

In the men's competition, Boucher won the 1,000m and the 1,500m and was third, behind the USSR's Sergei Fokichev and Japan's Yoshihiro Kitazawa, in the 500m. Tomas Gustafson of Sweden won the 5,000m by edging out the Soviet Igor Malkov by .02 seconds—imagine . . . a 3.1-mile race determined by two-hundredths of a second—but Malkov returned the favor by beating Gustafson in the 10,000m by .05 seconds. For the American men's team, Jansen and Thometz were fourth and fifth in the 500m, Thometz was fourth in the 1,000m, while Mike Woods was seventh in the 10,000m. Woods was a thirty-one-year-old anesthesiologist from Wisconsin who in 1982 had "staged a one-man, twenty-hour skate-a-thon" to save the West Allis track.[109] "It was a goal of mine to win a medal and I didn't do that," he said. "[But] I wanted to be competitive, and I achieved that. . . . [Remember,] it's still our three hundred Midwest kids out there in the cold in Milwaukee against two hundred thousand registered Soviet skaters. . . . I have to say I'm proud at what I've done. I finished seventh in the Olympics and how many people can say that?"[110]

Epilogue

The Seats of Zetra Hall

THE NINETEENTH of February was a busy day in Sarajevo. It was the thirteenth and final day of the 1984 Winter Olympics. It featured three events: in hockey, the vaunted Soviet team defeated Czechoslovakia; in the men's slalom, the American skiers Phil and Steve Mahre finished one-two; and in the men's 50km cross-country race, the Swedish skier Thomas Wassberg narrowly defeated his teammate Gunde Svan. There was a figure-skating exhibition in the evening, featuring, among others, Torvill and Dean, and a thirty-minute closing ceremony at Zetra Hall. Before a capacity crowd of eighty-five hundred people, forty-nine girls in white, holding placards, led forty-nine flag-bearers, one from each country, into the arena. There was *Jugoslavija*—the host country came first at the closing, according to custom— *Andora, Argentina, Australija,* all the way to the forty-ninth and final country *Velika Britanija* (Great Britain). Then came the athletes. The arena was too small for everyone, so each country was limited to six representatives. The organizers then played the Greek national anthem, signifying the games of ancient Greece, the Yugoslav anthem, and finally the anthem of Canada, the host country of the next Winter Olympics in Calgary.

At center ice Branko Mikulić and Juan Antonio Samaranch ascended a platform. Mikulić spoke first. "It is said that these Games were the best ever," he declared. "We gained precious experience. I hope that the next Games in Tito's Yugoslavia—when we get them again—will be even better."[1] The crowd roared its applause. Samaranch approached and said he was giving Mikulić the golden Olympic Order, the IOC's highest award. Rather than a plaque or a trophy, the Olympic Order was a thick gold chain that featured Olympic rings in the front and stylized olive branches that attached in the back. It was impressive. Samaranch thanked Mikulić profusely, then placed the award around his neck. The Sarajevo games were "a wonderful success," he said. "I am convinced . . . [they] will remain forever in our hearts and memories." But "it is my duty as president of the International Olympic Committee to declare the fourteenth Olympic Winter Games closed . . . *Doviđénja,* Yugoslavia. [Goodbye, Yugoslavia]. *Doviđénja, drago* Sarajevo. [Goodbye, dear Sarajevo]."[2] At that point, ten army cadets lowered the Olympic flag and carried it out of the arena. The Olympic flame was extinguished, the athletes hugged each other and shook hands, and the Sarajevo Olympics were over.

The games were a smashing success. Milton Richman, the longtime sports editor at UPI, insisted that Sarajevo's games were "beyond question . . . the best organized and most smoothly run" he'd seen in a quarter century. "[What] impressed me the most," wrote Richman, "is how the Yugoslavian people did everything possible, and some things that seemed impossible." The games were "without wrinkle from the Opening Ceremony right down to the closing one. Nothing was too difficult for them. . . . And when you tried to thank them, they smiled affably and said *nema problema.*"[3]

The press was nearly unanimous in its praise. "With a great deal of effort," wrote *Frankfurter Allgemeine Zeitung,* "the organizers succeeded in staging, from nothing, an event of worldwide importance." France's *L'Equipe* called it "an organizational feat," while Spain's *El Mundo Deportivo* wrote, "These white Olympiads [*sic*] may have been the best."[4] "From a world view," wrote the *Los Angeles Times* reporter Alan Greenberg, "the logistics of these Games couldn't have worked out much better. These were the first Winter Olympics ever held in a communist country, and some believed Yugoslavia would botch them. They were dead wrong. Buses ran on time. Taxis were plentiful. Computers provided up-to-the minute results. . . . [The] competition sites were first-class and well-staffed . . . [and] the Yugoslavs were gracious . . . [hosts]."[5]

By some accounts the people of Sarajevo were almost too hospitable. Waiters, on occasion, refused to accept tips. Shopkeepers in Baščaršija toasted customers with *šljivovica,* a potent plum brandy favored by Yugoslavs, and taxi drivers handed out cigarettes. "My son and daughter, age nine and twelve," one visitor wrote, "were nonplussed to find that when they rode in taxis alone, the taxi drivers often, as a sign of courtesy, offered them cigarettes. . . . Smoking is big in Sarajevo, but this big?"[6] In one well-known story, the *Detroit News* columnist Joe Falls jumped into a cab at Skenderija and told the driver he wished to be taken to the Latin Bridge, to the spot where Gavrilo Princip had shot Archduke Franz Ferdinand in 1914. When they got to the bridge and Falls attempted to pay the man, the driver said no, as in no charge. "I didn't know what to do," wrote Falls, "so I offered him my hand. He shook it . . . [and] smiled. . . . As I got out of the back seat, I looked at the roof of the car to see what kind of cab I was in. [But] there was nothing on the roof. Then, it hit me. I wasn't in a taxi at all; I had jumped into somebody's private car. As he drove away, I tried to call to him, to say thank you again, but he was gone. I thought to myself, 'If this was Detroit, he would have taken me to see Jimmy Hoffa.'"[7] When the photographer Red Grandy was caught in subzero temperatures on Mount Jahorina and was unable to take pictures, a concerned Yugoslav rubbed beeswax and camphor on his hands.[8]

"You got on a bus, and everyone got up to give you their seat," said Peter Ueberroth. "A little old lady got up, [and] offered me her seat, trying to explain in English. [They were] great people, just great people."[9] The chief organizer of the 1984 Summer Olympics in Los Angeles, Ueberroth was in Sarajevo to survey the games. So was Frank King, the head of the 1988 Calgary Olympic Organizing Committee. King was "wide-eyed," wrote the *Calgary Herald*. "Words like gigantic, tremendous, and mammoth poured from [his] lips" as he discussed the "Yugoslavian show."[10] King just couldn't believe the enthusiasm. The Yugoslavs were into it. "You could smell the spirit months before," said one resident. "The streets were alive day and night. . . . Everybody was really excited inside, everything was clean."[11]

Financially, the games were probably a wash. It's hard to tell. In October 1984 Mikulić claimed that Sarajevo's Olympic organizers had realized a $10.6-million profit on expenditures of $124.6 million.[12] But they had also received considerable contributions from the Yugoslav federal government and the republican and provincial governments as well as from Sarajevo itself. In addition, the Project for the Protection of Sarajevo's Human Environment, the massive taxpayer-funded urban renewal program, was not on the SOOC's books. It was a parallel project, which explains why, at the conclusion of the games, Olympic Village A at Mojmilo and the Press Village at Dobrinja became public housing complexes.[13]

Sarajevo's sports facilities went to a city-run tourist agency called ZOI'84, which was the Serbo-Croatian acronym for "Winter Olympic Games '84"— *Zimske olimpijske igre* '84. The agency oversaw the hotel, ski jumps, and cross-country runs on Mount Igman, the hotels and ski slopes on Mounts

Bjelašnica and Jahorina, various hotels within the city, as well as Zetra Hall and the bobsled and luge runs on Mount Trebević. It was ZOI'84's job to do what the SOOC had always wanted to do, that is, turn Sarajevo into a must-see tourist destination for westerners. Working hand in hand with Yugotours, a Yugoslavian state tourist agency, in December 1984, ZOI'84 began offering eight-day, all-inclusive ski packages with roundtrip airfare from New York for $598. During the high season, 10 January to 7 March, the price increased to $638, with two-week packages starting at $736.[14] Ridiculously cheap. By contrast, all-inclusive trips to Chamonix and Val-d'Isère, France, via Air France were upward of $1,200 a week. "Sarajevo was the best deal," said a tourist from Appleton, Wisconsin. "The price was $800 a person for ten days," including "three meals a day. France, Austria, and Switzerland were all over a thousand."[15] A California man was shocked to discover that a two-week trip to Lake Tahoe was more expensive than a two-week trip to Sarajevo, including airfare and a side trip to Dubrovnik.[16]

The promotion worked. That winter, ZOI'84 registered nearly 100,000 hotel stays, more than half by foreign tourists. In ski terms, the number was small; Saas-Fee in Switzerland booked 818,000 stays, St. Moritz over 1 million.[17] However, in 1985 Bosnia drew only 365,000 foreign tourists in total.[18] Thus, under the circumstances, 50,000 or 60,000 wasn't bad. "Before the Games, the only [people] who stopped here were on the way to the seaside," Ostoja Vukmirović, an official with ZOI'84, explained.[19] Now, they had come to Sarajevo to ski. Unfortunately, 1985 was Sarajevo's foreign tourist highpoint. The next year, the number of hotel stays increased by 16.8 percent and the number of Yugoslav guests rose by 40 percent, but foreigners didn't come.[20] "First of all, it's difficult to get here," said one visitor. "There aren't enough flights to Belgrade, and then you have to change planes to fly here. . . . You've got to be adventurous and be ready to roll with the punches. . . . The best way to describe it . . . [is] you're on your own."[21]

In 1986 Bosnia's new tourist chief—Bosnia had never had a tourist chief—was the former organizer of the games, Ahmed Karabegović. His official title was minister of tourism and catering. Savvy in a way few officials ever were, Karabegović knew that organizing a two-week sports festival, however grand, was completely different from organizing a tourist trade. That took time. "It isn't possible to [make Sarajevo into] a new tourist destination overnight," he wrote.[22] Nor was it simply a matter of hosting the Olympics and expecting the tourists to come. What Sarajevo needed was an entire infrastructure: tourist agencies in foreign cities that were from Sarajevo (and not just Yugoslavia), direct routes and better services from JAT, the Yugoslavian airlines, parking lots, filling stations, swimming pools. Whatever resorts in, say, Switzerland had, Sarajevo would need.

However, that required cash, cash that Bosnia, and even Yugoslavia, didn't have. By 1986 the country was $20 billion in debt. Its inflation rate was 85 percent, and its standard of living since 1980 had declined by 30 percent. There were 2.2 million unemployed. "We're living on credit," said a spokesman for a pen and pencil factory in Zagreb. "We don't know what's going to happen in the next five years, and we've already cut wages just to keep our workers on the job."[23] The root of Yugoslavia's problem, apart from borrowing, was a defunct political system in which each republic was a protectionist enclave. Croatia protected Croatian interests, Serbia Serbian interests, and so on. That meant each republic had its own central government, its own police and banking system, and its own plan of investment. The result was no central control, no planning, and a gridlocked, inefficient economic system with dozens of redundant industries. "Every republic [just] had to have its own steel mill and sugar factory," one politician remarked, "whether or not it . . . [had] the raw materials [for them]".[24]

In 1986 an article in the *New York Times* described a potato-processing plant built in Bosnia, where there were no potatoes; a tile-making factory in Macedonia that couldn't process local soils; and an aluminum factory in Croatia built over bauxite deposits that turned out not to exist. The article also noted that over the previous year Vojvodina had exported seven thousand tons of grain, while parts of Yugoslavia had actually imported grain.[25] Perhaps the greatest white elephant of them all was the *Metalurški kombinat Smederevo*, a.k.a. "the Sick Man of the Danube," a sprawling steel mill in Serbia with eleven thousand employees that rang up half of Serbia's foreign debt.[26] "Yugoslavia today desperately needs a political body . . . where the 'buck stops,'" wrote the scholar Bogdan Denitch, "where major economic decisions of general interest to the federation can be made and above all enforced."[27] That body, at least in theory, was Yugoslavia's nine-man collective presidency, the one that had ruled Yugoslavia since Tito's death in 1980. There was also the premier. Nominated by the republics and provinces and approved by both the presidency and the parliament, the premier was Yugoslavia's head of government. He or she led the legislative branch, while the collective presidency was its head of state. In 1986 the Yugoslav premier was Branko Mikulić.

Mikulić had been chosen, in part, because he had organized the 1984 Winter Olympics. Efficient, disciplined, and a leading proponent of federal versus republican authority, Mikulić introduced the first part of a three-part austerity package to combat inflation. He froze wages, cut prices, devalued the dinar to make exports cheaper, and introduced new legislation to close at least fifteen hundred loss-making companies. "We are very much aware that . . . these changes will amount to a . . . toughening of conditions for the average Yugoslav," said one of Mikulić's ministers. "And we know some social consequences could come. We are anticipating social problems."[28] What Mikulić didn't anticipate was a nationwide series of hundreds of strikes across professions in every republic and province. Once, while visiting an alpine ski competition in Kranjska Gora, Mikulić was refused service by the waiters at a restaurant. The Croatian parliament rejected his austerity program outright, while Slovenia's trade union council, a meeting of all its unions, demanded he resign.[29] Mikulić's economic policy doesn't take "the human factor into consideration," said one union rep. "We have to cut all that is unprofitable, but we can't leave workers [in] . . . the streets."[30]

In May 1988 Mikulić survived a no-confidence vote, but when parliament refused to adopt a further reform package that December, Mikulić resigned. He was replaced by Ante Marković, a centrist Croat politician who in January 1990 implemented a "shock therapy" stabilization program when the dinar's annual inflation rate hit 2,000 percent. "Simply counting money [is] difficult," wrote one journalist. "The million-dinar note is now worth a dollar," so people count money "by holding a finger over the long rows of zeroes on the bank notes."[31] To combat inflation Marković revalued the dinar, making it fully convertible for the first time since the Second World War, and pegged it to the German mark. He also tightened the money supply, freed prices, and froze wages, and by March 1990 inflation had dropped to just 8.4 percent.[32] However, in the words of Warren Zimmermann, the last American ambassador to what was a unified Yugoslavia, it was "too little and too late."[33] By this point, President Slobodan Milošević of Serbia had overthrown the provincial governments of Vojvodina and Kosovo and the republican government of Montenegro in a brazen attempt to recentralize Yugoslavia under Serbian control.

Milošević had been an apparatchik, a bureaucratic yes-man, but during the late 1980s had switched course and become a nationalist. His goal was simple: by controlling Serbia, the two provinces, and the Republic of Montenegro, he now had four seats in Yugoslavia's collective presidency and four delegations in parliament. Holding roughly half the votes and given the sizable Serb populations in Croatia and Bosnia, he could bend Yugoslavia to his will. At least that was the plan. But in appealing to Serb nationalism the opportunistic Milošević "had opened a Pandora's Box."[34] He'd seized power through a carefully controlled media and the coordinated use of rallies in which tens of thousands of Serbs, bussed in by Milošević, were told his version of the truth: Yugoslavia had imprisoned the Serbs. Indeed, the entire country, its government, and its constitution were a cryptofascist, CIA-inspired conspiracy, backed alternatively by Germany, Austria, the Vatican, the Freemasons, Hezbollah, and the Jews. "The media offensive of Milošević's Serbia," one author wrote, "resembled very closely the propaganda campaign of Nazi Germany." It was "so heated" and "so all-encompassing" that many Serbs "lost touch with reality" and were "ready to believe anything they were told."[35]

In late 1989, for example, when Slovene officials, fearing violence, banned a Serbian truth rally in Ljubljana, Milošević denounced the Slovenes for their "incomprehensible fascistic hatred," then ordered a boycott of Slovenian goods.[36] Although willing to stay in Yugoslavia, on their terms, the Slovenes favored a decentralized system in which no one republic or leader had control. Therefore, to protect Slovenia from Milošević, in September 1989 the Slovene parliament amended Slovenia's republican constitution to include multiparty elections, the first in Yugoslavia in nearly forty-five years, and the right to self-determination. If Milošević pushed too hard, Slovenia would secede.

Whereas Slovenia had, at most, 50,000 Serbs, however, Croatia had half a million. Bosnia had 1.3 million. Thus, if either republic attempted to leave Yugoslavia, there was going to be a war. "Milošević talked of Yugoslavia at the same time he asserted 'Serbia's right to statehood,'" one author explained. "The implication was that if Yugoslavia could not be turned back to what it [was] under Tito," Milošević "would fashion" a new state "encompass[ing] all Serbs."[37] To that end, in the summer of 1990 the Serb-controlled Yugoslav National Army (JNA) began sending guns to members of the Serbian Democratic Party (SDS), a radical nationalist Serb group in Croatia. In August, the SDS barricaded roads and occupied police stations in the Serb-majority district of Knin in order to set up an autonomous government there. By October, other districts had followed, including one bordering Serbia that bisected the Brotherhood and Unity Highway between Zagreb and Belgrade.

These Serb areas "will never be a part of [an independent] Croatia," said Knin's deputy mayor. "We're interested only in being part of Yugoslavia."[38]

Things grew worse in February 1991, when, like Slovenia, the Croatian parliament voted to "invalidate all federal laws within its territory."[39] Although not yet independent, Croatia was a sovereign state. But the Serbs told a different story. In March the republic's Serbian districts, known collectively as the Krajina, announced their secession from Croatia. Through the fall of 1991, the SDS, with support from the JNA and various Serb paramilitaries, cleansed the Krajina, a full one-third of Croatia's territory, of all non-Serbs. Thousands were killed, and over half a million people were displaced.

The pattern repeated itself in Bosnia. The SDS in Bosnia was led by a former psychiatrist named Radovan Karadžić, who rejected republican rule in order to set up six different Krajinas of his own. The SDS had taken part in Bosnia's first free elections and agreed, grudgingly, to a power-sharing arrangement in which the SDS, the Party of Democratic Action, a Muslim organization, and the Croatian Democratic Union had control. However, in October 1991, alarmed by JNA movements within Bosnia, the Bosnian parliament, with over seventy abstentions by Serbians, passed what it called a Memorandum of Sovereignty.[40] In response, Bosnia's Serb territories formed an independent ministate known as the Bosnian Serb Republic, or Republika Srpska, and prepared for war.

They prepared for war at the very moment Bosnian, Serbian, and Montenegrin athletes were competing as Yugoslavs at the 1992 Winter Olympics in Albertville, France. Technically, the three republics were still in Yugoslavia, though Macedonia was leaving the federation and Croatia and Slovenia were independent states. In January, both Croatia and Slovenia had been recognized by the European Community. They were also recognized by the Vatican and given provisional status as National Olympic Committees by the IOC.[41] With less than a month's preparation both sent teams to Albertville. "We've come here to participate," said the Croatian delegation chief, Sandra Dubravčić, "to show the world . . . that Croatia is not part of Yugoslavia anymore."[42]

A twenty-seven-year-old retired figure skater, Dubravčić was the same Sandra Dubravčić who in 1984 had ascended the steps at Sarajevo's Koševo Stadium and lit the Olympic flame. Now, she wanted nothing to do with Yugoslavia. Her teammates didn't either. The trainer, Ozren Müller, was a military ski instructor whose friend and skiing partner Davor Sefić had been killed defending Dubrovnik. However, in Albertville his alpine ski team stayed in the same Olympic Village as the Serbs. "I know they are not soldiers," explained Müller. "[They're] only athletes and members of [their] delegation, [but] I have nothing to say to these people. . . . I have too much hatred to be objective right now."[43]

Meanwhile, in Bosnia, the former Yugoslav republic was falling apart. In March 1992 Serb paramilitaries and Muslim–Croat militiamen exchanged fire in Bosanski Brod, a city on the border of Croatia. Serbs and Croats fought in Neum in Dalmatia, in Doboj in the Posavina region, and in Mostar in Herzegovina.[44] Serbs and Muslims fought in Goražde, to the east of the republic, while Serb forces attempted to blockade Sarajevo. War came to central Sarajevo in April 1992, when Serb paramilitaries took up positions at the Holiday Inn, the one built for the Olympics, and fired indiscriminately into a peace rally being held in front of the parliament.[45]

Elsewhere in and above the city, on its ridges, Muslim and Serb militias vied for control. The fiercest fighting occurred in Dobrinja, the series of apartment blocks that in 1984 had housed the Press Village. In May, Serb forces surrounded the settlement, and its residents began to starve. "There's been shooting and shelling there all the time," said a spokesman for UNHCR, a UN relief agency. In the absence of food, the residents "have been living on grass—ordinary grass."[46] There was one doctor; he operated in a basement and amputated limbs without an anesthetic. Relief came in June 1992, when Muslim forces liberated Dobrinja and the UN brought food.[47]

In Mojmilo, the housing district north of Dobrinja and the site of Olympic Village A, the fighting was equally intense. Here, Muslim and Serb forces fought for control of housing complexes and access to Mojmilo Hill, which overlooked Dobrinja. In June, Muslim forces captured the complexes and the hill, but the former village was destroyed. Immediately southeast of the city was Mount Trebević, the site of the bobsled and luge runs. From here, Serb forces pounded Sarajevo with impunity. In September 1992 the *New York Times* reporter Roger Cohen visited Position No. 8, a sniper post overlooking Sarajevo from which "the yellowish Holiday Inn" and "the Baščaršija market district" were "perfectly visible through telescopic sights." The view, wrote Cohen, was magnificent.[48]

Located behind Serbian lines and cut off from the city were Mounts Igman and Bjelašnica. The former sites of the Nordic events and men's alpine ski competitions, these were in Muslim hands and under the control of various warlords until August 1993, when they were captured by the Serbs. The two mountains had been Sarajevo's lifeline, especially Igman. Located across the airport southwest of the city, Igman was the only high ground immediately surrounding Sarajevo that wasn't held by the Serbs. It was also home to Igman Road, a treacherous mountain pass that went through Veliko Polje, the site of the 1984 cross-country and biathlon competitions, and on into Muslim territory. This was the road Igor Boras took in February 1993 on his way to the World Bobsleigh Championships in Austria (see chapter 1). Everything that went into or out of the city, including guns, went through Igman.

However, in August 1993, when Muslim forces from Bjelašnica and Igman left to fight the Croats in Herzegovina, the mountains were taken by the Serbs. The Serb commander was Gen. Ratko Mladić, who, a day or two after the fighting, took the UN chief in Bosnia, Gen. Francis Briquemont, on a tour of the summit. "Everything you see here is controlled by the forces of Republika Srpska," he said, surveying the region. "In peacetime, I never came here. It was too expensive."[49] The Serbs held Igman and Bjelašnica for two weeks but handed the area over to French UN peacekeepers when NATO threatened to strike. For the rest of the war, Igman and Bjelašnica were demilitarized zones, but the hotels there, including the former Olympic Village B, and the ski jumps and lift facilities were destroyed.

Mount Jahorina was on the Serbian side. Although just thirty minutes south of Sarajevo and within earshot of Serb artillery, the site of the women's alpine ski competition survived the war unscathed. In fact, the parliament of Republika Srpska often held its meetings at the Hotel Bistrica, the Olympic hotel on Jahorina. (It was here, in May 1993, that Serb representatives voted 51–2 against a UN peace plan.)[50] "The war situation makes it very hard to run this hotel and the Olympic Center here," the manager Drago Blagojević complained in an interview in 1993. "Thanks to [UN sanctions on Republika Srpska] it's been very hard to get spare parts for the wires and other technical equipment, and all the other supplies we need are very expensive. But we are managing as best we can."[51]

In 1994 Serb officials at Jahorina organized a mini-Olympics to commemorate the tenth anniversary of the 1984 Winter Olympic Games. It was bizarre. Standing in front of a so-called Serbian Olympic flame, Bosnian Serb dignitaries gave speeches, children sang of peace, and athletes from Republika Srpska, Serbia, and Montenegro competed in four events: the slalom, the giant slalom, cross country, and biathlon.[52] "We are fully aware we will not have a lot of participants because we are still not recognized as a state," said Ljubomir Žuković, the head of the Bosnian Serb Olympic Committee.[53]

As it stood, the IOC recognized only one National Olympic Committee in Bosnia, and that was the committee in Sarajevo. Led by a Croat politician named Stjepan Kljuić, the Olympic Committee of Bosnia and Herzegovina formed in June 1992 and sent athletes to the Barcelona Summer Olympics that July. Traveling by bus under armed escort, a delegation of twenty-six athletes and coaches arrived at Butmir International Airport in Sarajevo. From there they were flown to Barcelona by the UN.[54] "The most important thing for us is [to take] part," said Kljuić, "to show [that] we exist. . . . The results aren't important. You can't imagine [the] conditions our athletes [have been training] under. [They've been] fired on by snipers [and have had just] 1,000 calories a day to eat."[55]

Kljuić carried a copy of a booklet titled *Do You Remember Sarajevo?* that had been published by the Olympic Committee of Bosnia and Herzegovina specifically for circulation in Barcelona.[56] The first page read, "Sarajevo in the Year 1984." There were pictures of Zetra Hall, Skenderija, Koševo Stadium, the Holiday Inn, all in pristine condition. A later section, "Sarajevo in the Year 1992," showed the same buildings, now destroyed: a plume of smoke billowing from Zetra Hall, Zetra in ruins, the Holiday Inn with charred windows, Skenderija without a roof. There were pictures of other buildings too: the main post office, Olympic Village A at Mojmilo, the train station, the Olympic museum. Each was a mangled carcass, a blackened and burned out shell.

Zetra Hall had been bombed by the Serbs in May 1992, a scant two months before Barcelona. Firemen saved part of the building, but the arena had a gaping hole in the ceiling, lights dangled from wires, and the floor was exposed. Eventually, French peacekeepers commandeered the site, but twice each week a sixty-two-year-old Bosnian carpenter named Muhamed Cavdar carried away its seats. "I am a woodworker," Cavdar said in an interview in 1993. "We have permission from the city [to] go to Zetra to use the wood. . . . [We have] limited choices. It's either this or . . . nothing."[57] Having no coal or heating oil and limited in its use of natural gas, Sarajevo by the winter of 1993 had cut down its trees. There was no wood anywhere—literally, no wood.

Therefore, the residents of the city buried their dead in coffins *made from the seats of Zetra Hall.* There were so many dead—11,451, to be exact—and so few places to bury them that the residents used whatever green space they could find. "People were buried wherever there [was] space," said one peacekeeper, "usually late at night so that the Serb snipers couldn't see the funeral and open fire." It was like burying people "in the middle of Central Park."[58] In late 1992, as Lav Cemetery filled to overflowing, residents began using the soccer field next to the speed-skating oval at Zetra Hall to bury the victims. An entire family of six was buried here in one funeral in 1994.[59]

That year Zetra's speed-skating oval was supposed to have had its most famous visitor: Pope John Paul II. The aging pontiff had planned to visit Sarajevo during a ceasefire and to hold Mass for at least twenty-five thousand people on Zetra's pockmarked track. In September, Bosnian authorities built a stage and a ramp; they also mowed grass and removed debris from Sniper Alley, the pope's route from the airport, and flew in the pontiff's bulletproof car.[60] Two days before the Mass, however, Serb insurgents fired eleven artillery rounds into Sanac, a front-line suburb, and the pope's visit was called off.[61]

Indeed, Sarajevo had had several ceasefires, including one, in March 1994, when upward of twenty thousand people attended a soccer match between FC Sarajevo and a UN team at Koševo Stadium, the site of the Olympic opening ceremony in 1984. In a scene one writer described as worthy of inclusion in *Apocalypse Now,* British Coldstream Guards played "In the Mood," the classic Glenn Miller standard, while soldiers with machine guns guarded the pitch, and helicopters with antisniper teams circled overhead.[62] This particular ceasefire began in February 1994 after the Markale massacre, when a Serb mortar shell killed sixty-eight people in a crowded market in Sarajevo. NATO gave the Serbs an ultimatum: move your heavy guns at least twenty kilometers from the city or face airstrikes. The Serbs moved the guns and agreed to a ceasefire.[63]

Taking effect on 9 February, the ceasefire coincided with the tenth anniversary of the 1984 Winter Olympics. (The opening ceremonies had been on the eighth; the ceasefire was on the ninth.) At the time, Samaranch was in Lillehammer at the 1994 Winter Olympics when he announced suddenly that he and Jacques Rogge, the Belgian president of the Association of European Olympic Committees and the future Olympic president, would be visiting Sarajevo.[64] Samaranch had been planning the trip for months. In fact, he'd spent the past two years, ever since the Barcelona Olympics in July 1992, pushing an "Olympic Truce."

Based on the ancient Greek practice of *ekecheiria* ("holding of hands"), the Olympic Truce referred to a month-long period in which wars ceased and visitors were given free passage to and from Olympus. At its ninety-ninth session in Barcelona, goaded by the war in Bosnia, the IOC proposed a permanent ekecheiria, in which all combatants in every region of the world would honor a one-month ceasefire from the seventh day before an Olympics to the seventh day after it.[65] "We know it is nearly impossible," Samaranch admitted, "but it is the duty of the Olympic movement to try. If fighters stop for a few weeks, maybe [they'll] stop for a longer time, maybe forever."[66]

In all, 184 National Olympic Committees supported the proposal, which Samaranch sent to Secretary-General Boutros Boutros-Ghali at the UN. Samaranch hoped the UN would pass a resolution in which the organization's member states would observe the Olympic Truce, starting with Lillehammer. Passed by unanimous consent in October 1993, the resolution had sixteen cosponsors, including, most notably, Bosnia.[67] To solidify the truce, in December 1993 Samaranch met with President Bill Clinton, with the heads of the National Olympic Committees of Croatia and Serbia, and with the Bosnian presidents of each warring side: the Muslim Alija Izetbegović, the Serb Radovan Karadžić, and the Croat Mate Boban.[68] "We have begun talks with . . . [all] three parties," Samaranch assured the world, "and we are optimistic [the truce] . . . will be a success."[69] It wasn't.

The truce began on 5 February 1994. Within hours, a Serb shell obliterated the Markale market. It was an "atrocious [attack], a tragedy, an awful human drama," said Director-General François Carrard of the IOC. "But we are not giving up the truce, not at all."[70] Instead, Samaranch announced from Lillehammer that he would use Olympic funds to rebuild Sarajevo's venues as soon as the war was over. He then promised to match, "dollar-for-dollar, crown-for crown," any donations made by athletes to Bosnia.[71] At the games' opening ceremony, on 12 February, Samaranch asked viewers for a moment of silence before issuing a plea: "Please stop fighting. Please stop killing. Drop your guns."[72]

Over objections from his executive board, Samaranch flew to Sarajevo on 16 February, where he met with President Izetbegović and officials from the Olympic Committee of Bosnia and Herzegovina and toured Zetra Hall.[73] "I [took] . . . Mr. Samaranch to [center ice]," said Izudin Filipović, director of the Bosnian committee, the place where "ten years earlier he had closed the Olympic Games with . . . 'Doviđénja, drago Sarajevo.' This time, I got the impression that he couldn't speak . . . that the words stuck in his throat."[74] To memorialize the occasion, Filipović gave Samaranch a poster. It was white with black lettering and read, "Sarajevo: Olympic City, 1984–1994." The picture was of five Olympic rings in blood.[75] The next evening Samaranch returned to Lillehammer. There, he repeated his pledge and promised to be "a coordinating force" among governments, businesses, and nonprofit organizations that would one day aid Sarajevo. "We will help," he said, "with deeds, not words."[76]

In November 1995, when the Bosnian War ended with the signing of the Dayton Peace Accords in Dayton, Ohio, Samaranch sent Pere Miró, the deputy sports director of the IOC, to Bosnia. Miró's job was to survey the damage and to coordinate the reconstruction of one venue in particular—Zetra Hall. With contributions from the European Union, the City of Barcelona, the governments of the Netherlands and Norway, the International Skating Union, and a nonprofit organization known as the Humanitarian Sports Group, founded by the Norwegian speed skater and philanthropist Johann Olav Koss, the IOC completed the building in March 1999. It cost $20 million; the IOC's contribution was $11.5 million.[77]

The new Zetra Hall was beautiful. Home to the Bosnian Olympic Committee, the Sarajevo Olympic Museum, a gym, a shooting range, two cafes, and an arena, it was the nicest sports facility in Bosnia and one of the top facilities in the Balkans. It still is. Unfortunately, the reopening ceremony was a bust. Scheduled for the end of March 1999 and featuring a planned gala presentation by Samaranch and ice-skating performances by Katarina Witt and Torvill and Dean, the reopening was canceled because of the war in Kosovo.[78] Nevertheless, in November 1999 Torvill and Dean returned to Sarajevo. Taken on a tour of the city and its ruined Olympic venues, they were shocked by what they saw. Their city, their gray Olympic city, had been destroyed. "We came into contact with so many people there, and when you [heard] of people being killed, you wonder[ed] whether you talked with them or brushed shoulders with them," Dean commented. "We have wonderful memories of Sarajevo, and it's tragic [what happened there]."[79]

A common theme among athletes was dismay—dismay that Sarajevo had hosted the Olympics and then fought such a brutal civil war. "It was a shock to us," the former Yugoslav skier Jure Franko declared. "It was hard to believe that people who lived in . . . peace for fifty years could . . . [do those things] to each other."[80] Scott Hamilton reacted to the disaster by saying, "This was the place where my Olympic dream came true. . . . [To] see it bombed out, burned out, destroyed, you wonder: For what purpose? To what end?"[81] Phil Mahre admitted, "It's kind of hard to grasp. . . . You go to bed one night and your neighbor is your neighbor, and the next day he's your enemy. . . . We didn't see any of that tension when we were there."[82] Indeed, for most former Yugoslavs, and Bosnians in particular, the 1984 Winter Olympics are a marker, a symbol, the apotheosis of an earlier, idealized period in which Yugoslavia still existed and Serbs, Croats, and Muslims got along.

In 2001, for example, the gold medalist Debbie Armstrong returned to Sarajevo with the nonprofit group American Forests, whose Global ReLeaf project sought to restore Bosnian forests through the replanting of hundreds of thousands of trees.[83] "The thing that really struck me," she said, "having been there in '84 and having returned in '01, is that for them, the Olympics are like 9/11. There's pre-9/11 and post-9/11, and nothing [after that date] has ever been the same. That's their Olympics. It chokes me up to even talk about it, but in '01 I brought my medal with me. We met the mayor, and when I handed it to him he just stood there, staring at it, and then he started to cry. It was *that* powerful. I mean, it's just a medal, right? I certainly cherish it, but to him, it symbolized this glorious time, this time of peace and togetherness that'll never happen again."[84]

A resident of Sarajevo named Ismet Huseinović, a coppersmith in Baščaršija, agrees: "There has never been and will never be such an event in Sarajevo." By hosting the games, "we defended [the city's] honor." And not just the city's honor," he insists, "but [the honor of] . . . Yugoslavia." We "were all [in it] together."[85] In 2002 the Olympic Committee of Bosnia and Herzegovina attempted to bring people together once again by submitting a brave, yet unsuccessful bid for the 2010 Winter Olympics. Faced with poverty, unemployment, a divided political system with two competing entities, a destroyed infrastructure, and seventeen thousand peacekeepers on the ground, it had no chance.[86] The 2010 Winter Olympic Games went to Vancouver.

"It wasn't a realistic bid," said Said Fazlagić, an official with the Bosnian Olympic Committee, but "the goal, I think, was to take people's minds away from war and onto something else. In Bosnia, the games belong to everyone, regardless of religion. It doesn't matter what your political philosophy is either. It doesn't matter who you are or what your name is . . . the games belong to you. Just go outside. . . . Vučko is everywhere. You'll find Olympic signs in and around Sarajevo and in Republika Srpska too. That's because we all have such positive memories and wish, in some way, we'd host the Olympics again."[87]

POSTSCRIPT: *In December 2012 Muslim-controlled Sarajevo and Serbian-controlled East Sarajevo won a joint bid to host the 2017 European Youth Olympic Winter Festival, a kind of Junior Olympics. As the Bosnian journalist Vedat Spahović put it, the Olympics were "coming home."*[88]

Notes

Introduction

1. Alex Alvarez, *Governments, Citizens, and Genocide* (Bloomington: Indiana University Press, 2001), 144.

2. Igor Boras, interview by author, 10 July 2010. Hereafter all Boras quotes are from this interview unless otherwise noted.

3. John Pomfret, "The War Gives Authority to Criminals," *Philadelphia Inquirer,* 22 August 1992.

4. John Pomfret, "A Perilous Olympic Struggle," *Washington Post,* 17 January 1994.

5. "The Destruction of an Olympic Site," *San Francisco Chronicle,* 12 June 1992.

6. Gary Shelton, "War Follows Bosnian Team," *St. Petersburg Times* (Fla.), 13 February 1994.

7. William Oscar Johnson, "The Killing Ground," *Sports Illustrated,* 14 February 1994, 46.

8. Bill Glauber, "Peaceful Sarajevo Just a Memory," *Baltimore Sun,* 7 February 1994.

9. Jane Leavy, "In Sarajevo, Fond Memories Turned Bleak," *Washington Post,* 19 February 1994.

10. Susan Tyler Eastman, Robert S. Brown, and Karen J. Kovatch, "The Olympics That Got Real? Television's Story of Sarajevo," *Journal of Sport and Social Issues* 20.4 (November 1996): 377.

11. "IOC to Match Sarajevo Donations," *Fort Worth Star-Telegram,* 18 February 1994.

12. "Olympics Head Revisits Sarajevo, Offers Help to Besieged Bosnians," *St. Louis Post-Dispatch,* 17 February 1994.

13. Bill Livingston, "Closed Encounters: A Torch to Nagano, a Light for Sarajevo," *Cleveland Plain Dealer,* 28 February 1994.

14. Eastman et al., "The Olympics That Got Real?" 386–87.

15. Tony Chamberlain, "Sarajevans Weary, Proud," *Boson Globe,* 6 February 1984.

16. Jeff Hastings, interview by author, 9 August 2009.

17. Debbie Armstrong, interview by author, 17 September 2009; Murray Olderman, "Events in Sarajevo Changed World," *Nevada Daily Mail,* 3 February 1984.

18. "Agreement between the Organizing Committee of the XIVth Olympic Winter Games and the Coca-Cola Company," 19 March 1981, International Olympic Committee Archives, Lausanne, Switzerland, CIO JO-1984W-FIRM-CT, folder 206666.

19. "Olympics et cetera," *Milwaukee Journal,* 8 February 1984.

20. Johnson, "The Killing Ground," 51.

21. Robert J. Donia, *Sarajevo: A Biography* (Ann Arbor: University of Michigan Press, 2006), 248.

22. "Blade Reporter Will Give Her View of Olympics," *Toledo Blade,* 29 January 1984.

1. Athens, 1978

1. Lord Killanin, *My Olympic Years* (London: Secker and Warburg, 1983), 11.

2. Jack Ludwig, *Five Ring Circus* (Garden City, N.Y.: Doubleday, 1976), 9.

3. Barry Lorge, "Games Guardians," *Washington Post,* 9 February 1980.

4. Geoffrey Miller, *Behind the Olympic Rings* (Lynn, Mass.: H. P. Zimman, 1979), 23.

5. *Olympic Rules, Bye-Laws, and Instructions* (Lausanne: International Olympic Committee, 1976), 5.

6. For a brief review of how Coubertin first organized the IOC, see chapter 1, "The Baron's Dream," in Allen Guttmann, *The Olympics: A History of the Modern Games,* 2nd ed. (Champaign: University of Illinois Press, 2002), 7–20. See also John J. MacAloon, *This Great Symbol: Pierre de Coubertin and the Origins of the Modern Olympic Games* (Chicago: University of Chicago Press, 1981).

7. Miller, *Behind the Olympic Rings,* 27.

8. "Address by I.O.C. President Lord Killanin," IOC Archives, CIO SESS-080ES-CERE, folder 0099006.

9. John E. Findling and Kimberly D. Pelle, eds., *Encyclopedia of the Modern Olympic Movement* (Westport, Conn., 1996), 158.

10. Will Grimsley, "Scribe Asks: 'What Happened to the Games?' " *Spokane Daily Chronicle* (Wash.), 28 July 1976.

11. Killanin, *My Olympic Years,* 104.

12. Steve Cady, "Brundage's Last Hurrah," *New York Times,* 10 September 1972. For a biography of Brundage, see Allen Guttmann, *The Games Must Go On: Avery Brundage and the Olympic Movement* (New York: Columbia University Press, 1984).

13. "Olympic Terror Leaves 17 Dead," *St. Petersburg Evening Independent* (Fla.), 6 September 1972.

14. Red Smith, "Six Days Late, the Gasman Cometh," *New York Times,* 11 September 1972. For an examination of Brundage's response to the massacre and the public's reaction to it, see David Clay Large, *Munich 1972: Tragedy, Terror, and Triumph at the Olympic Games* (New York: Rowman and Littlefield, 2012), 243–48.

15. Bill Bruns, "Will Colorado Scrap Its Own 1976 Olympics?" *Life,* 3 November 1972, 81.

16. For an overview of Denver's failed Olympic bid, see Matthew Burbank et al., *Olympic Dreams: The Impact of Mega-Events on Local Politics* (Boulder: Lynne Rienner, 2001), 48–50.

17. "Denver Games Vetoed," *Reading Eagle* (Penn.), 8 November 1972.

18. Jerry Kirshenbaum, "Voting to Snuff the Torch," *Sports Illustrated,* 20 November 1972, 46.

19. Bruns, "Will Colorado Scrap Its Own 1976 Olympics?," 81.

20. Sam W. Brown, Jr., "Snow Job in Colorado," *New Republic,* 29 January 1972, 18.

21. "19th Hole: Readers Take Over," *Sports Illustrated,* 11 December 1972, 115.

22. Ludwig, *Five Ring Circus,* 35.

23. Cooper Rollow, "No Deficit at Montreal Olympics, Vows Mayor," *Chicago Tribune,* 11 February 1973. The $125-million figure was quoted in Ludwig, *Five Ring Circus,* 35.

24. David Minthorn, "Olympics' Cost Boom Far Exceeds Anticipated Mark," *Reading Eagle* (Penn.), 3 August 1972. For a comparison of Summer Olympic organizational costs, see Holger Preuss, *The Economics of Staging the Olympics: A Comparison of the Games, 1972–2008* (Northampton, Mass.: Edward Elgar, 2004).

25. Ludwig, *Five Ring Circus,* 35. Even worse, Drapeau had guaranteed certain key builders "cost-plus" contracts but failed to insist on a "do-not-exceed" clause. He guaranteed the company Zarolega, Inc., for example, a 12 percent profit on the first $30 million spent on the Olympic Village and 6 percent on anything above that. Therefore, with no real reason to limit costs, Zarolega spent and spent. See P. A. Bosela and N. J. Delatte, "Use of Failure Case Studies in a Construction Planning and Estimating Course," in Dana Ames et al., eds., *Structures Congress 2011* (Reston, Va.: ASCE Publications, 2011), 1134.

26. Steve Cady, "Montreal Olympics: A Billion-Dollar Photo Finish," *New York Times,* 28 March 1976.

27. Killanin, *My Olympic Years,* 122.

28. Cady, "Montreal Olympics: A Billion-Dollar Photo Finish."

29. "The Sky Isn't Falling, But Olympic Stadium Is," *Austin American-Statesman* (Tex.), 14 September 1991.

30. Doug Gilbert, "Another Confidence Vote Given Montreal Facilities," *Ottawa Citizen,* 3 February 1976.

31. "Killanin Suggests New Olympic Logo of Crossed Fingers," *Montreal Gazette,* 30 January 1976.

32. "Innsbruck Residents Unmoved by Games," *Montreal Gazette,* 29 January 1976.

33. "Costs Rise for Winter Olympics," *Toledo Blade,* 18 January 1976.

34. "Four Times Estimate, Winter Games Costly Too," *Spokesman-Review* (Wash.), 18 January 1976.

35. Jack Murphy, "Voracious Olympics: Survival Problem," *New York Times,* 4 April 1976.

36. See Peter Benesh, "The Olympic Games Fiasco: Who Needed It?" *Saskatoon Phoenix* (Canada), 31 July 1976; Murphy, "Voracious Olympics: Survival Problem"; and Arthur Daley, "Denver Is Out and Montreal Is Uneasy," *New York Times,* 30 November 1972.

37. Daley, "Denver Is Out and Montreal Is Uneasy."

38. For a discussion of Brundage's opposition to the Winter Olympics, see Guttmann, *The Games Must Go On,* 194–99.

39. Miller, *Behind the Olympic Rings,* 109.

40. " 'Winter Olympics Are Dead': Brundage Calls for End," *Palm Beach Post-Times* (Fla.), 20 August 1972.

41. Otto Schantz, "The Olympic Ideal and the Winter Games," in Norbert Muller, Manfred Messing, and Holger Preuss, eds., *From Chamonix to Turin* (Kassel, Germany: Agon Sportverlag, 2006), 46–47.

42. Les Brown, "Olympic Games Average 35% of the TV Audience," *New York Times,* 11 February 1976.

43. "Hamill Haircut Popular in US," *Miami News,* 29 March 1976.

44. Ray Holliman, "ABC's Olympic Television Coverage: It's Extravagant," *St. Petersburg Times* (Fla.), 17 July 1976.

45. "Olympic Flame Finally Lit," *Palm Beach Post* (Fla.), 18 July 1976.

46. Miller, *Behind the Olympic Rings,* 160.

47. "China and Olympism," *Olympic Review* 190/191 (August/September 1983): 584.

48. Guoqi Xu, *Olympic Dreams: China and Sports, 1895–2008* (Boston: Harvard University Press, 2008), 88. See also Alan Bairner and Hwang Dong-Jhy, "Representing Taiwan: International Sport, Ethnicity and National Identity in the Republic of China," *International Review for the Sociology of Sport* 46.3 (2011): 237–39.

49. Guttmann, *The Olympics: A History of the Modern Games,* 92.

50. "Canada, China Sign Huge Wheat Deal," *Milwaukee Journal,* 6 October 1973.

51. "Angry Olympic Officials Ready for Struggle with Canada," *Spokesman-Review* (Wash.), 7 July 1976.

52. Miller, *Behind the Olympic Rings,* 87.

53. "Mike Hughes, "The IOC Gives In; Taiwan Is Out," *St. Petersburg Times* (Fla.), 12 July 1976.

54. For an examination of the African-led boycott of the 1976 Montreal Games, see Courtney W. Mason, "The Bridge to Change: Apartheid Policy, South African Sport and the Olympic Boycott Paradigm," in Stephen R. Wenn and Gerald P. Schaus, eds., *Onward to the Olympics: Historical Perspectives on the Olympic Games* (Waterloo, Ontario: Wilfrid Laurier University Press, 2006), 285–97.

55. Hubert Mizell, "Africa Walkout: Another Political Black Eye," *St. Petersburg Times* (Fla.), 18 July 1976.

56. Ellen Lentz, "Germans: 'Socialist Victory,' " *New York Times,* 4 August 1976.

57. Bill Shirley, "At the Very End, American Women Swim to Gold," *Los Angeles Times,* 26 July 1976.

58. Joe Sargis, "Montreal Olympics Is Now History," *Ellensburg Daily Record* (Wash.), 3 August 1976.

59. Tim Burke, "Feeding the Dragon In Hope It Will Eat Us Last," *Montreal Gazette,* 13 July 1976; Steve Cady, "Killanin's 1980 Goal Is Olympics for All," *New York Times,* 3 August 1976.

60. Miller, *Behind the Olympic Rings,* 141.

61. "LA Favors the Games, If—" *Pittsburgh Press,* 11 September 1977.

62. "Former Olympics Supporter Says LA Should Withdraw Bid," *Eugene Register-Guard* (Oreg.), 31 May 1978. For a brief study of the unique commercial nature of the 1984 Summer Games, see Alan Tomlinson's "Los Angeles 1984 and 1932: Commercializing the American Dream," chapter in Alan Tomlinson and Christopher Young, eds., *National Identity and Global Sports Events: Culture, Politics, and Spectacle in the Olympics and the Football World Cup* (Albany: State University of New York Press, 2006), 163–76. See also Jules Boykoff, *Celebration Capitalism and the Olympic Games* (New York: Routledge, 2013), 29–32.

63. "Amateurism Still an Issue," *Spokesman-Review* (Wash.), 25 January 1976.

64. Miller, *Behind the Olympic Rings,* 137.

65. "L.A. Path Still Rocky," *Ellensburg Daily Record* (Wash.), 24 March 1978.

66. William Oscar Johnson, "A Flaming Olympic Mess," *Sports Illustrated,* 26 June 1978, 23, 26.

67. Miller, *Behind the Olympic Rings,* 49.

68. William Oscar Johnson, "History's New Imprint," *Sports Illustrated,* 22 March 1982, 51.

69. Jay Clarke, "Intriguing City Spies Olympic Gold," *Detroit Free Press,* 8 January 1984.

2. The Swedish Prince

1. R. J. Crampton, *Eastern Europe in the Twentieth Century* (New York: Routledge, 1994), 308.

2. According to the Organization for Economic Cooperation and Development, in 1978 Yugoslavia's per capita gross domestic product was $2,140. Portugal's was $1,900. See *OECD Economic Surveys: Yugoslavia* (Paris: OECD Publications, May 1980), summary table in front matter, and *OECD Economic Surveys: Portugal* (Paris: OECD Publications, July 1980), summary table in front matter.

3. John R. Lampe, *Yugoslavia as History,* 2nd ed. (New York: Cambridge University Press, 2000), 322.

4. Mile Stojić, "Branko Mikulic—Socialist Emperor Manqué," *Bosnia Report,* December–March 2006, www.bosnia.org.uk.

5. David Binder, "Yugoslavs Alert," *New York Times,* 28 February 1965.

6. David Binder and Vilko Zuber, "Yugoslavia to Pave Way for Tourists," *New York Times,* 7 July 1963.

7. Robert J. Donia, *Sarajevo: A Biography* (Ann Arbor: University of Michigan Press, 2006), 20.

8. Ibid., 13.

9. With its creation in 1918, Yugoslavia was originally known as the Kingdom of the Serbs, Croats, and Slovenes but changed its name to the Kingdom of Yugoslavia in 1929.

10. Jovan Ilić and Dušanka Hadži-Jovančić, *The Serbian Question in the Balkans* (Belgrade: University of Belgrade Faculty of Geography, 1995), 273.

11. Sabrina Ramet, *Nihil Obstat: Religion, Politics, and Social Change in East-Central Europe and Russia* (Durham: Duke University Press, 1998), 161.

12. Steven L. Burg and Paul S. Shoup, *The War in Bosnia-Herzegovina: Ethnic Conflict and International Intervention* (Armonk, N.Y.: M. E. Sharpe, 1999), 37.

13. Enver Redžić, *Bosnia and Herzegovina in the Second World War* (London: Frank Cass, 2005), 195.

14. Noel Malcolm, *Bosnia: A Short History* (New York: New York University Press, 1996), 201.

15. Statistics cited in Nicholas R. Lang, "The Dialectics of Decentralization: Economic Reform and Regional Inequality in Yugoslavia," *World Politics* 27.3 (April 1975): 314.

16. Malcolm, *Bosnia: A Short History,* 201–2.

17. Ante Čuvalo, *Historical Dictionary of Bosnia and Herzegovina* (Lanham, Md.: Scarecrow Press, 1997), 108–9.

18. Aleksander Trumić, "Space Planning for the 1984 Winter Olympics," *Survey – Sarajevo* 9.4 (1982): 429.

19. Takač wrote that Zečević visited the IOC in 1970, though Zečević insists he visited a year later, in 1971. See Zlatan Rasidagić, "Dr. Ljubiša Zečević: Kako smo dobili ZOI'84," BiH Ski, 10 July 2008, http://bihski.com.

20. Artur Takač, *Sixty Olympic Years* (Biel, Switzerland: Courvoisier-Attinger, 1998), 233.

21. Rasidagić, "Dr. Ljubiša Zečević: Kako smo dobili ZOI'84."

22. The $72-million figure was cited in a Sarajevo Olympic Organizing Committee pamphlet submitted to the IOC entitled "Sarajevo: Candidate XIVth Winter Olympic Games." See IOC Archives, CIO VIL-1984W-CORR, folder 10342.

23. Izet Kalkan et al., *Sarajevo: Projekat zaštite čovjekove okoline* (Novi Sad: Forum, 1982), n.p. See also Nesha Starcevic, "Turkish Goldsmith Donates a Kilogram of Gold for Games," *Gettysburg Times* (Penn.), 7 February 1984.

24. Kalkan et al., *Sarajevo: Projekat zaštite čovjekove okoline,* n.p.

25. Ahmed Karabegović, interview by author, 24 June 2010.

26. Kalkan et al., *Sarajevo: Projekat zaštite čovjekove okoline,* n.p.

27. Ibid., n.p.

28. Ahmed Karabegović, interview by author, 24 June 2010.

29. "Kako smo dobili ZOI'84."

30. The conditions for candidate cities wishing to host the games are spelled out in the Olympic Charter.

31. Organizing Committee of the XIVth Winter Olympic Games, *Final Report: Sarajevo '84* (Sarajevo: Oslobođenje, 1984), 104–9.

32. Leigh Montville, "How to Describe Sarajevo?," *Boston Globe,* 4 February 1984.

33. Leonard Shapiro, "Sarajevo," *Washington Post,* 5 February 1984.

34. Ron Goldwyn, "Been to Harrisburg, You've Seen Sarajevo," *Philadelphia Daily News,* 6 February 1984.

35. Barry Lorge, "Barry Lorge," *San Diego Union,* 5 February 1984.

36. Tom Coat, "Sarajevo Awaits Its Chance to Add to Olympic Legacy," *Evening Tribune* (Calif.), 30 January 1984.

37. Larry Wood, "There'll Be Less Trouble on Network," *Calgary Herald,* 31 October 1979.

38. Doug Gilbert, "Yugoslav New Top Planner for the Montreal Olympics," *Montreal Gazette,* 7 November 1972.

39. Doug Gilbert, "A Stadium 'Optimist' Says It Can Be Done," *Montreal Gazette,* 16 January 1976.

40. Ahmed Karabegović, interview by author, 24 June 2010.

41. Takač, *Sixty Olympic Years,* 234.

42. Ibid., 235.

43. Ibid., 234.

44. "Alpine Skiing Made Strong Comeback," *Reading Eagle* (Penn.), 23 January 1976; Morten Lund, "Portillo: Historic Queen of the Southern Hemisphere," *Skiing Heritage Journal* 15.1 (March 2003): 29.

45. Takač, *Sixty Olympic Years,* 234.

46. "Lake Placid Way Behind, Ski Official Claims," *Palm Beach Post-Times* (Fla.), 15 January 1977; "Innsbruck Offers Help, Not Escape," *Observer-Reporter* (Penn.), 18 March 1976.

47. Doug Gilbert, "Can Lake Placid Gear Down Olympics? Probably Not," *Montreal Gazette,* 17 February 1978.

48. "Minutes from the 80th Session of the International Olympic Committee, Athens, 17th–20th May 1978," 82, IOC Archives.

49. Ibid., 79.

50. Gilbert, "Can Lake Placid Gear Down Olympics? Probably Not."

51. Geoffrey Miller, *Behind the Olympic Rings* (Lynn, Mass.: H. P. Zimman, 1979), 49.

52. Gilbert, "Can Lake Placid Gear Down Olympics? Probably Not."

53. Takač, *Sixty Olympic Years,* 236.

54. Ibid., 236–37.

55. "Minutes from the 80th Session of the International Olympic Committee," 33, IOC Archives.

56. Ahmed Karabegović, interview by author, 24 June 2010.

3. Nobody Changes Light Bulbs

1. William Oscar Johnson, "A Trip East with West," *Sports Illustrated,* 24 October 1983, 94.

2. Ibid.

3. For a fascinating article on the role of jokes in Bosnia, see Srdjan Vučetić, "Identity Is a Laughing Matter: Intergroup Humor in Bosnia," *Spaces of Identity* 4.1 (2004): n.p., http://pi.library.yorku.ca.

4. Johnson, "A Trip East with West," 94.

5. "Information about Preparing the XIV Olympic Winter Games '84 (Short Report), January 1979," IOC Archives, CIO JO-1984W-RAPPO, folder 206533.

6. R. W. Apple Jr., "An Ailing Economy Worries Yugoslavs," *New York Times,* 20 February 1980.

7. Jens Stilhoff Sörensen, *State Collapse and Reconstruction in the Periphery: Political Economy, Ethnicity and Development in Yugoslavia, Serbia and Kosovo* (New York: Berghahn Books, 2009), 101 n. 18.

8. Mihailo Crnobrnja, *The Yugoslav Drama* (Montreal: McGill-Queen's Press, 1996), 112.

9. Raif Dizdarević, *From the Death of Tito to the Death of Yugoslavia* (Sarajevo: Šahinpašić, 2009), 73 n. 18.

10. Ibid.

11. John Darnton, "Yugoslavs Set for Tito's Death," *Calgary Herald,* 30 January 1980.

12. John Darnton, "After Tito the System Is Ready," *New York Times,* 18 January 1980.

13. John Darnton, "Eastern Europe After Tito," *New York Times Magazine,* 13 April 1980, 82.

14. David B. Richardson, "Yugoslavia after Tito: The Days Ahead," *U.S. News and World Report,* 25 February 1980, 35.

15. "Tito in History," *Pittsburgh Post-Gazette,* 5 May 1980.

16. "Yugoslavia: 'Nothing Will Surprise Us' Drills Show Readiness," *Lewiston Morning Tribune* (Me.), 3 March 1980; "Tito's Illness Revives Worries of War," *Lakeland Ledger* (Fla.), 28 January 1980.

17. "Soviets Vow Respect in Yugoslav Affairs," *Pittsburgh Post-Gazette,* 18 November 1976.

18. Bernard D. Nossiter, "U.N. Votes 104–18 to 'Deplore' Soviet Moves in Afghanistan," *New York Times,* 15 January 1980.

19. Ahmed Karabegović, interview by author, 24 June 2010.

20. Howard Cosell and Peter Bonventre, *I Never Played the Game* (Boston: G. K. Hall, 1986), 518.

21. Vic Ziegel, "Arledge Changed Way We View Sports Today," *New York Daily News,* 6 December 2002.

22. Fred Rothenberg, "Wide World Celebrates 20th Anniversary," *Boca Raton News* (Fla.), 23 April 1981.

23. Roone Arledge, *Roone: A Memoir* (New York: Harper Collins, 2004), 72.

24. Jay Sharbutt, "ABC's Olympics Given Top Rating," *Sarasota Journal,* 28 July 1976.

25. Doug Gilbert, "Hockey TV Ratings an Olympic Shock," *Montreal Gazette*, 20 February 1976.

26. John J. O'Conner, "How ABC Got to the Top," *New York Times*, 19 October 1977.

27. Alan Richman, "Competitive Broadcaster: Roone Pinckney Arledge, Jr.," *New York Times*, 27 September 1979.

28. "Letter from Arthur A. Watson, President NBC Sports, to International Olympic Committee," IOC Archives, CIO JO-1984W-TVR, folder 204704.

29. Edwin McDowell, "The Russian Bear Has a White Trunk," *New York Times*, 27 January 1980.

30. "Report on the Meeting between the IOC and the Representatives of the Sarajevo OCOG, Lausanne, 20th May 1980," IOC Archives, CIO JO-1984W-REUN, folder 206567.

31. Robert K. Barney et al., *Selling the Five Rings* (Salt Lake City: University of Utah Press, 2004), 185.

32. Geoffrey Mason, interview by author, 30 July 2009.

33. "Report by the IOC Representatives on Their Visit to Sarajevo Regarding Television Negotiations with the American Broadcasting Companies, 21st–24th January 1980," IOC Archives, CIO JO-1984W-TVR, folder 204704.

34. Peter Ueberroth, *Made in America* (New York: William Morrow, 1985), 53.

35. Barney, *Selling the Five Rings*, 84.

36. Ibid., 104.

37. Ibid., 118.

38. Michael Payne, *Olympic Turnaround* (Westport, Conn.: Praeger, 2006), 25.

39. Anita Verschoth, "Carrying the Torch," *Sports Illustrated*, 13 April 1981, 70.

40. Ueberroth, *Made in America*, 68.

41. "Report by the IOC Representatives on Their Visit to Sarajevo Regarding Television Negotiations with the American Broadcasting Companies, 21st–24th January 1980."

42. Fred Rothenberg, "ABC Gets TV Rights to Sarajevo Olympics," *Youngstown Vindicator* (Ohio), 3 February 1980.

43. "Report on the Meeting between the IOC and the Representatives of the Sarajevo OCOG, Lausanne, 20th May 1980"

44. See "Payment Schedule," in "Agreement between the International Olympic Committee and the Organizing Committee of the XIV Olympic Winter Games—Sarajevo 1984—and ABC Sports, Inc.," IOC Archives, CIO JO-1984W-TVR-CT, folder 204721.

45. Organizing Committee of the XIVth Winter Olympic Games, *Final Report: Sarajevo '84* (Sarajevo: Oslobođenje, 1984), 171.

46. "Agreement between the Organizing Committee of the XIVth Olympic Winter Games Sarajevo 1984 and Mizuno Corporation," IOC Archives, CIO JO-1984W-FIRM-CT, folder 204735.

47. "Information about Preparing the XIV Olympic Winter Games '84 (Short Report), January 1979."

48. Jack Anderson, "Yugoslavia: Will Soviets Divide/Conquer?" *Sarasota Tribune*, 3 March 1980; Eric Bourne, "Yugoslavs Keep Cool—Despite Soviet Moves," *Christian Science Monitor*, 21 January 1980; Apple, "An Ailing Economy Worries Yugoslavs."

49. "Yugoslavia Battles 30 pct. Inflation," *Youngstown Vindicator* (Ohio), 30 September 1980.

50. David Binder, "Yugoslav Feel the Pinch of Economic Curbs," *New York Times*, 7 November 1982; "Yugoslav Shoppers Have to Fight for Their Soap," *Daily Reporter* (Iowa), 9 April 1983.

51. "Yugoslav Shoppers Have to Fight for Their Soap."

52. "Yugoslav Airlines' Flights Curtailed by Fuel Shortage," *BBC Summary of World Broadcasts*, 15 October 1981.

53. "Shortage of Raw Materials and Fuel," *BBC Summary of World Broadcasts*, 5 March 1981; "Electricity Supply Situation," *BBC Summary of World Broadcasts*, 14 January 1982.

54. John B. Oakes, "Yugoslavia(s)," *New York Times*, 25 June 1982.

55. R. W. Apple Jr., "Sarajevo Awaiting a Change of Image," *New York Times*, 24 February 1980.

56. "In Brief: Preparations for the 1984 Winter Olympics in Sarajevo" Tanjug News Agency, 19 January 1981.

57. "Officials Absolved of Blame," *Calgary Herald*, 5 December 1980; "In Brief: Radio Sarajevo on the 1984 Olympics," Tanjug News Agency, 9 November 1982.

58. "Lake Placid 1980: XIIIth Olympic Winter Games," in John E. Findling and Kimberly D. Pelle, eds., *Historical Dictionary of the Modern Olympic Movement* (Westport, Conn.: Greenwood Press, 1996), 295.

59. "Inquiry on Olympic Buses Opens," *New York Times*, 4 March 1980.

60. "The Only Amateurs at Lake Placid Are the Organizers," *Eugene Register-Guard* (Oreg.), 18 February 1980.

61. Ray Grass, "Many Olympic Tickets Are Unsold," *Deseret News* (Utah), 19 February 1980.

62. Eddie MacCabe, "It's Official: Placid Bus System a Disaster," *Ottawa Citizen*, 18 February 1980.

63. "Olympic-sized Woes at Games," *Wilmington Morning Star* (N.C.), 18 February 1980.

64. Hubert Mizell, "Winter Olympics a Disaster on Skis and Skates," *St. Petersburg Times* (Fla.), 20 February 1980.

65. Stan Abbot, "An Extravaganza Touched by Absurdity," *Anchorage Daily News*, 25 February 1980.

66. Ahmed Karabegović, interview by author, 24 June 2010.

67. "Remarks by Mr. Cyrus Vance," *Olympic Review* 149 (March 1980): 109.

68. Lord Killanin, *My Olympic Years* (London: Secker and Warburg, 1983), 177–78.

69. Barry Lorge, "Killanin Would Buy Summer Time," *Washington Post*, 19 February 1980.

70. Ueberroth, *Made in America*, 83. "USOC President Blasts Carter," *Palm Beach Post* (Fla.), 22 April 1980.

71. "USOC President Blasts Carter."

72. "Recommendation In, But USOC Isn't Talking," *Spokesman-Review* (Wash.), 16 March 1980.

73. Dick Schneider, "Lay Says Ignore Russia's Ivan, Misha," *Lakeland Ledger* (Fla.), 16 March 1980.

74. John Darnton, "Belgrade Visitors Pair Off for Talks," *New York Times*, 8 May 1980.

75. "Tito's Epochal Funeral," *Time*, 19 May 1980, 33.

76. "Brezhnev Upstages Carter in Yugoslavia," *Palm Beach Post* (Fla.), 8 May 1980.

77. Lord Killanin, *My Olympic Years*, 209.

78. Ibid., 214.

79. John R. Short, *Global Metropolitan: Globalizing Cities in a Capitalist World* (London: Routledge, 2004), 96; Alfred E. Senn, *Power, Politics, and the Olympic Games* (Champaign, Ill.: Human Kinetics, 1999), 186.

80. Christopher Booker, *The Games War* (London: Faber and Faber, 1981), 78.

81. "Soviets Report Afghan Team Killed," *Montreal Gazette*, 16 July 1980.

82. "Little Shame and Less Olympic Glory," *Guardian* (UK), 19 July 1980.

83. *World Economic Outlook, April 1985* (Washington: International Monetary Fund, 1985), 160; Anders Aslund, *Building Capitalism: The Transformation of the Soviet Bloc* (New York: Cambridge University Press, 2002), 49.

84. Cited in Nicholas Evan Sarantakes, *Dropping the Torch: Jimmy Carter, the Olympic Boycott, and the Cold War* (New York: Cambridge University Press, 2010), 245.

85. "U.S. Athletes Split on Carter's Embargo Plan," *Daytona Beach Morning Herald* (Fla.), 21 January 1980.

86. Joe Gergen, "L.A. Has Come a Long Way since the Games in 1932," *Record* (N.J.), 23 July 1984.

87. David B. Kanin, *A Political History of the Olympic Games* (Boulder: Westview Press, 1981), 148.

88. George Will, "Balkans Still Boiling," *Victoria Advocate* (Tex.), 14 April 1984.

4. No Amount of Slivovitz

1. Tom Mackin, *Making Other Plans* (Bloomington, Ind.: AuthorHouse, 2009), 246.

2. "Promotion of Bjelašnica," *Sarajevo '84* 3 (May 1982): 27.

3. Peter Baumgartner, "The Olympic Winter Games 1984 in Sarajevo," *Olympic Review* 159 (January 1981): 17.

4. For an excellent study of Yugoslavia's youth labor brigades, see Dragan Popović, "Youth Labor Action (*Omladinska radna akcija*) as Ideological Holiday-Making," in Hannes Grandits and Karin Taylor, *Yugoslavia's Sunny Side* (New York: Central European Press, 2010), 279.

5. Ibid., 279–80.

6. "The Olympic Gold for the Young Builders," *Sarajevo '84* 6 (December 1983): 36.

7. Bob Ottum, "They Were Real Troopers," *Sports Illustrated*, 14 March 1983, 82.

8. "Yugoslavian City Battles Olympic Hitches," *Miami Herald*, 6 February 1983.

9. Velemir Vuksic, *Tito's Partisans, 1941–45* (Oxford, U.K.: Osprey, 2003), 43.

10. Ottum, "They Were Real Troopers," 86.

11. Jan Steler, "Thoughts on the Construction of Combined Runs," *Olympic Review* 187 (May 1983): 312–13.

12. Steven C. Smith, *A Heart at Fire's Center* (Berkeley: University of California Press, 1991), 303.

13. Bob Ottum, "Now Bring on the Torch," *Sports Illustrated*, 14 March 1983, 90.

14. Organizing Committee of the XIVth Winter Olympic Games, *Final Report: Sarajevo '84* (Sarajevo: Oslobođenje, 1984), 126.

15. "Accommodation of Olympic Family," IOC Archives, CIO JO-1984W-HEBER, folder 204627.

16. "Liste des personnalités invités par le Président Samaranch aux XIVes Jeux d'hiver a Sarajevo," IOC Archives, CIO JO-1984W-INVIT, folder 204650.

17. Sabahudin Selesković, interview by author, 25 June 2010.

18. "The Hotel for the Olympic Family," *Sarajevo '84* 3 (May 1982): 52; "Jako, jako smo zadovoljni!" *Olimpiski Informator* 22 (October 1983): 1–2.

19. Kosuke Inagaki, "Lausanne: 'Olympic Capital' Steeped in IOC History," *Asahi Shimbun*, 25 August 2013.

20. David Miller, *Olympic Revolution: The Biography of Juan Antonio Samaranch* (London: Pavilion Books, 1992), 36.

21. Joanna Davenport, "Monique Berlioux: Her Association with Three IOC Presidents," *Citius, Altius, Fortius* 4.3 (Autumn 1996): 17. See also Kenneth Reich, "Berlioux Lost Control When Samaranch Was Named IOC President," *Los Angeles Times*, 3 June 1985.

22. Ahmed Karabegović, interview by author, 25 June 2010. The IOC member Ashwini Kumar of India insists that during Samaranch's trip to Sarajevo in 1983, Berlioux "was not even listening" to the president. See Miller, *Olympic Revolution*, 35.

23. For an examination of Samaranch's role in assisting the SOOC, see Robert K. Barney et al., *Selling the Five Rings* (Salt Lake City: University of Utah Press, 2004), 191–93.

24. "Winter Olympics Financing Causes Disagreement," *Borba*, 17 June 1982, translated and summarized in the Foreign Broadcast Information Service (FBIS) *Daily Report* (Eastern Europe), FBIS-EEU-82-126, 30 June 1982. See also Kate Meehan Pedrotty, "Yugoslav Unity and Olympic Ideology at the 1984 Sarajevo Winter Olympic Games," in Grandits and Taylor, *Yugoslavia's Sunny Side*, 353.

25. The Olympic contribution figures come from "XIV Olympic Winter Games Sarajevo 1984," *Yugoslav Survey* 25 (November 1984): 18. The "planned" contribution for all of Yugosla-

via was 2,423,900,000 dinars, of which Bosnia and Sarajevo contributed 1,640,000,000 dinars (67.66 percent), the federal government 210,000,000 dinars (8.66 percent), and the republics and provinces 573,900,000 dinars (23.67 percent).

26. For the dinar exchange rate in 1982–83, see Biljana Stojanović, "Exchange Rate Regimes of the Dinar 1945–1990: An Assessment of Appropriateness and Efficiency," paper presented at the Second Conference of the South-Eastern European Monetary History Network, 13 April 2007, www.oenb.at. The exchange rate in January 1984 was listed in SOOC's *Press Bilten* of 26 January 1984. IOC Archives, CIO JO-1984W-BULLE, folder 204684.

27. John R. Lampe, *Yugoslavia as History,* 2nd ed. (New York: Cambridge University Press, 200), 328.

28. "Table Summaries of the Television Contracts Re: XIVth Winter Games," IOC Archives, CIO JO-1984W-TVR, folder 206567.

29. Pedrotty, "Yugoslav Unity and Olympic Ideology,: 354.

30. "Mikulic Speaks at Sarajevo on Olympics Significance," Tanjug Domestic Service, 28 December 1980, in FBIS *Daily Report* (Eastern Europe), FBIS-EEU-80-252, 30 December 1980.

31. "Information about Preparing the XIV Olympic Winter Games '84 (Short Report), January 1979," IOC Archives, CIO JO-1984W-RAPPO, folder 206533; "Committee Adopts Winter Olympics Cost Estimates," *Borba,* 25 December 1980, in FBIS *Daily Report* (Eastern Europe), FBIS-EEU-81-005, 8 January 1981; "How Much Will the XIV Winter Olympic Games Cost?" *NIN,* 4 January 1981 (article translation in IOC Archives, CIO JO-1984W-FINAN, folder 204617).

32. "'Misinformation' about Winter Olympics Refuted," Tanjug Domestic Service, 25 January 1983, in FBIS *Daily Report* (Eastern Europe), FBIS-EEU-83-018, 26 January 1983.

33. Leonard Shapiro, "Road to Olympics Steep but 'Sarajevo Is Ready,'" *Washington Post,* 21 November 1983.

34. "XIV Olympic Winter Games Sarajevo 1984," 18.

35. SOOC's agreement with Coca-Cola was signed in March 1981. See "Agreement," IOC Archives, CIO JO-1984W-FIRM-CT, folder 206666.

36. "XIV Olympic Winter Games Sarajevo 1984," 18.

37. Izet Kalkan et al., *Sarajevo: Projekat zaštite čovjekove okoline* (Novi Sad: Forum, 1982), n.p.

38. "XIV Olympic Winter Games Sarajevo 1984," 19.

39. Nesha Starcevic, "Turkish Goldsmith Donates a Kilogram of Gold for Games," *Gettysburg Times* (Penn.), 7 February 1984.

40. The donations were listed in SOOC press releases entitled "Till the Beginning of the Games," IOC Archives, CIO JO-1984W-CP, folder 204690. See "Donation—Willer Gobelin Tapestry," 2 April 1983; "Medical Care—Diagnostic Instrument for the Orthopedic Clinic," 6 April 1983; "Donation Funds of Yugoslavs Living in France," 18 May 1983. See also "Donators," *Sarajevo '84* 5 (March 1983): 43.

41. Starcevic, "Turkish Goldsmith Donates a Kilogram of Gold for Games."

42. Boris Boskovic, "Letter from Belgrade," *World Press Review* 31.6 (June 1984): 46.

43. Hal Piper, "Amateurs? Try the Yugoslav Hosts," *Spokesman-Review* (Wash.), 4 December 1983.

44. Eddie MacCabe, "Yugoslav Pride Shows as Winter Games Draw Near," *Ottawa Citizen,* 3 February 1984.

45. "Getting There Not Half Fun," *Vancouver Sun,* 9 December 1981.

46. "Sarajevo Fog Causes Problems," *Spokesman-Review* (Wash.), 23 December 1982.

47. Mark Nolan, "Sarajevo Ready for the Games," *Lawrence Journal-World* (Kans.), 29 October 1983.

48. "'Stear' and 'Kahlbacher' Maintain Olympic Roads," in the press release "Till the Be-

ginning of the Games," 21 September 1983, IOC Archives, CIO JO-1984W-CP, folder 204690; Organizing Committee of the XIVth Winter Olympic Games, *Final Report: Sarajevo '84,* 142, 187.

49. "Sarajevo Fog Causes Problems."

50. Nesha Starcevic, "Problems Arise for Winter Olympics," *Gettysburg Times* (Penn.), 8 February 1983.

51. Maxine Sevack, "Podborski Slips to Second on Scary Downhill Slope," *Globe and Mail* (Toronto), 29 January 1983.

52. Ibid.

53. "Skiing Star Seriously Hurt," *Windsor Star* (Canada), 27 January 1983; "Fall Knocks Mueller Out of Downhill," *Montreal Gazette,* 27 January 1983; Ottum, "They Were Real Troopers," 82.

54. "Yugoslavian City Battles Olympic Hitches."

55. "Athletes, Organizers, and Facilities Pass the Test," *Sarajevo '84* 5 (March 1983): 20

56. Jeff Hastings, interview by author, 9 August 2009.

57. Ottum, "They Were Real Troopers," 90.

58. Piper, "Amateurs? Try the Yugoslav Hosts."

59. Ottum, "They Were Real Troopers," 77.

60. "Inspects Olympic Site," Belgrade Domestic Service, 30 May 1983, in FBIS *Daily Report* (Eastern Europe), FBIS-EEU-83-106, 1 June 1983.

61. Leigh Montville, "How to Describe Sarajevo?," *Boston Globe,* 4 February 1984.

62. "Report on Technical Matters of the XIV. Olympic Winter Games as a Result of the Visit to Sarajevo 11th–20th February 1983," IOC Archives, CIO JO-1984W-VISIT, folder 204703. See also Sigge Bergman, "Snow in Sarajevo a Guarantee of Success," *Olympic Review* 197 (March 1984): 206.

63. "Report from Visit to Sarajevo October 8–11th 1983," IOC Archives, CIO JO-1984W-VISIT, folder 204743.

64. Frederick Kempe, "Yugoslavs Climb Olympic Mountain," *Wall Street Journal,* 15 June 1983; Leonard Shapiro, "Sarajevo," *Washington Post,* 5 February 1984.

65. "Swathed in Splendor, the Games Officially Open," *St. Joseph Gazette* (Mo.), 9 February 1984.

66. Jane Leavy, "Pomp, Happy Circumstances Open Games," *Washington Post,* 8 February 1984.

5. Up Close and Personal

1. "Rock n' Rollin [*sic*] Brings His Message to Fans," *Sarasota Herald-Tribune,* 23 January 1984.

2. Will Grimsley, "Rock n' Rollen Back after Being Arrested," *Gainesville Sun* (Fla.), 14 February 1984.

3. "Sarajevo Tries Hard to Be Safe This Time," *Chicago Tribune,* 31 January 1984.

4. Mary Thornton, "FBI Probing 19 Terrorists Gangs Alleged in U.S.," *Washington Post,* 7 May 1984; Kenneth Reich, "U.S.-based Terrorism Threat Cited," *Los Angeles Times,* 5 October 1983.

5. Gail Bass and Brian Michael Jenkins, "A Review of Recent Trends in International Terrorism and Nuclear Incidents Abroad," report prepared for the Sandia National Laboratories by the Rand Corporation, Santa Monica (Calif.), April 1983, www.dtic.mil.

6. Milton Richman, "Gold Medal for Yugoslavs," *Lodi News-Sentinel* (Calif.), 22 February 1984.

7. Patrick F. R. Arhsien and R. A. Howells, "Yugoslavia, Albania, and the Kosovo Riots," *World Today* 37.11 (November 1981): 420–21.

8. Sabrina P. Ramet, *The Three Yugoslavias: State-Building and Legitimation, 1918–2005* (Bloomington: Indiana University Press, 2006), 301–2

9. "Fire at Pristina Plastics Factory," *BBC Summary of World Broadcasts,* 16 December 1983; "Irredentist Incident in Stuttgart: Yugoslav Protest to FRG," *BBC Summary of World Broadcasts,* 21 November 1983; "Explosions in Pristina Centre," *BBC Summary of World Broadcasts,* 21 November 1983; "Sarajevo Games Security Tightening," *Ottawa Citizen,* 21 January 1984.

10. Ashwini Kumar to Monique Berlioux, "XIVth Winter Games—Security," letter written 9 September 1983, IOC Archives, CIO JO-1984W-SECUR, folder 204746.

11. Michael White, "U.S. Foiled as Hijack 'Leader' Vanishes," *The Guardian* (UK), 14 October 1985; Michael Young, "Did Mahmoud Abbas Finance the 1972 Munich Olympic Takeover?," *Slate,* 24 July 2003.

12. Ahmed Karabegović, interview by author, 24 June 2010.

13. Hal Bock, "Sarajevo Anxious to Please," *Lewiston Journal* (Me.), 30 January 1984; "Tanks, Soldiers at Olympics Site," *Times-Union* (Ind.), 31 January 1984.

14. Marie Alkire, interview by author, 8 May 2009.

15. Josh Thompson, interview by author, 17 May 2009.

16. Daryl F. Gates with Diane K. Shah, *Chief: My Life in the LAPD* (New York: Bantam Books, 1992), 241.

17. Thomas D. Elias, "The Olympic Rumor Mill," *Lodi News-Sentinel* (Calif.), 19 June 1984.

18. "Beautification Big Deal in L.A. Now," *Lawrence Journal-World* (Kans.), 8 July 1984; Dave Zirin, "Want to Understand the 1992 LA Riots? Start with the 1984 LA Olympics," *Nation,* 30 April 2012, www.thenation.com.

19. Craig Whitney, "Moscow Dissidents Flee Olympic Games," *New York Times,* 11 May 1980; "Officials Target Criminals, Homeless as Games Approach," *Waycross Journal-Herald* (Ga.), 21 March 1996.

20. Gates, *Chief: My Life in the LAPD,* 241.

21. Aziz Hadžihasanović, *1984. Olimpijada trijumfa i šansi* (Sarajevo: Rabic, 2010), 72.

22. "Restaurant Closed for Gouging Actor," *Palm Beach Post* (Fla.), 15 February 1984.

23. "Whitneys Will Fete Olympics at Sarajevo, Bosnia Bash," *Palm Beach Daily News* (Fla.), 30 December 1983; "People and Things," *Milwaukee Journal,* 7 February 1984.

24. Kit Konolige, *The Richest Women in the World* (New York: Macmillan, 1985), 299.

25. John Corry, "TV: ABC's Coverage of the Winter Olympics," *New York Times,* 11 February 1984.

26. David Crook, "ABC Set to Launch Video Orgy for Winter Games," *Los Angeles Times,* 6 February 1984.

27. Skip Myslenski, "ABC Overcooks Its Sarajevo Soufflé," *Chicago Tribune,* 21 February 1984.

28. Andy Rooney, "TV at Its Best in Sarajevo," *Chicago Tribune,* 16 February 1984.

29. Lee Margulies, "Up Close with 'Up Close' Creators," *Los Angeles Times,* 8 August 1984.

30. William Taafe, "Adding That Personal Touch," *Sports Illustrated,* 30 July 1984, 42.

31. Fred Rothenberg, "ABC to Take Home Some Olympic Gold, Too," *The Day* (Conn.), 12 August 1983.

32. Mike Duffy, "Networks Load Big Guns for First Sweeps Week," *Ottawa Citizen,* 4 February 1984.

33. "Did ABC Spend Its $91.5 million on a Dud?" *Spokesman-Review* (Wash.), 16 February 1984.

34. Bill King, "Olympic Memory Too Vivid for ABC," *Ocala Star-Banner* (Fla.), 11 February 1984.

35. David Anderson, "'Sarajevo' as a TV Sitcom," *New York Times,* 12 February 1984.

36. Neil Amdur, "Arledge Weathers the Storm," *New York Times,* 19 February 1984.

37. Dave Goldberg, "Weather, U.S. Hockey Team Force U.S. to Cut Back Coverage," *Lawrence Journal-World* (Kans.), 10 February 1984.

38. Will Grimsley, "ABC's Arledge: He Holds Olympic TV in His Hands," *Spokesman-Review* (Wash.), 15 February 1984.

39. "Games No Hit on TV," *Montreal Gazette,* 13 February 1984; "ABC Taking a Beating in Olympic Ratings," *Gainesville Sun* (Fla.), 11 February 1984; John Carmody, "The TV Column," *Washington Post,* 13 February 1984.

40. Brian Biggane, "ABC's Ratings Skate toward the Top," *Palm Beach Post* (Fla.), 15 February 1984.

41. Mike Duffy, "Olympic Ratings Near Disaster for ABC," *Ottawa Citizen,* 15 February 1984.

42. "Olympics Score in Nielsen Ratings," United Press International, 15 February 1984.

43. Biggane, "ABC's Ratings Skate toward the Top."

44. "Ratings Mixed for Olympics," *New York Times,* 21 February 1984.

45. Bill Abrams, "All Three Networks Declare a Victory in February Ratings," *Wall Street Journal,* 5 March 1984.

46. David Carey, "ABC May Face an Olympic Load of Make-Goods," *Adweek,* 20 February 1984.

47. Bill Abrams, "ABC Advertisers in Olympics Will Get Free Time," *Wall Street Journal,* 14 March 1984.

48. Rick Warner, "Olympic Coverage: Fine Form," *Free Lance-Star* (Va.), 13 February 1988.

49. For a history of Radio Free Europe and Radio Liberty, see A. Ross Johnson and R. Eugene Parta, eds., *Cold War Broadcasting: Impact on the Soviet Union and Eastern Europe* (Budapest: Central European Press, 2010). See also Arch Puddington, *Broadcasting Freedom: The Cold War Triumph of Radio Free Europe and Radio Liberty* (Lexington: University of Kentucky Press, 2003).

50. Marat Gramov to Juan Antonio Samaranch, letter written 9 January 1984, IOC Archives, CIO JO-1984W-ACCPR, folder 204421.

51. James L. Buckley, "Let Radio Free Europe Send Its Team to the Olympics, Too," *Los Angeles Herald Examiner,* 4 April 1984.

52. Will Grimsley, "Roby, Roosevelt U.S. Link to Olympics," *Gettysburg Times* (Penn.), 16 July 1980.

53. "South Africa May Rejoin Olympics," *Lewiston Tribune* (Me.), 24 May 1982.

54. "Draft Preamble and Resolution of Executive Board Regarding Accreditation of Radio Free Europe," n.d., IOC Archives, CIO JO-1984W-ACCPR, folder 204426.

55. "Yachtsman Called Soviet 'Patsy' in Olympic Radio Battle," *Lakeland Ledger* (Fla.), 10 February 1984.

56. "Board for International Broadcasting," entry in Christopher H. Sterling, ed., *Encyclopedia of Radio* (New York: Taylor and Francis, 2004), 1:297–98.

57. "Time to Phase Out a Cold War Relic," *Lewiston Morning Tribune* (Me.), 4 April 1972.

58. Organizing Committee of the XIVth Winter Olympic Games, *Final Report: Sarajevo '84* (Sarajevo: Oslobođenje, 1984), 134–35.

59. "Death Won't Disrupt Olympics," *Los Angeles Times,* 10 February 1984.

60. "Morning Briefing: A Biathlete Fires Shots in Print," *Los Angeles Times,* 14 February 1984.

61. Sabahudin Selesković, interview by author, 25 June 2010.

6. Do You Believe in Debacles?

1. Craig R. Whitney, "The Soviet Union Builds a Grand Design for Athletics; Professional Amateurs," *New York Times,* 10 February 1980.

2. For an interview with Al Michaels and a video clip of the final five minutes of the "Miracle on Ice" hockey game, see Darren Rovell, "Miracle on Ice: One-on-One with Al Michaels, 30 Years Later," CNBC.com, 22 February 2010, www.cnbc.com.

3. Wayne Coffey, *The Boys of Winter* (New York: Three Rivers Press, 2005), 242.

4. Frank Brown, "Soviets Win Hockey Challenge Cup," *Times-News* (N.C.), 12 February 1979.

5. "Jubilant Yanks Shock Soviets," *Windsor Star* (Canada), 23 February 1980.

6. As a former executive director of USA Hockey put it, the "Miracle on Ice" in 1980 was "the most transcending moment in the history of our sport in this country. For people who were born between 1945 and 1955, they know where they were when John Kennedy was shot, when man walked on the moon, and when the USA beat the Soviet Union in Lake Placid." See Kevin Allen, "College Kids Perform Olympic Miracle," ESPN Classic, n.d., http://espn. go.com.

7. "Hockey as Good as Gold in USA," *Sarasota Herald-Tribune,* 25 February 1980.

8. Frank Corkin, "They Cried Tears of Hockey Joy," *Morning Record and Journal* (Conn.), 27 February 1980.

9. "Americans Hail Hockey Victory," *Youngstown Vindicator* (Ohio), 23 February 1980.

10. Robert D. McFadden, "Cheers Resound Across Nation," *New York Times,* 23 February 1980.

11. "Olympians Honored," *Ellensburg Daily Record* (Wash.), 25 February 1980.

12. "Olympic Hockey Teammates Part Sadly," *St. Petersburg Times* (Fla.), 26 February 1980.

13. E. M. Swift, "Playing in a Dream World," *Sports Illustrated,* 12 December 1983, 90.

14. Matt Castello, "Lou Vairo: Coach of the Month," HockeyBarn, 22 January 2009, www. hockeybarn.com.

15. Ibid.

16. Leavy, "The Coach; Sweet Lou: the Soul on Ice," *Washington Post Magazine,* 5 February 1984, 22.

17. John Powers, "Test of Medal," *Boston Globe,* 27 January 1984.

18. George Vecsey, "A Hockey Coach Grows in Brooklyn," *Anchorage Daily News,* 5 February 1984.

19. Leavy, "The Coach; Sweet Lou: the Soul on Ice."

20. Castello, "Lou Vairo: Coach of the Month."

21. Soviet game schedules as well as team and player records compiled by the website Hockey CCCP International, www.chidlovski.com.

22. Randy Starkman, "26 Touring Soviet Stars to Play 6 NHL Teams," United Press International, 25 December 1982.

23. *The USSR Olympic Team* (Moscow: Fizkultura i Sport Publishers, 1984), 179; Robert McKenzie, "Soviet System Gets Close Look from Canadians," *Globe and Mail* (Toronto), 2 February 1982.

24. McKenzie, "Soviet System Gets Close Look from Canadians."

25. John F. Burns, "Full-time Goal for Soviet Team," *New York Times,* 25 December 1983.

26. Hubert Mizell, "Sparks Will Fly If Americans Meet Soviets in Hockey Final," *St. Petersburg Times* (Fla.), 18 February 1980.

27. Geoffrey Caldwell, "International Sport and National Identity," in Eric Dunning and Dominic Malcolm, eds., *Sport: Issues in the Sociology of Sport* (London: Routledge, 2003), 15.

28. "Hockey Escape of the Century: Stastnys Land in Quebec," International Ice Hockey Federation, n.d., www.iihf.com.

29. Eric Duhatschek, "Russians Are Coming in Two Years," *Calgary Herald,* 9 June 1983.

30. Jeff Merron, "Russians Regroup on Other Side of Red Line," ESPN.com, 14 February 2002, http://sports.espn.go.com.

31. Christopher Young, "Wife of Soviet Hockey Star Attacks Coach," *Toronto Star,* 2 February 1989.

32. Gary Mason, "Coach Tikhonov: Hated and Unrepentant," *Vancouver Sun,* 15 November 2002.

33. David Johnston, "Soviet Supermen Mere Mortals After All," *Montreal Gazette,* 28 December 1985.

34. John Gugger, "Soviet Hockey Team Opens Up a Bit," *Toledo Blade,* 26 February 1988.

35. Mason, "Coach Tikhonov."

36. Dave Bidini, *The Best Game You Can Name* (Toronto: McClellan and Stewart, 2005), n.p.

37. Milt Dunnell, "Tikhonov the Terrible Really a Nice Guy, Son Says," *Toronto Star,* 4 April 1994.

38. Coffey, *The Boys of Winter,* 244.

39. Mason, "Coach Tikhonov."

40. Alan Robinson, "Khabibulin Hopes to Get Medal This Time," *Kingman Daily Miner* (Ariz.)," 14 February 2002.

41. "Getting Axe? Tarasov in Doghouse," *Ottawa Citizen,* 16 May 1969.

42. Burns, "Full-time Goal for Soviet Team."

43. "Soviets Haunted by Olympic Nightmare," *Pittsburgh Post-Gazette,* 3 April 1980.

44. Lawrie Mifflin, "U.S. Hockey Team Faces a Tough Task," *New York Times,* 18 September 1983; "Career in Doubt over Shoplifting," *Windsor Star* (Canada), 15 December 1983.

45. Burns, "Full-time Goal for Soviet Team."

46. "Badali Pressure Lawton to Sign with North Stars," *Ottawa Citizen,* 5 August 1983.

47. Ray Didinger, "Men of Winter," *St. Petersburg Independent* (Fla.), 12 December 1983.

48. Kevin Dupont, "Goalie, 18, Answer Critics," *New York Times,* 15 October 1983.

49. Lou Vairo, interview by author, 18 August 2012.

50. Jack Fall, "A New Departure toward Arrival," *Sports Illustrated,* 28 March 1983, 47.

51. Didinger, "Men of Winter."

52. John Feinstein, "Together Again: U.S., Soviet Hockey on Tour," *Washington Post,* 9 December 1983.

53. Jane Leavy, "U.S. Hockey Team: The Shadow of a Shout," *Washington Post,* 29 September 1983.

54. Swift, "Playing in a Dream World," 94.

55. John Husar, "1980 Glory Weighs on the Kids of 1984," *Chicago Tribune,* 10 December 1983.

56. Michael R. Gordon, "Ex-Soviet Pilot Still Insists KAL 007 Was Spying," *New York Times,* 9 December 1996.

57. William, Schneider, "Reagan Is the Real Winner in This Crisis," *Los Angeles Times,* 18 September 1983.

58. Frank J. Prial, "Protesters March on Soviet Mission," *New York Times,* 3 September 1983.

59. "Angry Protesters Storm Soviet Compound," *Washington Post,* 5 September 1983.

60. "Vodka Boycott Spreading," *Los Angeles Times,* 16 September 1983; George Ramos, "Soviet Ship Focus of L.A. Harbor Protest," *Los Angeles Times,* 7 September 1983.

61. "Soviet Team's Tour Officially Canceled," *Washington Post,* 17 September 1983.

62. Kevin DuPont, "Downing of Jet Has Tangled Soviet–U.S. Sports Exchange," *New York Times,* 21 September 1983.

63. Gordon Edes, "U.S.-Soviet Hockey Game at Forum Is Off," *Los Angeles Times,* 17 September 1983.

64. John Husar, "Hockey: Is This U.S. Team As Good As Gold?" *Chicago Tribune,* 9 December 1983.

65. "U.S.-Soviet Series to Begin Dec. 9," *Chicago Tribune,* 27 October 1983.

66. "U.S. Olympic Player Defends Soviet Tour," *Ottawa Citizen,* 3 November 1983.

67. "U.S.-Soviet Hockey Game Is Criticized in Cincinnati," *Los Angeles Times,* 15 December 1983; Robert McGill Thomas Jr., "Fighting Words," *New York Times,* 12 December 1983.

68. John Husar, "Soviets Rip U.S.," *Chicago Tribune,* 12 December 1983.

69. Ray Didinger, "Hockey Helps Warm U.S.-Soviet Relations," *Reading Eagle* (Penn.), 26 December 1983.

70. Ibid.

71. "U.S. Olympic Skaters Show Russians They Got What It Takes to Repeat Title," *Telegraph Herald* (Iowa), 13 December 1983.

72. Al Morganti, "Impossible Mission Overcame USA Icers," *Boca Raton News* (Fla.), 13 February 1984.

73. Kevin Mulligan, "Team USA Putting Hopes on Thin Ice," *Philadelphia Daily News*, 7 February 1984.

74. "Eligibility Rules Take Center Stage," *Observer-Reporter* (Penn.), 7 February 1984.

75. Milton Richman, "Open Olympics a Possibility," *Ellensburg Daily Record* (Wash.), 7 February 1984.

76. Hal Bock, "Rules Being Bent," *Argus-Press* (Mich.), 6 February 1984.

77. Gyle Konotopetz, "Gloves Come Off in Olympic Fight," *Calgary Herald*, 22 November 1983.

78. Eddie MacCabe, "Canada's Heavy Artillery Armed for Hockey War," *Ottawa Citizen*, 4 February 1984.

79. "Eagleson Challenges Status of Two U.S. Gold Medalists," *Montreal Gazette*, 27 January 1984.

80. Andrew Podnieks, *Canada's Olympic Hockey Teams* (Toronto: Doubleday, 1997).

81. Lou Vairo, interview by author, 18 August 2012.

82. John Husar, "U.S. Hockey Loss Imperils Medal Hopes," *Toledo Blade* (Ohio), 8 February 1984.

83. Al Morganti, "Canada Puts Shadow over U.S. Chances," *Miami Herald*, 8 February 1984; Al Morganti, "Loss Hurts, but U.S. Still Has a Chance for the Gold," *Philadelphia Inquirer*, 8 February 1984.

84. "Soviets, Czechs Ready for Hockey Showdown," *Reading Eagle* (Penn.), 19 February 1984.

85. "Canada Awaits Czechoslovakia Showdown," *Montreal Gazette*, 14 February 1984.

86. Jane Leavy, "U.S. Hockey Dream Ends," *Toledo Blade*, 10 February 1984.

87. Bob Verdi, "It'd Take a Miracle," *Chicago Tribune*, 10 February 1984.

88. Rich Hofmann, "Czechs Bid U.S. Hockey Team a Rather Rude 'Gute-bye,'" *Evening Tribune* (Calif.), 10 February 1984.

89. Al Morganti, "Hockey Team Falls to Czechoslovakia," *Philadelphia Inquirer*, 10 February 1984; Hofmann, "Czechs Bid U.S. Hockey Team a Rather Rude 'Gute-bye.'"

90. "Vairo on Hot Seat," *Star Phoenix* (Canada), 13 February 1984; Chris Jenkins, "Tie Puts U.S. in the Tank," *San Diego Union*, 12 February 1984.

91. Leigh Montville, "No Miracle This Time," *Boston Globe*, 10 February 1984; Morganti, "Hockey Team Falls to Czechoslovakia."

92. "U.S. Hockey Team Returns to Small Crowd, No Flags," *Gainesville Sun* (Fla.), 21 February 1984.

93. Chris Jenkins, "Team USA Can't Even Beat Norway," *San Diego Union*, 12 February 1984.

94. Lou Vairo, interview by author, 18 August 2012.

95. "Team Canada Will Play Cautiously against Mighty Soviets," *Montreal Gazette*, 17 February 1984.

96. John Powers, "Make No Mistake About It: Soviets Atone," *Boston Globe*, 20 February 1984.

97. "U.S. Hockey Team Returns to Small Crowd, No Flags."

7. Nine Times First Place

1. Letter from Shirley McBurney to Juan Antonio Samaranch. February 1984, IOC Archives, CIO JO-1984W-Prote, folder 204709.

2. Dave Anderson, "Subtract Figure Skating," *New York Times*, 16 February 1984.

3. Ibid.

4. Brian R. Sala, John T. Scott, and James F. Spriggs III, "The Cold War on Ice: Constructivism and the Politics of Olympic Figure Skating Judging," *Perspectives on Politics* 5.1 (March 2007): 17–29.

5. Ibid., 25.

6. Rick Talley, "Soviet Judges Put on Ice," *Chicago Tribune*, 2 June 1977.

7. "Politics Still Decides Figure Skating Titles," *Sarasota Journal*, 9 February 1976.

8. "Francis Ignores Devilish Record," *Leader-Post* (Canada), 15 February 1980.

9. "Politics Still Decides Figure Skating Titles."

10. For a (still confusing) review of how figuring skating was scored, see L. E. Sadovskii and A. L. Sadovskii, *Mathematics and Sports* (Providence: American Mathematical Society, 2000), 40–44.

11. Fred Rothenberg, "Figure Skating Scoring System Too Complicated," *Lewiston Evening Journal* (Me.), 2 February 1977.

12. Dick Schaap, *The 1984 Olympic Games* (New York: Random House, 1984), 58.

13. Randy Harvey, "It's Compulsory, But Is It Necessary?" *Los Angeles Times*, 8 January 1988.

14. "Skating Is Paced by Viennese Girl," *New York Times*, 26 February 1969.

15. "I'm Unbeatable, Schuba Declares," *St. Petersburg Times* (Fla.), 4 February 1972.

16. Ibid.

17. Donald Kaul, "Winter Olympics a Yawn a Minute," *Lakeland Ledger* (Fla.), 24 February 1988.

18. Dorothy Hamill and Deborah Amelon, *A Skating Life* (New York: Hyperion, 2007), 76.

19. Bob Ottum, "Wow! Power," *Sports Illustrated*, 6 February 1984, 92.

20. Scott Hamilton, *The Great Eight: How to Be Happy (Even When You Have Every Reason to Be Miserable)* (Nashville: Thomas Nelson, 2008), 7.

21. Ibid., 8.

22. Ibid., 38.

23. Ottum, "Wow! Power," 102.

24. Frank Litsky, "Champion in Quest for New Image," *New York Times*, 7 March 1983.

25. Jerry Crowe, "Hamilton Wins Again; Sarajevo is Next," *Los Angeles Times*, 22 January 1984.

26. Beverly Ann Menke, *Don Laws: The Life of an Olympic Figure Skating Coach* (Lanham, Md.: Scarecrow Press, 2012), 116.

27. Kurt Andersen, "This One Figures to Be on Ice," *Time*, 30 January 1984, 50.

28. "Hamilton Finds Figures 'Satisfying Challenge,'" *Toledo Blade*, 14 February 1984.

29. "Hamilton Figuring on Gold after Leading Compulsories," *Palm Beach Post* (Fla.), 14 February 1984.

30. Michael Farber, "Brian Orser Set to Collect a Medal in Figure Skating," *Montreal Gazette*, 15 February 1984.

31. Alan Greenberg, "After Wavering, He Waves the Flag," *Los Angeles Times*, 17 February 1984.

32. Scott Hamilton with Lorenzo Benet, *Landing It: My Life On and Off the Ice* (New York: Kensington Books, 1999), 175.

33. Greenberg, "After Wavering, He Waves the Flag."

34. Michael Farber, "Orser Settles for Skating Silver," *Montreal Gazette*, 17 February 1984.

35. "Button Figures on Hamilton," *Chicago Tribune*, 13 February 1984.

36. Ibid.

37. Frank Litsky, "Miss Zayak's Triples Stirring Controversy," *New York Times*, 9 March 1981.

38. Neil Amdur, "'Zayak Rule' Causes Concern," *New York Times*, 18 January 1984.

39. E. M. Swift, "The Thinner Was the Winner," *Sports Illustrated*, 14 February 1983.

40. "Tiffany Chin Takes First in Singles," *Evening News* (N.Y.), 14 December 1980.

41. Neil Amdur, "Outlook Is Shiny and Goals Are Set for Tiffany Chin," *New York Times,* 13 February 1984.

42. Katarina Witt with E. M. Swift, *Only with Passion* (New York: Public Affairs, 2005), 24.

43. Brian Schmitz, "The World's in Love with Katarina Witt," *Spokesman-Review* (Wash.), 22 February 1988.

44. Rick Reilly, "Behold the Shining Star of the GDR," *Sports Illustrated,* 20 January 1986.

45. Katarina Witt, "The Stasi Watched My Every Move," *Mirror* (London), 24 March 2012; Jere Longman, "Shadow of East Germany Lingers," *New York Times,* 14 February 2010.

46. Tony Paterson, "Stasi Files Reveal Witt Was Willing Accomplice," *Telegraph* (London), 5 May 2002.

47. Katarina Witt, "World Champion in Budapest 1988," interview featured in biography page of Katarina Witt's official website, n.d., http://en.katarina-witt.de.

48. Frank Litsky, "Miss Sumners Leads Skating," *New York Times,* 16 February 1984.

49. Jane Leavy, "Sumners Figures It's Gold," *Washington Post,* 16 February 1984.

50. Jane Leavy, "Sumners, Witt: Test of Nerves," *Washington Post,* 18 February 1984.

51. "Sumners Drops to Second Spot," *Lewiston Daily News* (Me.), 16 February 1984.

52. Alan Greenberg, "A Faulty Finish Finishes Sumners; Witt Wins Gold," *Los Angeles Times,* 19 February 1984.

53. Ibid.

54. U.S. Olympic Committee, *A Basic Guide to Figure Skating* (Torrance, Calif.: Griffin, 2002), 100.

55. "Canadian Pair Falls Out of Race for Olympics Skating Medal," *Montreal Gazette,* 11 February 1984.

56. Phil Hersch, "They Saved the Best for When It Mattered Most," *Telegraph Herald* (Iowa), 13 February 1984.

57. Susan Reiter, "Ice Dancing: A Dance Form Frozen in Place by Hostile Rules," *Dance Magazine,* 1 March 1995, 46–47.

58. Ibid.

59. Dan Barnes, "Last Compulsory Dance?" *Leader-Post* (Canada), 20 February 2010.

60. James Christie, "Duchesnays Dance Up a Storm," *Globe and Mail* (Toronto), 7 March 1990.

61. John Hennessy, *Torvill and Dean* (London: David and Charles, 1984), 51.

62. Jayne Torvill and Christopher Dean, *Torvill and Dean: The Autobiography of Ice Dancing's Gold Medal Winners* (Secaucus, N.J.: Carol, 1998), 65.

63. Ibid.

64. Hennessy, *Torvill and Dean,* 70.

65. Bob Ottum, "Just the Perfect Couple," *Sports Illustrated,* 7 November 1983, 35.

66. Hennessy, *Torvill and Dean,* 103.

67. Beverley Smith, "Torvill, Dean Take Dancing to Lofty Limits," *Globe and Mail* (Toronto), 22 March 1984.

68. Jane Leavy, "Ice Dancing's Royal Pair Proper Revolutionaries," *Washington Post,* 12 February 1984.

69. Allan Greenberg, "Royalty on Ice," *Los Angeles Times,* 12 February 1984.

70. Jack Guinn, "Ravel's *Bolero* Gets Ratings of '10,'" *Chicago Tribune,* 10 March 1980.

71. Pamela Andriotakis, "Bo Derek's 'Bolero' Turn-On Stirs Up a Ravel Revival," *People,* 31 March 1980, 79.

72. Torvill and Dean, *Torvill and Dean,* 103–4.

73. Ibid., 112.

74. Neil Norman, "Torvill and Dean: In from the Cold," *Independent* (UK), 8 January 2006.

8. The *Nasenbohrer*

1. William Oscar Johnson, "They Saved the Best for Last," *Sports Illustrated,* 27 February 1984, 18.

2. Ibid.

3. "Johnson Nearly Paid the Price for Jail Stop," *Daytona Beach Morning Journal* (Fla.), 19 February 1984.

4. Dennis Collins, "Johnson's Words Turn to Gold," *Eugene Register Guard* (Oreg.), 17 February 1984.

5. Georges Joubert, "How Bill Johnson Won the Gold," *Skiing* 37.1 (September 1984): 201.

6. William Oscar Johnson, "Rub-a-Dub-Dub, He Was Splashier in the Tub," *Sports Illustrated,* 28 January 1985, 38.

7. "Johnson Nearly Paid the Price for Jail Stop."

8. Dave Anderson, "Flip Side of the Gold," *New York Times,* 17 February 1984; Laurence Shames, "Reckless," in Mark Bryant ed., *Out of the Noösphere: Adventure, Sports, Travel, and the Environment* (New York: Simon and Schuster, 1992): 44.

9. "Johnson's Turnaround," *Palm Beach Post* (Fla.), 17 February 1984; Gregory Lewis, "Bill Johnson: Skiing's Lone Ranger," *Skiing* 37.1 (September 1984): 175.

10. Mathew Fisher, "Fog, Heavy Snow Lead to Ski Upset," *Globe and Mail* (Toronto), 16 January 1984.

11. Ibid.

12. "Bill Johnson Nearly Falls, Wins Lauberhorn Downhill," *Los Angeles Times,* 16 January 1984.

13. Fisher, "Fog, Heavy Snow Lead to Ski Upset."

14. John Husar, "Olympics: U.S. Skier Just Can't Convince the Experts," *Chicago Tribune,* 6 February 1984.

15. "Johnson Makes Good on Threat," *Youngstown Vindicator* (Ohio), 17 February 1984.

16. Dan Barrerio, "Johnson: Skier Puts Up without Shutting Up," *Reading Eagle* (Penn.), 17 February 1984; Matthew Fisher, "U.S. Skier Almost Unbeatable," *Globe and Mail* (Toronto), 7 February 1984.

17. Samuel Abt, "One Year Later, Bill Johnson Hasn't Mellowed," *Spokesman-Review* (Wash.), 26 January 1985.

18. Phil and Steve Mahre with John Fry, *No Hill Too Fast* (New York: Simon and Schuster, 1985), 20.

19. Lewis, "Bill Johnson: Skiing's Lone Ranger," 172.

20. Matthew Fisher, "Skiers Criticize Downhill Run," *Globe and Mail* (Toronto), 2 February 1984.

21. Seth Masia, "Float Like a Butterfly, Sting Like a Bee," *Ski* 48.8 (April 1984): 44.

22. Matt Fisher, "Easy Riders Have Edge," *Globe and Mail* (Toronto), 8 February 1984.

23. Denis Collins, "Johnson Has Best Time in Ski Practice," *Washington Post,* 6 February 1984.

24. Barrerio, "Johnson: Skier Puts Up without Shutting Up."

25. "Fresh Snow Greets Olympics," *Lodi News-Sentinel* (Calif.), 6 February 1984.

26. "Winter Games Not Misnamed," *Washington Post,* 13 February 1984.

27. Jennifer Woodlief, *Ski to Die: The Bill Johnson Story* (Cincinnati: Emmis Books, 2005), 14.

28. John Skow et al., "The High and Mighty," *Time,* 27 February 1984, 83; Woodlief, *Ski to Die,* 15.

29. Johnson, "They Saved the Best for Last," 17.

30. Michael Strauss, "Cheeky Skier Strikes Gold," *Palm Beach Post* (Fla.), 19 February 1984.

31. Woodlief, *Ski to Die,* 22.

32. "Johnson Good on Downhill Promise," *Ottawa Citizen* (Canada), 16 February 1984.

33. Skow et al., "The High and Mighty," 83.

34. Denis Collins, "Johnson Keeps His Golden Promise," *Washington Post,* 17 February 1984.

35. John Tagliabue, "U.S. Captures Its First Gold For Downhill," *New York Times,* 17 February 1984.

36. "Johnson Fits Flamboyant Style of Downhill," *Sarasota Herald-Tribune,* 17 February 1984.

37. Johnson, "Rub-a-Dub-Dub," 36.

38. Woodlief, *Ski to Die,* 84.

39. Bill Donahue, "End of the Run," *Outside,* 2 January 2002, www.outsideonline.com.

40. Brian Maffly, "Johnson Not Fazed by Slow Comeback," *Salt Lake Tribune,* 3 January 2001; Ray Grass, "Johnson Still Trying to Recapture '84 Glory," *Deseret News* (Utah), 11 February 2001.

41. E. M. Swift, "Last Run," *Sports Illustrated,* 16 April 2001, 53.

42. Grass, "Johnson Still Trying to Recapture '84 Glory."

43. Bill Pennington, "The Mountain Had Other Plans," *New York Times,* 6 April 2001.

44. Ibid.

45. Woodlief, *Ski to Die,* 225.

46. Tom Archdeacon, "Johnson Searches for Life He Lost," *Dayton Daily News* (Ohio), 15 February 2002.

47. "Skier Bill Johnson's Health in Decline," *Seattle Times,* 9 February 2012.

48. See "Alpine Ski World Cup Downhill Men's Races," Alpine Ski Database, www.ski-db.com.

49. Pat Graham, "Strokes Decimate Daring Downhiller," *Columbus Dispatch* (Ohio), 9 February 2012.

50. Nick Howe, "Tamara McKinney: The Enigma, the Racer, the All-Time Winner," *Skiing Heritage* 10.1 (March 1998): 33.

51. Matthew Fischer, "Skier Armstrong Takes Giant Step for U.S.," *Globe and Mail* (Toronto), 14 February 1984.

52. Nicholas Howe, "Sarajevo '84," *Women's Sports* 6.2 (February 1984): 52.

53. Denis Collins, "Armstrong: From the B Team to an A Plus," *Washington Post,* 13 February 1984.

54. Nicholas Howe, "A Natural Force Named Armstrong," *Skiing* 37.3 (November 1984): 119.

55. William Oscar Johnson, "Have Fun! Have Fun! Have Fun!" *Sports Illustrated,* 20 February 1984, 21.

56. Nicholas Howe, "If It's Friday, It Must Be Lenggries," *Skiing* 35.3 (November 1982): 101–2.

57. Terry Richard, "Seattle Ski Racer Has Olympic Goal," *Oregonian,* 2 December 1984.

58. Paul Buker, "Relatives Hail Armstrong's Gold Medal in Giant Slalom," *Oregonian,* 14 February 1984.

59. "Two Avalanches Follow Ski Trials," *Palm Beach Post* (Fla.), 8 February.

60. Bob Verdi, "Scott Calls Shot, Armstrong Fires," *Chicago Tribune,* 14 February 1984.

61. Skip Myslenski, "Armstrong Driven to Relive Magic Moment of '84," *Chicago Tribune,* 25 November 1987.

62. "U.S. Men's Skiers Bid Falls Shy," *Telegraph Herald* (Iowa), 14 February 1984.

63. Ray Sons, "Armstrong's Golden Slalom Enriches U.S.," *Reading Eagle* (Penn.), 14 February 1984; Collins, "Armstrong: From the B Team to an A Plus."

64. "Americans Go Wild on First Gold," *Ottawa Citizen* (Canada), 14 February 1984.

65. Bob Lochner, "What Happened to the U.S. Team's Burning Desire?" *Pittsburgh Press,* 16 February 1984.

66. Phil and Steve Mahre, *No Hill Too Fast,* 18.

67. Woodrow Paige Jr., "Mahres Approach Last Shot," *Anchorage Daily News*, 14 February 1984; John Mossman, "Phil Mahre Has Mellow Attitude," *Spokesman-Review* (Wash.), 11 February 1984; and Lochner, "What Happened to the U.S. Team's Burning Desire?"

68. Bob Sudyk, "Phil and Steve Mahre: As Exciting as a Case of Ex-Lax," *Anchorage Daily News*, 15 February 1984.

69. "A Biathlete Takes a Few More Shots," *Los Angeles Times*, 17 February 1984.

70. Phil and Steve Mahre, *No Hill Too Fast*, 81–82.

71. "Mahre Wins World Cup Championship," *Deseret News* (Utah), 28 March 1981.

72. John Fry, *The Story of Modern Skiing* (Lebanon: University Press of New Hampshire, 2006), 144.

73. "Double Trouble," *Anchorage Daily News*, 31 January 1982.

74. Bill Tanler, "The Mahre Brothers: Doing It Their Way," *Ski* 42.3 (November 1977): 62–63.

75. William Oscar Johnson, "Double Trouble on the Slopes," *Sports Illustrated*, 18 January 1982, 93.

76. Ibid.

77. John Husar, "Leading the U.S. to the Top," *Chicago Tribune*, 19 October 1983.

78. Gregory Lewis, "Phil Does It Again," *Skiing* 36.1 (September 1983): 172.

79. Johnson, "Double Trouble on the Slopes," 40.

80. "Double Trouble," *Anchorage Daily News*, 31 January 1982.

81. Dave Anderson, "Mahres Needed Nothing But Snow," *Spokesman-Review* (Wash.), 3 December 1981.

82. Bob Lochner, "Cash to Be Made at Sarajevo," *Los Angeles Times*, 5 February 1984.

83. Leonard Shapiro, "Bank on It: Big Money Makes the Circuit, Too," *Washington Post*, 5 February 1984.

84. "Agreement Reached on Olympic Flame," *Pittsburgh Post-Gazette*, 4 May 1984.

85. "Skiing," *Chicago Tribune*, 29 October 1983.

86. "Stenmark Justifies Income," *Star-Phoenix* (Canada), 11 February.

87. Ken Shulman, "Going Up the Downhill Slope," *New York Times*, 27 January 1992.

88. John Mossman, "Mahre Doesn't Miss Stenmark," *Daily News* (Ky.), 12 February 1984.

89. Mossman, "Phil Mahre Has Mellow Attitude."

90. Dave Anderson, "For Yugoslavia, A Hero," *New York Times*, 15 February 1984.

91. Dave Kindred, "Dreams Turn to Drudgery for Phil Mahre," *Miami News*, 15 February 1984.

92. "British Couple Perfect in Seizing Gold," *Sarasota Herald-Tribune*, 15 February 1984.

93. Norm Clarke, "Top Two U.S. Racers Miss Gates," *Lewiston Journal* (Me.), 17 February 1984.

94. Phil and Steve Mahre, *No Hill Too Fast*, 23.

95. Bob Lochner, "Mahre Brothers Pull Off a Twin Killing in Slalom," *Los Angeles Times*, 20 February 1984.

96. Ibid.

9. The "Minor Sports"

1. W. D. Frank, "Cold Bullets, Hot Borders: The Shooting War that Russia Won," *Ski Heritage* 21.2 (June 2009): 39.

2. Lawrie Mifflin, "Costly Biathlon," *New York Times*, 18 August 1983.

3. David Chamberlain, "Biathlon: An Ex-Soldier, a Pacifist, and a Green-Chile Rancher? What Kind of Team Is This?" *Sport*, February 1984, 36.

4. Mifflin, "Costly Biathlon."

5. Jill Lieber, "Ready, Aim . . . Medal!" *Sports Illustrated*, 23 February 1987, 54.

6. "Lugers, More Often Than Not, Are Losers," *Anchorage Daily News*, 7 February 1976.

7. J. D. Reed and Steven Holmes, "Marching to Their Own Beat," *Time*, 30 January 1984, 50.

8. "Interested in Trying Out for the Luge Team?" *Spokesman-Review* (Wash.), 6 February 1983.

9. Tim Rockwood, ed., *Research Information for the XIV Olympic Winter Games* (New York: ABC Sports, 1983), 3:232.

10. David Wallechinsky, *The Complete Book of the Winter Olympics* (New York: Little, Brown, 1993), 158.

11. "U.S. Ski Team Talented, Potential for Greatness," *Bangor Daily News* (Me.), 24 November 1983; "Flying Finn Shatters Jump Mark," *Spokesman-Review* (Wash.), 16 January 1983.

12. Dave Seminara, "Vinko Bogataj and the Ecstasy of Defeat," realclearsports.com.

13. Tony Chamberlain, "The Agony of Recurrence," *Boston Globe*, 13 February 1984.

14. Mike Harden, "Agony of Defeat to Continue for Wide World Wonder," *Columbus Dispatch* (Ohio), 9 October 1987.

15. Bob Verdi, "Agony of Defeat," *Pittsburgh Press*, 13 February 1984.

16. Greg Windsperger, interview by author, 28 August 2009.

17. Jeff Hastings, interview by author, 9 August 2009; Ray Didinger, "U.S. Hopes Soar with Hastings," *Philadelphia Daily News*, 26 January 1984.

18. They didn't pay for them either. Established in 1978, the USOC was a 501(c)(3) not-for-profit corporation with limited resources. It gave money to each Olympic sport according to that sport's "perceived popularity." Since minor sports weren't popular and had few participants and even fewer sponsors, USOC funding was slight. See Wanda Ellen Wakefield, "Out in the Cold: Sliding Sports and the Amateur Sports Act of 1978," *International Journal of the History of Sport* 24.6 (2007): 787. See also, Reed and Holmes, "Marching to Their Own Beat," 50.

19. "Winter Olympic Preview: U.S. Squad Looking Good," *Pittsburgh Press*, 27 January 1980.

20. Peter Bayer, "Biathlon at the Winter Olympics," in *50 Years of Biathlon, 1958–2008* (Salzburg: International Biathlon Union, 2008), 35.

21. John Morton, interview by author, 31 July 2009.

22. Beth Bragg, "These Soldiers Tell Ski Stories," *Anchorage Daily News*, 24 July 2003.

23. Jim Carr, "Biathlon Interest Booming," *Nordic World*, December 1978, 23.

24. Marie Alkire, interview by author, 8 May 2009.

25. Jim Jerome, "In Sarajevo, the Most Eloquent Quest Wasn't for Gold," *People*, 27 February 1984, 35–36.

26. In 2013 the American biathlete Tim Burke tied Thompson by winning a silver medal in the 20km race at the World Biathlon Championships in the Czech Republic.

27. Josh Thompson, interview by author, 17 May 2009.

28. Ibid.

29. Marie Alkire, interview by author, 8 May 2009.

30. William Oscar Johnson, "Some Win and Some Luge," *Sports Illustrated*, 2 February 1976, 31.

31. "Lugers, More Often Than Not, Are Losers"; Bill Shirley, "U.S. Finds Tough Sledding in Olympic Luge," *Los Angeles Times*, 15 February 1980; and Johnson, "Some Win and Some Luge," *Sports Illustrated*, 2 February 1976, 31.

32. "'Luge' Doesn't Throw a Curve to Spelling Bee Champion," *Palm Beach Post* (FL), 1 June 1984.

33. Mark Godwin, "And Just What Is Luge?" *Anchorage Daily News* (AK), 8 February 1980.

34. "Lugers, More Often Than Not, Are Losers."

35. Jane Gross, "Inflexible Flying," *New York Times*, 10 February 1980.

36. John Freeman, "If You Love the Luge or Boggle at the Bobsled, Set the Set on CBS," *San Diego Union-Tribune*, 13 February 1994.

37. Thomas Boswell, "Winter's Daredevils Have No Fear," *Washington Post*, 12 February 1980.

38. Steve Goldstein, "Top U.S. Luger Is Committed to Going Downhill Fast," *Philadelphia Inquirer,* 12 January 1984.

39. Ron Rossi, interview by author, 13 May 2009.

40. John Powers, "California Dreamin': Bonny Warner Tackles Luge," *Boston Globe,* 6 February 1984.

41. Johnette Howard, "Mountains of Cash Help U.S. Near Olympics Peak," *Detroit Free Press,* 8 January 1984.

42. "Luge Team Molds 12 Nervy Pioneers," *New York Times,* 4 February 1983.

43. Alexander Wolff, "They Plan to Do Some Tough Sledding," *Sports Illustrated,* 5 December 1983, 36.

44. Goldstein, "Top U.S. Luger Is Committed."

45. John Powers, "The Olympics: Luge," *Boston Globe,* 18 December 1983.

46. Rich Hofmann, "Luger Has His Moment with Flag to Wave," *Evening Tribune* (Calif.), 9 February 1984; Barry Lorge, "U.S. Flag Carrier Nearly Gets Carried Away at Sarajevo," *San Diego Union,* 9 February 1984.

47. Tom Callahan, "The Sweet Scene in Sarajevo," *Time,* 13 February 1984, 62.

48. Barry Lorge, "Have You Heard about the Lonesome Luger?" *San Diego Union,* 6 February 1984; Denis Collins, "Olympian Heights Are Out of Sight for Some," *Washington Post,* 6 February 1984.

49. Rich Hoffman, "Making the Team—Puerto Rico Has Tucker in Luge," *Philadelphia Daily News,* 7 February 1984.

50. Bill Lyon, "Solitary Training Skier for Egypt Spent 40 Days in Desert Cave Preparing for the Olympics," *Philadelphia Inquirer,* 7 February 1984.

51. Collins, "Olympian Heights Are Out of Sight for Some."

52. James Davidson, "Jamaican Bobsledders Head Oddball List," *Deseret News* (Utah), 13 February 1988.

53. Gregg Patton, "Brothers Dag and Ricardo Burgos Spangen Are Cross Country Skiers from Guatemala," *USA Today,* 23 February 1988.

54. John Kekis, " 'The Eagle' Soars Like Never Before," *Miami Herald,* 14 December 1988.

55. Chris Jenkins, "They're Just a Few of this Winter's . . . Olympic Oddities," *San Diego Union,* 21 February 1988.

56. Bill O'Brian, "San Diego's Contribution to These Games," *Evening Tribune* (Calif.), 4 February 1984.

57. Steve Goldstein, "Bobsledders Need to Ride the Fine Line," *Philadelphia Inquirer,* 17 January 1984.

58. Jim Sarni, "Bobbing for Gold," *Sun-Sentinel* (Fla.), 10 January 1988.

59. Richard Sandomir, "Analyst Informed by Saddest Experience," *New York Times,* 14 February 2010.

60. "Stuntman Killed in Bobsled Accident," *Los Angeles Times,* 18 February 1981.

61. Goldstein, "Bobsledders Need to Ride the Fine Line."

62. "Olympic Bobsled Has Six More Mishaps," *New York Times,* 6 January 1980.

63. "Sports," *Boston Globe,* 26 February 1980.

64. Michael Wilbon, "Not a Member of the Club," *Washington Post,* 20 February 1992.

65. "Sport: The Cigarski Is Smoking," *Time,* 20 February 1984, 69; John Powers, "Bobsled: Cinderella Sailors," *Boston Globe,* 6 February 1984.

66. "Bobsledders Want Truce in Stampede," *Spokane Chronicle,* 17 February 1984; "Skullduggery on Bobsled Run," *Montreal Gazette,* 3 January 1984.

67. Powers, "Bobsled: Cinderella Sailors."

68. Reed and Holmes, "Marching to Their Own Beat," 50–51.

69. "US Bobsled Team Acquires Swiss Driver's Quick Sled," *Boston Globe,* 15 February 1984; Tom Callahan, "Something to Shout About," *Time,* 27 February 1984, 79.

70. Jeff Hastings, interview by author, 9 August 2009.

71. "Medal Snatched from U.S. Grasp," *San Diego Union*, 12 February 1984; Steve Goldstein, "Motivation Taken Away, Ahern Still Hits Ski Trail," *Philadelphia Inquirer*, 13 February 1984.

72. Barry Lorge, "Barry Lorge," *San Diego Union*, 12 February 1984.

73. Mike Madigan, "Two Nordic Restarts Draw U.S. Complaints," *Pittsburgh Press*, 12 February 1984; "U.S. Team Blasts Jump Judges for Negating Nordic Results," *Miami Herald*, 12 February 1984.

74. Denis Collins, "In Fallout of Jump, Ahern is 17th," *Washington Post*, 13 February 1984; Goldstein, "Motivation Taken Away, Ahern Still Hits Ski Trail."

75. Katherine Springer, "America's Top Ski Jumper Feels No Pressure," *Schenectady Gazette*, 4 February 1984.

76. Jeff Hastings, interview by author, 9 August 2009.

77. Mitch Albom, "Ski Jumping: Ways Are Newer, Dangers Fewer. But It's Still the Only Way to Fly," *Sport*, February 1984, 53.

78. Al Morganti, "Any Medal Would Be a Leap for Ski Jumpers," *Philadelphia Inquirer*, 19 January 1984.

79. Greg Windsperger, interview by author, 28 August 2009.

80. Jane Leavy, "Hastings Looks, Leaps, and Loves It," *Washington Post*, 30 January 1984.

81. Bob Lochner, "Ski Jumper Just Misses Bronze," *Anchorage Daily News*, 19 February 1984.

82. Bob Michals, "'Agony of Defeat' Now Brings Smiles," *Palm Beach Post* (Fla.), 17 February 1984.

83. Tony Chamberlain, "Nykaenen Rockets Past Hastings," *Boston Globe*, 19 February 1984.

84. Steve Goldstein, "On Skis, Koch Cuts Solitary Trail," *Philadelphia Inquirer*, 8 January 1984.

85. Kenny Moore, "A Fire Burns Fiercely within Him," *Sports Illustrated*, 6 February 1984, 45.

86. Goldstein, "On Skis, Koch Cuts Solitary Trail."

87. "Koch Looks at the Bright Side," *Miami News*, 11 February 1984.

88. Fred McMane, "Speed Skaters Help U.S. Avoid Disaster," *Sarasota Journal* (Fla.), 18 February 1980.

89. "Speed Skaters Save U.S. from Embarrassment," Telegraph-Herald (Iowa), 18 February 1980; "Skaters Soothe Smarting U.S. Pride," *Sarasota Herald-Tribune*, 15 February 1968.

90. John Powers, "German Uprising: Establishing Special School and Aiding Athletes Financially Has Given GDR the Olympic Edge," *Boston Globe*, 24 July 1988.

91. Danielle Keefler, "Three East German Champions Set the Standard in Women's Speed Skating," *Maclean's*, February 1988, 110.

92. Steven Ungerleider, *Faust's Gold: Inside the East German Doping Machine* (New York: St. Martin's Press, 2001), xv.

93. The allegations against Enke were made during the *Andere Tijden Sport* episode "De drieklapper van Yvonne," which aired in January 2010. The episode is available at http://nos.nl.

94. Ungerleider, *Faust's Gold*, 90–91.

95. Scott M. Reid, "Early Effort to Drug Test Olympic Athletes Kept Secret," *Orange County Register* (Calif.), 1 August 2009.

96. Cathy Breitenbucher, "Speed Skaters Administered Rigid Drug Tests," *Milwaukee Sentinel*, 10 January 1984.

97. Chad Finn, "Ohno Wins Bronze, Record Seventh Medal," *Boston Globe*, 20 February 2010.

98. "U.S. Speed Skaters Hope to Overcome Youth, Inexperience," *Palm Beach Post* (Fla.), 1 February 1984.

99. Will Grimsley, "Heiden 'Burned Out,'" *Lewiston Journal* (Me.), 6 February 1984.

100. Mike O'Brien, "Gold Medal Ice Rink Slated to Close," *Harlan Daily Enterprise* (Ky.), 21 May 1982.

101. Mike Kupper, "Will Bickering Chill U.S. Speed Skating Effort?" *Milwaukee Journal*, 29 December 1983.

102. Joe Gergen, "Medal Shutout May Hurt Speed Skating in U.S.," *Anchorage Daily News*, 19 February 1984.

103. "Cold War of Speed Skaters," *Chicago Tribune*, 3 February 1984.

104. Alan Greenberg, "Eric Heiden Is Back, But, Unfortunately, ABC's Got Him," *Los Angeles Times*, 7 February 1984.

105. "Skaters Lack a Heiden, But Rank Even with Europeans," *Boca Raton News* (Fla.), 10 January 1984.

106. Lorne Zeiler, *Hearts of Gold* (Vancouver: Raincoast Books, 2004), 47.

107. John Korobanik, "Boucher Predicts Gold in Speed Skating," *Ottawa Citizen*, 8 February 1984.

108. Phil Hirsch, "Karin Enke Makes Quick Dash to Gold," *Miami News*, 10 February 1984; Denis Collins, "Enke's First Gold May Start a Rush," *Washington Post*, 10 February 1984.

109. Bud Lea, "U.S. Speed Skaters Are Undertaking Olympian Task," *Milwaukee Sentinel*, 30 November 1983.

110. Gergen, "Medal Shutout May Hurt Speed Skating in U.S."

Epilogue

1. Alan Greenberg, "Sarajevo: Things Smooth from Start to Finish," *Los Angeles Times*, 20 February 1984.

2. "Closing Ceremony of the XIVth Olympic Winter Games," *Olympic Review* 197 (March 1984): 146; Greenberg, "Sarajevo: Things Smooth from Start to Finish"; Frank Litsky, "Skating and Song as Flame Goes Out," *New York Times*, 20 February 1984.

3. Milton Richman, "Gold Medal for the Yugoslavs," *Lodi News-Sentinel* (Calif.), 22 February 1984.

4. "As Seen in the Press," *Olympic Review* 197 (March 1984): 146.

5. Greenberg, "Sarajevo: Things Smooth from Start to Finish."

6. Kenneth Reich, "Sarajevo Lesson: Perhaps Olympic Ideals Still Live," *Los Angeles Times*, 21 February 1984.

7. Joe Falls, *Joe Falls: 50 Years of Sports Writing* (Champaign, Ill.: Sports Publishing, 1997), 115–16.

8. Interview with Red Grandy, "Crashing the 1984 Sarajevo Olympics for *Stars and Stripes*," North Country Public Radio, n.d., www.northcountrypublicradio.org.

9. Rich Hofmann, "A City with a Host of Worries," *Philadelphia Daily News*, 10 April 1984.

10. Don Collins, "Optimism Buoys Olympic Organizers," *Calgary Herald*, 23 February 1984.

11. Jim Muir, "Olympic Legacy in Sarajevo Ruined by War," *Christian Science Monitor*, 2 February 1994.

12. "Sarajevo Winter Olympics Show Healthy Profit," *Los Angeles Times*, 20 October 1984.

13. "Housing: Poor Sarajevo People Await Olympic Apartments," *Tri-City Herald* (Wash.), 19 February 1984.

14. Frank Riley, "Sarajevo Builds on Games," *Los Angeles Times*, 11 November 1984.

15. Larry Gerber, "Olympics Changed Sarajevo for the Better," *Daily News* (Ky.), 1 February 1985.

16. Milton Nieuwsma, "Sarajevo, Out of Fog, Into Future," *Chicago Tribune*, 13 April 1986.

17. "Sarajevo Pursues Dream," *Calgary Herald*, 16 July 1985; Aubrey Diem, *Switzerland: Land, People, Economy* (Waterloo, Ontario: Media International, 1993), 193.

18. Anton Gosar, "Structural Impact of International Tourism in Yugoslavia," *GeoJournal* 19.3 (October 1989): 280.

19. Ibid.

20. Ahmed Karabegović, "Tourism in Bosnia and Herzegovina: Affirmation of New Spaces," *Sarajevo'84* (February 1987): 5. This particular *Sarajevo'84* was the official "Yugoslav Review for Tourism and Cultural Heritage" and was different, apparently, from the previously cited *Sarajevo'84*, a multi-issue SOOC magazine published from 1981 to 1984.

21. Paula Butturini, "Four Years Later, Olympic Spirit Lingers in Sarajevo," *Daily News of Los Angeles,* 14 February 1988.

22. Karabegović, "Tourism in Bosnia and Herzegovina."

23. Fergus M. Bordewich, "Yugoslavia since Tito," *New York Times,* 13 April 1986.

24. Sonja Licht, "Civil Society, Democracy, and the Yugoslav Wars," in Metta Spencer, ed., *The Lessons of Yugoslavia* (New York: Elsevier Science, 2000), 114.

25. Bordewich, "Yugoslavia since Tito."

26. Cited in Jasmina Udovički and Ivan Torov, "The Interlude: 1980–1990," in Jasmina Udovički and James Ridgeway, eds., *Burn This House: The Making and Unmaking of Yugoslavia* (Durham: Duke University Press, 2000), 104.

27. Bogdan Denitch, *Limits and Possibilities: The Crisis of Yugoslav Socialism and State Socialist Systems* (Minneapolis: University of Minnesota Press, 1990), 54.

28. Jackson Diehl, "Yugoslavia's New Leader Has Yet to Take Hold," *Washington Post,* 8 December 1986.

29. Viktor Meier, Yugoslavia: *A History of Its Demise* (New York: Routledge, 1999), 102.

30. Mathis Chazanov, "Workers Joke, But Yugoslavian Economy Isn't Funny," *Los Angeles Times,* 21 March 1987.

31. Rone Tempest, "Yugoslav Leader Says Regime Is Secure," *Los Angeles Times,* 24 January 1990.

32. David Binder, "Prime Minister Is Bullish on Yugoslavia's Economic Changes," *New York Times,* 5 March 1990.

33. Warren Zimmermann, *Origins of a Catastrophe* (New York: Times Books, 1996), 43.

34. Mihailo Crnobrnja, *The Yugoslav Drama* (Buffalo: McGill-Queen's University Press, 1996), 106.

35. Christopher Bennett, *Yugoslavia's Bloody Collapse* (New York: New York University Press, 1995), 97.

36. "Yugoslavia Slides Deeper in Ethnic Conflict," *Glasgow Herald* (Scotland), 23 May 1989.

37. Stevan K. Pavlowitch, "Serbia, Montenegro, and Yugoslavia," in Dejan Djokić, ed., *Yugoslavism: Histories of a Failed Idea, 1918–1992* (Madison: University of Wisconsin Press, 2003), 69.

38. Ian Trayner, "Circles of Mutual Hatred Trap Serbs and Croats," *Guardian Weekly* (London), 19 May 1991.

39. Baine Harden, "Croatia Rejects Federal Control in Struggle for Independence," *Guardian* (London), 22 February 1991.

40. Steven L. Burg and Paul S. Shoup, *The War in Bosnia-Herzegovina: Ethnic Conflict and International Intervention* (Armonk, N.Y.: M. E. Sharpe, 1999), 104; Laura Silber, "Bosnia Declares Sovereignty," *Washington Post,* 16 October 1991.

41. "IOC Gives Slovenia a Chance," *Daily Mail* (London), 18 January 1992.

42. Dan Daly, "For Croats, Participation Alone Makes for Good Show," *Washington Times,* 15 February 1992.

43. Harvey Araton, "Croatia Competes from the Heart and Not for Medals," *New York Times,* 15 February 1992.

44. Richard Meares, "Widespread Clashes Reported in Croatia and Bosnia," *Reuters News,* 22 March 1992.

45. Marcus Tanner, "Capital Sarajevo Racked by Serb-Muslim Strife," *Independent* (London), 7 April 1992.

46. "Troops Should Intervene, Says Envoy," *Hamilton Spectator* (Canada), 13 July 1992.

47. Hugh Pain, "Battered Sarajevo Suburb Gets Food, But Ordeal Not Over," Reuters News, 12 July 1992.

48. Roger Cohen, "Serbian Snipers Content to Let Sarajevo Just Bleed," *New York Times,* 16 September 1992.

49. Maud S. Beelman, "Bosnian Serb General Shows Off His Mountain," Associated Press, 6 August 1993.

50. Dusan Stojanovic, "War Drums Echo in Mountain Valley," Associated Press, 6 May 1993.

51. Joel Brand, "Serbs Hope for Skiing Bonanza," *Times* (London), 18 October 1993.

52. Tim Judah, "Besiegers Play at Olympics Outside Contested Capital," *Times* (London), 15 February 1994.

53. "Bosnian Serbs Organize Shadow Olympics," Reuters News, 3 February 1994.

54. Martin Nesirky, "Olympic Paradise for Bosnians after Sarajevo Fall," Reuters News, 15 July 1992.

55. Nicole Martiche, "Hungry But Happy, Bosnian Olympic Team Is Complete," Agence France-Presse, 25 July 1992.

56. Olympic Committee of Bosnia-Herzegovina, *Do You Remember Sarajevo?* (Sarajevo: Svjetlost, 1992). See IOC Archives, JO-1984W-CNO, folder 206586.

57. Mark Milstein, "Sarajevo's Olympic Seats Are Now Coffin Boards," *Seattle Times,* 5 August 1993.

58. Philip Shenon, "A Postwar Shortage in Sarajevo: Space for Graves," *New York Times,* 21 April 1996.

59. "Sarajevans Bury Family as Shells Whistle Overhead," Reuters News, 6 January 1994.

60. Kurt Schork, "Sarajevo Rearranges the Rubble for Pope's Visit," Reuters News, 6 September 1994.

61. "Dismay in Sarajevo as Pope Calls Off Visit," *Independent* (UK), 7 September 1994.

62. Linnet Myers, "Bosnian Capital Gets Kick from Soccer as War Lulls," *Orange County Register* (Calif.), 21 March 1994.

63. John Kifner, "Serbs Agree to Give Up Heavy Guns," *New York Times,* 10 February 1994.

64. "Samaranch Set for Sarajevo," Agence France-Presse, 9 February 1994.

65. "Appeal of the International Olympic Committee in Favour of the 'Olympic Truce,'" *Olympic Review* 299 (September 1992): 429.

66. Stephen Wilson, "Sports News," Associated Press, 9 December 1993.

67. Dave Stubbs, "An Olympic Truce," *Montreal Gazette,* 29 October 1993.

68. "Samaranch Seeks Clinton Help on Olympic Truce," Reuters News, 17 December 1993; "I Want to Be in Sarajevo for the 10th Anniversary of the Games," *Olympic Review* 315 (January–February 1994): 17.

69. "Samaranch Calls for Olympic Truce," *Press Association,* 29 October 1993.

70. Dave Stubbs, "IOC Still Seeking Olympic Ceasefire," *Calgary Herald,* 7 February 1994.

71. Alister Doyle, "IOC to Match Athletes' Donations to Sarajevo," Reuters News, 17 February 1994.

72. John Powers, "Opening Up to Troubled World," *Boston Globe,* 13 February 1994.

73. "Board against Sarajevo Trip," Agence France-Presse, 10 February 1994.

74. Interview, "Izudin Filipović, Director of the BH Olympic Committee," part of the online interview collection "FAMA: Siege of Sarajevo 92–96," n.d., www.famacollection.org.

75. "Samaranch's Somber Sojourn to Sarajevo," *Chicago Sun-Times,* 17 February 1994.

76. Melissa Turner, "IOC Chief Pledges to Back Efforts for Rebuilding Facilities in Sarajevo," *Atlanta Journal,* 17 February 1994; "IOC Promises Help for War-Torn Sarajevo," Xinhua News Agency, 17 January 1995.

77. "Sarajevo 2010? Collateral Damage," *Sports Illustrated,* 5 April 1999, 30.

78. "Strife in Sarajevo: Reopening for 1984 Olympic Venue Postponed," *CNN Sports Illustrated*, 29 March 1999, http://sportsillustrated.cnn.com.

79. Jim Caple, "Crowd Gives Free Skate High Marks," *Buffalo News*, 27 February 1994.

80. Anna Callaghan, "Sarajevo 30 Years Later: From Games to War and Back," *Seattle Times*, 8 February 2014.

81. Nadine Brozan, "Chronicle: Olympic Champion Hopes Beauty Will Return to Sarajevo," *New York Times*, 19 February 1993.

82. Callaghan, "Sarajevo 30 Years Later."

83. "ReLeaf Returns to Sarajevo," *American Forests* 106.4 (Winter 2001): 11.

84. Debbie Armstrong, interview by author, 17 September 2009.

85. Rusmir Smajilhodzic, "Thirty Years after Olympics, Sarajevo Mourns Brotherhood Lost," Dawn.com, 17 February 2014, www.dawn.com.

86. Christopher Condon, "Sarajevo's New Dream of Olympic Glory," *Businessweek*, 30 January 2002, www.businessweek.com.

87. Said Fazlagić, interview by author, 10 June 2010.

88. Vedat Spahović, "Olimpijske igre se vraćaju kući," Al Jazeera Balkans, 8 December 2012, http://balkans.aljazeera.net.

Index

66, 95, 150–51, 163; background of, 56; loan to SOOC and, 56; proposed Olympic Truce, 7, 161–62; quarrel with Berlioux, 56; trip to Sarajevo in 1994, 7, 161–62; RFE/RL dispute and, 74

Sanac, Bosnia, 161

Sandberg, Tom, 141

San Diego, California, 137

San Diego Union, 32, 93

Saneyev, Viktor, 22

San Juan, 136

Sapporo, Japan, 31, 33; competition with Gothenburg and Sarajevo for Olympic bid, 32–36; suitability as 1984 Olympic site, 34

Sapporo Winter Olympics (1972), 33–34, 98, 132

Sarajevo, 3; bid for 2010 Winter Olympics, 164; city's decision to bid for Sarajevo Olympics, 29–31; civic improvements of, 30–31, 58; demographic makeup of, 7, 8, 27–28; destruction of Olympic sites in, 158–61; ethno-religious neighborhoods of, 27; foreign descriptions of, 8, 32; joint bid for 2017 European Youth Olympic Winter Festival, 164; origin of city, 26; and pollution, 31; post-Olympics tourism and, 153–54; selection as host city, 35–36; transportation improvements for, 51, 60; under Austro-Hungarian Empire, 27; under Ottoman Empire, 26–27; and World War I, 28. *See also* Sarajevo Winter Olympics (1984)

Sarajevo Haggadah, 4

Sarajevo Olympic Museum, 160, 163

Sarajevo Olympic Organizing Committee (SOOC), 40, 42, 44–45, 61–63, 127, 152–54; construction of Olympic facilities, 51–59, 62. *See also* Karabegović, Ahmed; Lukač, Pavle; Sarajevo; Sarajevo Winter Olympics (1984), Takač, Artur; Zečević, Ljubiša

Sarajevo Winter Olympics (1984): closing ceremony of, 150–51; competition with Gothenburg and Sapporo for Olympic bid, 32–36; death of Andropov during, 75–76; estimated profit from games, 152; issues of funding for, 38, 45–46, 56–58; mascot

of, 51, 60, 164; nostalgia for, 6–7, 163–64; number of participants in, 7, 63; official sponsors of, 8, 44, 58; opening ceremony of, 63–64, 72, 90, 151; praise for organization of, 150–52; pre-Olympic competitions of, 59–62; press coverage of, 54, 75; RFE/RL dispute and, 74–75; sale of broadcast rights for, 40–44, 57; security measures for, 65–68; Soviet invasion of Afghanistan and, 40, 48; Tito and, 38–39; torch run of, 63; weather issues of, 59–62, 72, 116, 121. *See also* American Broadcasting Company (ABC); Sarajevo; Sarajevo Olympic Organizing Committee (SOOC)

Saranac Lake, New York, 138

Sawbridge, Janet, 108

Scandinavia, 33, 35–36, 132

Scandinavium arena (Gothenburg, Sweden), 34

Schladming, Austria, 121

Schmidt, Helmut, 48

Schoenbrunn, Gabie, 146, 149

Schoene, Andrea, 145–46, 61

Schuba, Beatrix, 98

Scott, John T., 96

Scripps Howard National Spelling Bee, 134

Seattle, Washington, 120

Sefić, Davor, 157

Seibert, Michael, 73

Selesković, Sabahudin, 55, 76

Selezneva (Larisa) and Makarov (Oleg), 106

Senate Foreign Relations Committee, 74

Senegal, 137

Seoul, South Korea, 87

Serbia, 38, 56, 63, 66, 154; and boycott of Slovenian goods, 156; and creation of Yugoslavia, 28; and rise of Slobodan Milošević, 155–56; and World War I, 27. *See also* Yugoslavia

Serbian Democratic Party (SDS), 156–57

Serbo-Croatian language, 28, 63

7-Eleven, 23

7-Eleven pro-am cycling team, 148

Seyfert, Gabriele, 103

Shields, Brooke, 103

Shoup, Paul S., 28

Simoneau, Dan, 143

Jason Vuic is a writer and historian who specializes in the social and cultural history of Cold War–era Yugoslavia. A former Rotary Ambassadorial Scholar at the University of Novi Sad, Serbia, and Fulbright Scholar at the Institute of Ethnology and Folklore Research in Zagreb, Croatia, Vuic holds a bachelor's degree in history from Wake Forest University, a master's degree in history from the University of Richmond, and a doctorate in Balkan and East European history from Indiana University. He is a former assistant director of the Center for Slavic and East European Studies at Ohio State University. He lives in North Carolina with his wife, Kara.